© 2003

Published by Celtic FC Limited

Designed by Celtic FC Limited
Printed by The Print People

Edited by Paul Cuddihy and Joe Sullivan

ISBN: 0-9544954-1-1

Contents

Acknowledgements.. 9

Foreword by Martin O'Neill..........................11

Introduction: We marched with O'Neill........... 13

1. Memories of Seville...................................... 18

2. FC Basel... 45

3. FK Suduva.. 56

4. Blackburn Rovers...73

5. Celta Vigo.. 91

6. VfB Stuttgart.. 108

7. Liverpool.. 126

8. Boavista... 159

9. The UEFA Cup final......................................179

10. Fans' memories of Euro campaign.....................208

11. Post-match reaction.................................... 283

Route to the UEFA Cup final........................... 288

Campaign statistics...................................... 294

This book is dedicated to the tens of thousands of Celtic supporters who made the trip to Seville to support the team, and to the millions of others worldwide who were there in spirit.

Acknowledgements

THANKS must go, first and foremost, to the players, management and backroom staff of Celtic Football Club. It was their efforts throughout the season which took us to Seville, giving Celtic fans a whole variety of unforgettable experiences along the way. They wore the Hoops with distinction and we followed them with pride.

Putting this book together has been a labour of love, although tinged with disappointment over what might have been. The contributions from Celtic fans all over the world, particularly their memories of Seville, have been entertaining and emotional, and our thanks to each and every person who sent in their stories. Our apologies for not being able to include every single story, but to have attempted to do so would have probably led to the biggest book in publishing history.

The people who work in the Celtic Newsroom are in a privileged position. We work for the club we support and get to follow the team at home and abroad, reporting on Celtic for the *Celtic View*, the official club website and CelticTV. Each of the chapters in this book has been written by a different member of the Newsroom team, offering a distinctive insight into our UEFA Cup run, round by round.

Our thanks to SNS for their work in photographing our European adventure all the way from Suduva to Seville. Their images will help rekindle many fond memories. In particular, thanks to Alan Harvey of SNS for his work in covering the build-up to the UEFA Cup final and the game itself for Celtic.

Thanks to Scott Munro, Ryan McGraw, George Johnston and Dave Ure at First Press Publishing for their help in producing this book, and to the *Daily Record* for use of their pictures.

Thanks to Brian Sharp of DP21 for his help in the printing of this book.

Last, but by no means least, our thanks to the people of Seville. Their warmth, friendliness and hospitality in welcoming 80,000 Celtic supporters to their city helped make the occasion a special one and forged a lasting bond between Celtic Football Club and the city of Seville

Foreword

IT would have been a pleasure and a privilege to have written the foreword to this book in celebration of our victory in the UEFA Cup final. That this is not the case is a source of disappointment to me.

Our performance in Seville was absolutely magnificent. Every player gave their all in trying to win the trophy and I am sure the Celtic supporters were very proud of their team. I know that I was extremely proud of the players.

In football., you often get what you deserve from a game, but that night at the Estadio Olimpico, I thought we deserved more..

To have played as well as we did against a team of the quality of Porto, and to have twice come from behind, says much about this group of players. We looked the stronger team as the game progressed and it was unfortunate that we were reduced to ten men when Bobo Balde was ordered off.

I said at the time, and it was well documented, that Porto's time-wasting tactics and play-acting were a source of frustration, and the reaction of the Celtic fans when they went up to receive the trophy says everything about how they were perceived.

I also spoke of the relative youth of the referee, which suggested a lack of experience at that level, and certainly a strong referee was needed to deal with some of Porto's unsportsmanlike behaviour.

Ultimately, what the history books will record is that we did not win the UEFA Cup in season 2002/03. But our achievement in reaching the final is something that all Celtic supporters should be immensely proud of.

We picked ourselves up from the disappointment of losing to FC Basel in the Champions League qualifier to make an impact in the UEFA Cup. Along the way we defeated some top quality sides from the best leagues in Europe – Blackburn Rovers, Celta Vigo, VfB Stuttgart, Liverpool and Boavista – and we thoroughly deserved to take our place in the final.

Our supporters have also been magnificent, following the team from Lithuania all the way through to the final in Seville, and your backing of the team in the final was exceptional.

It is ironic that, in probably the most memorable season in my time at Celtic, that we have ended up without a trophy to show for our efforts, but I know you will agree with me when I say that I could not have asked for any more from the players. They gave everything, both domestically and in Europe, and deserved more for those efforts.

However, this book remains a celebration of a great UEFA Cup campaign and I'm sure it will bring back some good memories of a great season.

MARTIN O'NEILL
May 2003

Introduction

We marched with O'Neill

by Paul Cuddihy

THERE are few words which can adequately describe what happened at the 2003 UEFA Cup final, though the phrase 'astonishingly brilliant' does come to mind.

An estimated 80,000 Celtic supporters travelled from all corners of the globe to Seville to cheer on the Bhoys against FC Porto. That more than half of them did not have tickets for the match makes it all the more remarkable. True, it's been 33 years since Celtic reached a European final, but the scale of the support which descended upon the southern Spanish city was truly extraordinary.

Is there another football club anywhere in the world which could have mobilised such a vast army of fans, prepared to make such sacrifices to attend a game, or even just be in the city where the match was taking place? This is a rhetorical question, of course. The rest of the football world discovered what Celtic supporters have always known – that Celtic Football Club is a unique institution in the world of sport. Its very foundation gave it a special character and created an emotional bond between club and supporter which transcends the mere act of following a football team or any other sporting institution.

The victory over Boavista in Portugal put Celtic into the UEFA Cup final, where they would meet Boavista's city rivals, Porto, victors over Lazio in the other semi-final. Our re-emergence on the European stage captured the imagination of supporters everywhere and sparked a frenzy as people chased tickets, travel and accommodation, or at least one of these three; as long as fans could get to Spain, to be part of this gathering of Celtic's worldwide family, then that would be enough.

It also heralded a three-week period when Seville and all things Spanish gripped Celtic fans. Who could forget the game at Ibrox just over two days after the win over

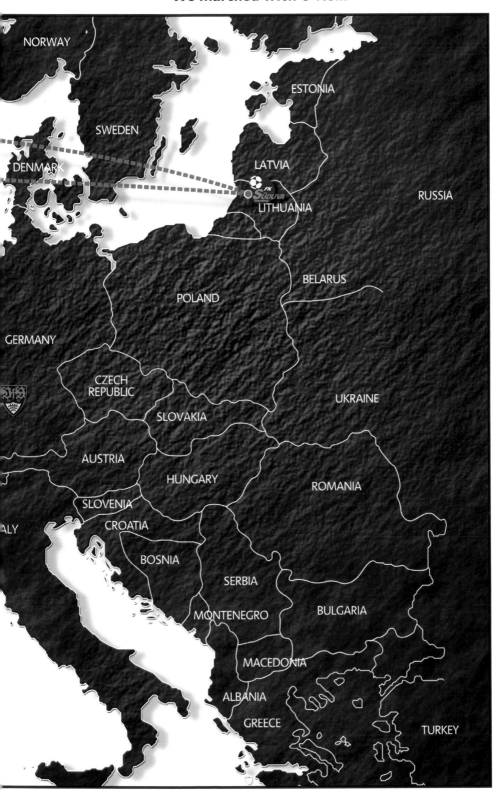

The Road to Seville

Boavista? It was a vital league match where anything other than victory would leave our rivals in an almost unassailable position at the top of the table. That we won, and won convincingly, says everything about our players – their ability and their character – but the character of the Celtic fans also came to the fore that day as we turned Ibrox into a massive beach party.

People turned up wearing sombreros, and shades, with lilos, towels and passports in tow, and they greeted the arrival of the teams on to the park with a shower of beach balls that reigned down from the Broomloan Road Stand. There were even stories of fans turning up in their swimwear – and that included one guy wearing a bikini!

It was an incredible end to a season which had started with great expectations of another Champions League adventure, which were quickly dashed by FC Basel. Whether many people at that time believed that we would subsequently reach the UEFA Cup final is unlikely, but as Martin O'Neill's side marched through the tournament – FK Suduva, Blackburn Rovers, Celta Vigo, VfB Stuttgart, Liverpool and Boavista – more and more Celtic supporters began to think that this was our season – our name was on the cup.

It began with the visit of FK Suduva. The Lithuanian side offered little resistance, although the 8-1 home victory in particular was a timely confidence booster following the disappointment of FC Basel.

Next up was the first of two Battle of Britains as Graeme Souness brought his Blackburn Rovers side to Celtic Park. We won the first leg courtesy of a Henrik Larsson goal – who else? – yet, in defeat, an arrogance seemed to possess Blackburn and their manager. The phrase 'Men against boys' certainly came back to haunt them at Ewood Park.

Celta Vigo were our next opponents and proved an extremely tough team. Again, it took a Larsson goal to give Celtic a narrow lead, and while the Spaniards scored twice at home, a brilliant John Hartson strike was enough to see Martin O'Neill's men through on away goals. It also meant that, for the first time in 23 years, there would be European football after Christmas at Celtic Park.

The draw wasn't getting any easier for Celtic. Having eliminated a team from the Premiership and La Primera Liga, it was now the turn of Germany's Bundesliga to put forward a side in the shape of VfB Stuttgart.

A 3-1 victory at home, minus an injured Larsson, followed by two early away goals in Germany, put the Hoops through, though a spirited second-half comeback from Stuttgart gave them a 3-2 victory on the night and ensured a nervous last few minutes for the Celtic fans in the Gottlieb-Daimler Stadium.

Special praise must go to the Stuttgart fans, who welcomed the travelling Celts with warmth and hospitality and took the defeat of their team with good grace and sportsmanship.

Now we faced another Battle of Britain, this time in the shape of Liverpool, and again, Celtic were being dismissed by observers down south. Henrik Larsson was back for this game and took less than two minutes to open the scoring. However, an equaliser from Emile Heskey gave Liverpool a vital away goal, and set Celtic a tough task at Anfield.

That night in Liverpool was a memorable one for the Celts, as goals from Alan Thompson and a wonder strike by Hartson secured a 2-0 victory, silenced the critics

We marched with O'Neill

and put Celtic in the semi-final of the UEFA Cup. Boavista were all that stood between Martin O'Neill's men and a place in the final. The Portuguese side might not have been the best we had faced during the campaign but they were certainly one of the toughest. A 1-1 draw at Celtic Park gave us a tough challenge for the return leg but we had Henrik Larsson and that was to prove the difference. The Super Swede's goal with 12 minutes to go was enough to give Celtic victory and a place in the UEFA Cup final … It was like a dream and now only Porto stood between us and the reality of the UEFA Cup.

Of course, the famous 'V' factor surfaced; every team we played in the competition up to and including the semi-final, contained a 'V' in their name. With the final being played in Seville, it seemed as if the fates had conspired to give us this triumph.

That we didn't win the UEFA Cup is now recorded in football's history books for all time. Yet, there was triumph for Celtic – a triumph of the spirit. There is not a single Celtic supporter, either among those who made it to Seville or from those who cheered on the Bhoys from afar, who would have swapped the experience for anything. Trebles can come and go but a European final will last forever.

This view has been echoed in post-match comments from the players and manager, which says much about the experience and, indeed, the impact the green and white army had on everyone connected with the club.

It is still disappointing, even heartbreaking, to think back on the final and realise that we didn't win. We deserved it – the fans and most definitely the players and manager. They gave everything for the cause in the Estadio Olimpico and their efforts, in the final and throughout the campaign, were appreciated by supporters.

It has been one of the strangest close seasons I can ever remember, when optimism still reigned supreme despite the absence of a trophy to show for the efforts of the season, both domestically and in Europe. And it is this optimism and Celtic pride which we have tried to capture in this book.

To achieve as broad a spectrum of the Celtic spirit as possible, various members of the Celtic Media team have given their own personal insight into the endeavours of the Bhoys by each 'adopting' one of the hurdles thrown in Celtic's path to Seville from August 14, 2002 through the entire 280 emotion-packed days to May 21, 2003.

While it charts the campaign, from our elimination in the Champions League by FC Basel, right through to the UEFA Cup final against Porto, this book also records the stories of Celtic supporters and their favourite memories of this European adventure. Not surprisingly, most of these stories come from Seville. Tales of ticket searches and travel plans, of meeting up with old friends and new faces in Seville … and of the excitement, joy, despair and, ultimately, pride at what we saw in the Estadio Olimpico.

It was 33 years since Celtic last reached a European final, far too long for a club of our size and stature. Getting to the 2003 UEFA Cup final caught the imagination of supporters. We might have been told that it was great for Scottish football – and I suppose it was – but this was primarily, and most importantly, a triumph for Celtic Football Club.

It was astonishingly brilliant. Enjoy re-living it.

Chapter One

Memories of Seville

ON the plane back from Portugal, I was still numb and searching for my true feelings about the match. Anger at Porto's diving, frustration at their timewasting but, at the same time, my chest was swollen with pride at the team's magnificent efforts.

Flicking through June's *Esquire* magazine, I read an article about Real Madrid called 'Defeat is not an option' and came across a poetic quote from Jorge Valdano, Real's Director of Football. Talking about the contrasting approaches taken by Manchester United and Lazio to respective past championship decider matches, he talked of Manchester United's "generosity and courage" compared with Lazio's "mean, anxious, measured and fearful" approach in the same situation. He then wrote a line that summed up exactly how I felt about the UEFA Cup final – *"I'd rather die like Manchester United than live like Lazio."*

FRANK DEVOY

HAVING booked the tickets pre the Liverpool game on Uefa.com, I was relieved that I was finally on my way. There had been many stops and starts where panic would set in and I now believed this to be over, although I would be happier when I was standing in the Estadio Olimpico.

The stops and starts included trying to get my tickets to go over to Seville, where would I go? Cadiz? Portugal? Costa Del Sol? In the end I booked for Torremolinos in the Costa Del Sol. I had to book for myself and the girlfriend while a mate from work was constantly on the phone: "Book this. How about that? Can you get this?" I thought I was gonna crack up a few times but I never.

The Boavista game was a nightmare. I don't know how many times I had sums flashing through my head, thinking about how much I had spent to get to Seville and momentarily thinking that it was wasted … Then up popped the King of Kings.

We flew down to Gatwick on the Sunday. When we arrived you would have thought it were Glasgow, the number of Hoops there. We dozed for six hours waiting for our connecting flight to Malaga. Arriving in Malaga, the rumours started that all the buses were fully booked and there were no trains left! How were we going to get from Malaga to Seville, 130 miles away?

As I said I was now on my way, heading down a relatively straight and modern motorway with my scarf tied to the outside of the car. Every second car that went by was beeping their horns in appreciation, not to mention all the buses full of fellow Celtic supporters. My guts were starting to turn. I felt like I did on my first game at Parkhead just three short years ago.

We parked at a hotel right at the very beginning of Seville and for those of you who were there, you will know that the stadium is about 15 miles away. We walked through the streets, more and more amazed with the sea of green and white round every corner. We joined in with the party at the cathedral and the square in the hope to meet my mate Les who had flown in that morning and was sitting next to us. We arranged to meet but then the phone lines went down so there was no chance.

We started to walk to the stadium, still not believing that it was as far as it was. No taxi wanted to stop, but when we arrived I met Les and all of a sudden it seemed worthwhile – we were at the Estadio Olimpico and it felt like Christmas. We entered the stadium as the gates opened and were there three hours before kick-off. The blister on my heel felt like the size of a football but when the King of Kings scored that first goal all was forgotten. Pure joy!

The result never turned out the way we wanted it and the walk back to the car was the longest three hours I have known, not to mention the drive home, but when I woke up the next morning I remembered why it was so good to be a Celtic supporter and that the Bhoys had done us proud.

Could defeat ever taste so sweet again? I will never forget my first European travel, only to find Paradise.

STEVEN FORSYTH, (Lisbon Lions Stand)

I TRAVELLED over from Australia for the game, having only managed to get a week off my work, so the whole trip has gone by so quickly. But a moment on the Tuesday before the match will live with me forever. I had just secured my ticket, which was being couriered from Glasgow to Seville by my sister, and taking hold of the ticket was a major cause for celebration for me.

I had secured a ticket earlier, only for it to fall through. Then I got another one, and it fell through too. On receiving the ticket I quickly rejoiced with about three or four pints of sangria and we headed off to the Charlie and the Bhoys gig in the park.

After quite a few more sangrias and some unbelievably large vodkas I was in party mode. The drunk-sounding compere was attempting to lead the Celtic support into a few tunes, and I heard him shout "Who do you want to see?" The crowd responded: "BILLY McNEILL!!" Again he repeated "Who do you want to see?"

"BILLY!" I was losing it at this stage and was screaming at the top of my voice. I couldn't think of anyone else in the world at that point in time that I wanted to see more than Billy McNeill. Then who do I see walking towards me – Big Billy. I was delighted. My sister grabbed him, I grabbed him and we thrust a camera into his face and got the shot. Billy hugged us then breezed on towards the stage and appeared

The Road to Seville

in front of the thousands to the tune of *You'll Never Walk Alone* – always a tearjerker but in this case I was inconsolable, slumped to my knees. It was all too much, but I quickly straightened myself up with a few more jugs of sangria and went on to have the night of my life – which incidentally ended on Sunday!

GERRY O'NEILL

IT starts with lucky white heather, lucky white heather. I had the best time in my life in Seville thanks to the Bhoys. We flew from Glasgow to Luton to Gibraltar, then hired a car from Gibraltar to drive on to Seville.

We parked the car at 8:30am on Wednesday in Seville. then we went off to have the most enjoyable day ever, watching the match in a bar. On returning to the car at 12:30am, my brother and I discovered the car window was broken and all our personal luggage had been stolen. Three police stations later, still no English-speaking policemen to report the incident. We decided to travel back down to Gibraltar and report the break-in there.

On returning to Glasgow, I put my film in to get developed, which was left in the car ashtray. I was informed by the store on Monday, June 2 that they had lost my film. I e-mailed their customer services to inform them of the importance of the film, which contained my snaps of the Bhoys in Seville.

They phoned me the next day and told me they are going to sent an apology and a £25 voucher, which I will give to charity, so I can keep a photocopy of the voucher and show my children and my grand-children my memories of Seville in years to come.

JOSEPH DENNISON

AS my son Jesper and I watch Celtic play Boavista in the semi-final of the UEFA Cup, I knew I was on my way to Seville if we managed to win. Then up pops Henrik late in the game to send Celtic fans around the world in to raptures of joy. 2-1 on aggregate and we are off to Seville! So who else is coming along? Gerry and Tommy Butler and Gerry's Irish mate Steve Brennan, who was based in Dublin.

We had been promised tickets for the game and so we arranged the trip. Flying from Glasgow and staying in the Santa Cruz district of Seville, it was all starting to sound great. As usual, nothing ever goes to plan and this was always going to be the case with a game of such importance! The week before we are due to fly out, there's a problem with our tickets, and to make matters worse everyone in Scotland and every Celtic supporter around the world seems to want to go to Seville for our first European final in 33 years. Gerry has started to whine constantly!

The day before the game and we are flying out of Prestwick instead of Glasgow, which is now in overload! So we get to bed early and up again at 2:30am and ready to leave at 3am for the airport. I'm already exhausted. I creep around the house getting ready, while the family sleeps soundly. It's time to put on the ceremonial gear – kilt, Hoops jersey and make ready the sombrero! Gerry arrives at the house and we walk out in to the darkness of the early morning, but even now at 3am the birds are singing. Don't they ever sleep?

We're off and already we are warming up with the CD blasting *Hail! Hail! The Celts Are Here*. We arrive at Prestwick to find the concourse engulfed by waves of Celtic fans all decorated in the Green and White Hoops. It's already a spectacle and

Memories of Seville

we haven't even left Scotland! We take off as the light rain of a Scottish darkened morning starts to hit the windows of our plane and before you know it we're there. The doors of the aircraft open to see us met by a searing heat that sweeps in to the cabin and immediately puts a smile on your face. 'Seville here we come.'

We head by bus for our drop-off point – the Plaza De Toros in Seville. The bus is hot and the traffic is slow and we start to realise how many Celtic fans are actually here in the city, passing many buses packed with fans crawling through the streets. It's a great reception from the Seville locals, who wave at us and are all smiling. I don't think they realise just how big this pilgrimage is going to be and maybe we don't either? Then we start to spot the Porto supporters as we near the centre and it's already a party as they wave and chant at us.

We drop our bags at the hotel and then stop in the nearest square to have an ice-cool beer. How nice that glides down your throat in the searing 30-degree heat that has greeted us in Seville. We are all parched and this has put new life back in to aching legs! While sitting there we admire the beautiful people, both men and women, of Seville as they pass by us. We admire the tanned skin and then compare them to our white legs showing under our kilts and shorts. As we start to take in the atmosphere around the city centre with only hours before kick-off, you can feel the excitement building in the air. Everywhere you look people of all ages, gender and nationalities are chanting and singing the Celtic songs and you could be at Parkhead if it wasn't for the sun, palm trees and truly wonderful Andalucian architecture that surrounds us. The Porto fans are doing their best to take us on but it's not good enough and they concede by trying and join in, what a carnival this is.

It's not long now before the big occasion so we head back to the hotel to cool down with a shower and then it's off again on the long walk to the stadium. Many thousands of fans both Celtic and Porto are now making their way along the route together, with songs being heaved out by tired lungs after hours of singing and a colourful parade of green and blue tops merging against the white-washed walls and clear blue skies of Seville.

The local people are lining the street to watch this spectacular and colourful procession take its route to the main walkway along the river, Rio Guadalquivir and across the bridge towards the stadium. We are now within touching distance of the Estadio Olimpico and the excitement is at fever pitch and the expectations of so many fans from Portugal and Scotland are only moments away from either being realised or being dashed. What is our fate, I wonder to myself as I walk through the crowds?

We arrive and as we come up through the gates to the main stadium we are met by a wall of noise and colour that I have never even heard or seen at Parkhead, where we are known for being able to put on a show! It's incredible and I have butterflies in my stomach as the songs start to pile out from both ranks of supporters. Gerry, Tommy and I have ended up in the Porto end but thankfully it's good-humoured.

Gerry comments on the light within the stadium and remarks, "This special continental light," and he's right. It is a strange light with a big red sun setting behind the glass walls at the dug-out side of the stadium. It's a bit surreal, having left the rain only a number of hours ago back in Scotland!

The game's underway and the chanting starts, but what is apparent is the heat is still stifling and I am boiling just watching these guys play football, so what must it be like down there in the cauldron and heat of the action? All around there is noise and colour, as people to my left in the Porto end are holding up blue pieces of cardboard, and to my right the Celtic fans, row upon row climbing up in to the evening sky, with banners festooned across the trackside and hanging from every possible visible point.

All square at 2-2, with Henrik proving his worth again and it's pulsating stuff. Into extra-time and there's no let-up in the action. Disaster! They score in the second period and it's 3-2 and they hold on to win. Our players looked drained and I feel washed out! I look around and watch grown men wipe away the tears from their sun-baked faces, and supporters from both sides are wrapped up in all kinds of emotions of both joy and despair. They don't know what to say or do, just hug! A Porto fan holds out his hand and we shake and then I'm pulled close and he says, "Celtic are great." I feel my eyes start to well up. It's all getting too much, so we depart the stadium, leaving the Porto fans to celebrate their victory.

It's an even longer walk back to the hotel and there's an eerie quiet that follows us as we trudge along the riverside. Nearly 80,000 Celtic fans in Seville and not one arrest – what an accolade for our fans. The next day it's time to fly home and to debate what went wrong, but one thing we all agree on is that our thanks must go to Martin O'Neill and to the Celtic players for making this dream trip a reality, and although the result didn't go our way, we did ourselves proud in Seville.

As Gerry dropped me off at home my mind started to wander to the next pilgrimage. How long it will be before we do it again? Hopefully it won't be too many years and I hope that it was a trip that my son Jesper and I could make together. Time to hang up the sombrero, Porto scarf and UEFA flag for another year and sit back with a cup of tea and dream of our next glorious adventure.

NICK PRICE, Edinburgh

GETTING the match tickets, hotel and flights into Spain seemed the hardest part over and done with. We had managed to get flights from Luton to Malaga and arrived at Waverly Station with happy anticipation of the days ahead. I had checked and double-checked with GNER that there would be no rail-works that weekend.

Unfortunately, someone at GNER had been lying through his or her teeth and there was not one single train heading south! Coaches were laid on, but by the time one of these things pulled into Luton, the whole trip would have been up in smoke. With neither the two of us holding a driver's licence, the only option left open to us was a lift from Sully's hungover and angry Dad.

When we eventually arrived at Luton Airport, things were looking up – cheering on the Celts was Nadine Coyle from the band Girls Aloud. Soon the place was teaming with fans and the camera crew from some reality TV show was having a field day. There was some good-natured banter with the air-hostess but the question on most people's lips was; why was millionaire jockey, Tony McCoy flying on EasyJet? As soon as the plane hit the runway, every fan aboard broke into 'Hail, Hail, the Celts are here', the first of many magical moments on an unforgettable trip.

The next day was spent trying to sort out travel from Malaga to Seville; there was not one bus or train to be had. We had even heard of people taking taxis but, as Euros dwindled, this was not an option. The Gremlins and Old Nick, whatever you want to call it, were still trying to put a spanner in the works. I remembered the

Memories of Seville

Germans who I wrote about for the *'Vorsprung Durch Celtik!'* article in the *Celtic View* were flying into Malaga. It was Matthias Kist to the rescue. Luckily Matthias had hired a minibus for himself and five other German Celts, with room for two more and fortune seemed on our side.

The marvel of Seville got more surreal with every step, it took a while to take it in. Just how many clubs in the world could bring a support like this and, not only that, but also one that could crack a smile from the Spanish Police? This was not just a mass exodus of Scots; it soon became apparent that our German companions were not our only international support. Celtic flags and accents from every corner of the globe spilled over onto the streets of Seville – New York, Canada, Australia, France and Bosnia were just a few of the ones we noticed. Some travelled for days on what seemed like a religious pilgrimage. The religious aspect was most apparent around the breathtaking Cathedral that for one day at least, was a mass of green and white hoops.

Within minutes of getting there I had met my old headmaster, Mr Dames of St Thomas of Aquinas, and a neighbour from down the street. There were fans bumping into each other who hadn't seen each other for ten years. Soon the fountains were flooding with Hoops and Tony Hamilton was on hand to capture the magic with the CelticTV film crew. What seemed like minutes later, Jackie Bird appeared and a bunch of us didn't need much persuading to pile in behind her for a live broadcast back home to *Reporting Scotland*.

While the German fans were ticketless, one of them had a contact at UEFA who had managed to get a spare ticket, with the promise of another later in the day. When the ticket materialised, it was between two of the more dedicated German fans for the golden brief. These guys had been to away to Vigo, Stuttgart and Boavista together, they didn't want to miss the final. Matthias and Harry decided that the only fair way to deal with the situation was to toss a coin. At this point Sully whispered to me that if the ticket were between him and me, he would sell the ticket and watch the game with a crate of beer under the big screen. If I knew Sully, he would have been half way to the stadium by now and no mistake, but fortunately we had tickets.

Just before Harry and Matthias tossed the coin, a local Spaniard had put on a fake Hoops top and decided to try and pickpocket some Celts by mingling into the crowd. When the affronted Glaswegian caught the Spaniard in the act, the local produced a knife. Fortunately the Spanish Police were down on him like a ton of bricks, with their batons doing cartwheels and the faultless Celtic fan made his way back to the comfort of his friends.

When the coin was eventually spun into the air, it was Harry who won the golden ticket. Matthias' face was tragedy personified. After offering our condolences, with time marching on we decided to head to the stadium. It has to be said UEFA should be rapped for a number of reasons – number one being the directions to the game were non-existent. We eventually managed to hail a taxi and reaching the stadium was like eventually arriving at the Promised Land.

It was like a who's who of Celts as we made our way in. There where shouts of "gonnae no dae that", for one of the sidemen from *Still Game* and *Chewin' The Fat,* perhaps for the millionth time that day. He didn't care though, he was as happy as the rest of us. Bernard Ponsonby was getting backslapped and tussled in a playful and good-natured manner by the fans. Even though we knew our tickets were for real, after some of the luck we had, there was always the lingering thought that the red light would flash on our way in but thankfully there was a flash of green and we were joining the party. Amazingly the Porto end was already full but slowly and surely the Estadio Olimpico began to resemble a home game for Celtic. The fans singing *You'll Never Walk Alone,* the huddle and the whole experience in general was ten times more heightened than any domestic game and more emotive for obvious reasons. Families and best friends might have been in different countries but everyone's hopes and dreams were united for one night only.

After the game emotions were running high. I think the Porto fans were amazed that the Celtic fans were still singing, some of the Porto support even began to chant Celtic; a truly marvellous moment. One Celtic fan decided to vent his frustration as he passed a tree, after a few disconnected slaps, the Hoops' fan broke down, only to start hugging the tree, apologising for his outburst. Obviously the dehydration has got to many of us and no wonder. At half-time there was not a drop of water in the stadium. I could not believe we were being ripped off for cups of ice. I had found an old bottle of water in my bag you could have boiled a Pot Noodle with.

Some fans were walking like John Wayne, obviously the chaffing had kicked in for many of us, walking for miles in all that heat! Many fans slept that night in the streets of Seville, sleeping where they fell, some had lost their friends, their passport and their flight but they didn't really care. For many of us it took days to sink in, it was like shock. Loosing everything else for many was conceivable but losing the cup just wasn't an option.

It was as if a malevolent force prised the thing from us and for many, that's what happened. The older guys seemed to take it on the chin better, full of stories of 1966 when Celtic reached the semi-final of the Cup-Winners' Cup, only to be pipped by Liverpool. The following year, however, we came back and won Europe's greatest prize.

Amazingly, the next day certain members of the press, the usual suspects, actually had the audacity to have a go at us. Not long ago, a European final seemed impossible, now Celtic look like contenders and can give anyone a game. We may have our detractors but over and above all we've got our footballing pride back with a bucketload of memories and that is something that will exalted throughout the world. For many, this wasn't the end but the beginning of a brave new chapter in the Celtic story.

RICHARD PURDEN

THE Omen: Got myself convinced that we would win after realising (in a moment of alcohol-fuelled inspiration) that my son, Calum, would be 2 years, 313 days old on the day of the final. When I sat on my Daddy's knee watching the 1967 European Cup final, I was, you've guessed it, 2 years, 313 days old.

Friendly thieves: My mate's brother got mugged in Seville while looking for a taxi. The bandits ran off with his wallet, containing cash, flight tickets, passport and, most importantly, his match ticket. Moments later, they returned his wallet minus cash and match brief, but still with passport and flight tickets. Even the Sevilla muggers were friendly! And no-one used the ticket!

International language: In a very posh coffee and cake shop near the

PRE-MATCH TENSION: *Celtic captain Paul Lambert and Henrik Larsson take in the atmosphere at the Estadio Olimpico ahead of the UEFA Cup final*

GHIRL POWER: *Richard Purden bumped into Nadine Coyle of pop band, Girls Aloud, at Luton Airport, and the Derry girl wished the Bhoys all the best in Seville*

WE'LL WALK A MILLION MILES: *this Celtic fan was prepared for any eventuality, including swimming to Seville if necesary, in order to get to the UEFA Cup final*

Memories of Seville

Cathedral, overrun with Hoops of course, it was five deep at the bar while, strangely, the ice cream counter was not so busy. Nevertheless one wee boy was being overlooked for service by the ice cream counter staff. He told his Mum who had been queuing for a drink for ages. In exasperation she stormed over to the ice cream counter and demanded, "Gonnae gie the wean an ice cream!" Which, naturally enough, the girl behind the counter understood perfectly.

GRAHAM SILCOCK

I WILL admit to having a lump in my throat and a tear in my eye when the Celtic fans inside the stadium sang *You'll Never Walk Alone* **in such rousing fashion as the Porto supporters celebrated their win.**

The Porto fans were struck dumb by the sight and sound of the green and white choir, then paid a generous and spontaneous tribute to the Celtic fans by applauding the hooped hordes for their loyalty and passion. In doing so they brought great credit upon themselves. If I live to be 100, I will never forget that moment. It encapsulated everything that is wonderful about Celtic, their fans, and football itself.

MARTIN G. HANNAN, Sports Writer, Scotland on Sunday

AS a Celtic fan looking back on a pleasing season with reasons to be cheerful, but one without a trophy in the cabinet, words fail me. To put it into football rhyming slang, and to paraphrase the opening of A Tale of Two Cities: It was the George Best of times, it was the Geoff Hurst of times.

We were never servile in Seville, and we were in-for-the-kill at Kilmarnock, but it was not to be. The gods that smiled on us over nine months pregnant with promise, chose to sneer when it mattered most. Life's a beach, and then you cry.

Sure, there are worse things in life than sloping off to Malaga in May and slumming it for three nights in a four-star hotel to see the Celtic compete in a European final for the first time in 33 years. Is that Malaga, or was I drinking heavy? Even if the bus taking you to the hotel you booked up for skirts that building and deposits you in one round the back that's still work-in-progress. There are worse things than forgetting to lift the bar from your mobile phone and being unable to get an outside line from your hotel room. Being incommunicado is better than being dumbstruck, and most of us were left speechless after a full-throttling, throat-constricting sojourn in Spain.

How do you take defeat, sir? One lump or two? There are worse things than losing dramatically on the domestic stage on goal difference to a team you dominated and outshone on the European stage. Worse things, too, than coming within five minutes of beating one of the most talented teams on the Continent. Even, if that team stand – or rather lie – accused of blatant playacting, flagrant diving, and vagrant time-wasting.

But there can't be many things worse than the frustration of watching the clock tick away on a brilliant performance in the Estadio Olimpico while an opposition player does his stretching exercises in your penalty box after scoring what proves to be the winning goal. That was the most surreal moment of a surreal experience. That's when I realised I was in Seville AND watching *The Bill*. In this episode a major robbery was in progress and the police were nowhere to be seen. Or rather, they were looking the wrong way. They should have been rooting out the den of thieves on the pitch rather than watching the crowd for trouble that would never come.

Derlei was booked for time-wasting for his breathtaking – to say the least - display of effrontery, but he should have faced a ten-year stretch for a crime against humility. He'll be laughing all the way to the bank when his exercise video comes out next month. But Derlei wasn't the only Porto player in no hurry to play ball. No sooner were his hamstrings back to their best than his keeper went down outside his own penalty box and stayed down so long he was pronounced dead - to shame. Up to that point several Portuguese men-o-war had been in a tug-of-war for a variation on the traditional Man of the Match Award.

They were competing for the less familiar prize of Mat of the Match, a fireside rug – or beach mat - given to the player who can take a tumble and stay down longest, also known as "doing a Coisty". Their goalkeeper, Vitor Baia, won hands down. MON (the Hoops!) himself timed Baia's bye-byes at 2 minutes and 20 seconds, the longest lie-down on record. At least brilliant Brazilian playmaker Deco deserved his plaudits. His team-mates were on the deck often enough to make you wonder if they were going for gold in Olympic Diving.

None of the old belly-flop at the local baths for these guys. It was world class. According to Spanish police, a Mr D. Balde, c/o Celtic Park, was cited as a witness. Mr Balde had attempted to execute a citizen's arrest on one of the suspects and was mistakenly apprehended and cautioned by the authorities.

This is to take nothing away from Porto ... except the cup they stole. While the Old Bill - as those watching at home can testify - were worrying about villains in villas and yobs with yachts, the crime of the century was being carried out right under their blue noses. The real crooks of the Costa del Sol were walking away with the best of gear in football booty, bold as you like. The getaway car was a team coach. Crafty or what? Interpol were alerted but failed to pick up the perpetrators at the airport. They couldn't catch the culprits at customs either, despite the use of sniffer dogs trained to detect the scent of champagne and silver. Rumour has it that the UEFA Cup final is to be the subject of a Crimewatch Special.

Okay, I admit Porto started well against a nervous Tic, and they have some superb skill in their side, but fair's fair, and that's not the way they played. Their un-sporting behaviour left a scar on the face of the beautiful game. When we were young, we played a game called Best man Shooter, where one kid went shooter and the rest had to pick the way they wanted to go – bazooka, bren gun, or beretta. The shooter then picked the best fall guy, the one who went down in the most dramatic fashion, and he'd be shooter next time round.

This game was usually played with the marksman at the bottom of a grassy knoll and his victims at the top, so they could fit in a few spectacular twists and turns on their way down. A few Porto players had evidently enjoyed this childhood pastime too, and they were able to pretend to roll down a hill on flat ground.

According to legend, Seville was founded by Hercules, and commentators are right to say that Celtic's efforts were Herculean. But it's Hercule Poirot whose services were needed after the game. "We wiz robbed" is the oldest excuse in the world, I know, but when the crime is carried out in front of 50,000 spectators and witnessed by a worldwide audience of 500 million there must be a Danny McGrain of truth to it. The coast of Spain close to Seville isn't called the Costa del Crime for nothing, and it was the scene of floodlit robbery on May 21. Security was tight, as were many of the supporters.

The first time I went abroad I had my back-bin tanned and had to walk home, so I've always kept a tight rein on my wallet. That's my story and I'm sticking to it. Before the game, there were the usual warnings about pickpockets. What the police didn't tell us was that they'd be sporting football strips and be aided and abetted by an official. Apparently the Guardia Civil questioned the Slovakian referee for several hours after the match before charging him with wasting police time. The ref later blew the whistle on police brutality, but the cops claim he took a dive on the station steps.

Seville has won itself another European final in 2005, this time the Champions League. I hope to be back for that to cheer on the Hoops, but I also hope UEFA and the stadium bosses can get their act together. Simple things like buying a programme or getting a drink in the searing heat were made difficult if not impossible by poor service.

The catering was of the kind you'd expect to find at a jumble sale or a school disco. Behind temporary hoardings a handful of staff served from boxes. For safety reasons all drinks had to be poured so that soft drinks containers could not be used for purposes other than those for which they were intended. But the upshot was that while the queue was ten-deep those serving took forever to pour cups of coke by hand. Then they ran out of first water, then coke. I was faced with the absurd spectacle of having to buy beer to wet my whistle by the end of the match. It was on a treble chance trip to the toilet, programme vendor, and refectory-style drinks outlet that I missed Henrik's second goal. I ran upstairs to catch the celebration. Get with the programme UEFA. Let's have seat-by-seat vendors like they do at baseball matches in the States. They're way ahead over there when it comes to catering for major sporting events.

You'll never walk alone, but many supporters, myself included, travelled alone to Seville because friends and family couldn't get tickets. By contrast, those without tickets travelled together and watched the game together. The rollercoaster ride on the bus from the hotel to the stadium was unforgettable. The fact that there was an actual rollercoaster outside the stadium was obviously a way of coming down. And who will forget the chaos in the coachpark after the match? After 90 minutes of searching for your bus, and finally finding it, you felt as if you'd won the cup. These celebrations were repeated all over the coach park. Result.

Seville was brill, and we'll be back. When you've got a grown man either side of you in tears, crying for their Momo and their Bobo, one sombre in a sombrero, the other sniffling behind sunglasses, you know you're standing shoulder-to-shoulder with the greatest – and greetiest – fans in the world. Funny enough, I was dry-eyed till I saw the cover of the last *Celtic View* of the season. I wasn't sure how they'd handle that bruising finale, but when I saw those indelible images of the smiling faces of players who gave all they had and then some I have to fess up and say I was in pieces. A lot of people blew their summer holiday kitty on that last roll of the dice. When your girlfriend puts your trip on her visa on the understanding that it's the trip of a lifetime it's hard to say we'll be back next year. "I thought you said it was a once-in-a-lifetime opportunity?" "Well, yes, but if MON gets the money for another couple of signings and ..."

The Road to Seville

Celtic's opponents were guilty as sin of gross time-wasting, but the net result of going to Seville was never a waste of time. Portugal continues to haunt Paradise. If the cup-winning team of 1967 fought like lions in Lisbon, then there was something of the wildcat too in the side that came so close to matching them in Seville against a Portuguese outfit who should have been wearing masks. There is a member of the cat family that suits the Celts who played with pride in Spain. The 'serval' is a tawny black-spotted long-legged African tiger-cat. It takes its name from the Portuguese word 'cerval', meaning 'deerlike'.

Deerlike is as good a way as any of describing the spring-heeled headers of Hooray Henrik that took us to the gates of glory. The Bhoy Wonder didn't deserve a runners-up medal. He should have been kissing the cup while Porto picked up their flip-flop divers-down medals. The Lisbon Lions remain unsurpassed in terms of achievement, but the Servals of Seville will never be forgotten. Here's hoping Henrik goes on to score more goals in European finals than Tommy Gemmell.

WILLY MALEY

TACKY tourists? Us? Hell no! Excusing the milk bottle white legs, lobster red foreheads, and bottles of beer in hand, we were sophisticated travellers, who were indistinguishable from the locals.

We even spoke the lingo, well three words – *'Donda Esta Estadio?'* Enough to get by, so we were informed, and three words that our self-appointed leader made frequent use of as we paraded through the streets of Seville on our way to the final of the UEFA Cup 2002/03 – Yes, Celtic FC were there.

This is what it's all about, I thought to myself, as our posse joined forces with many other hoop-wearing sophisticated travellers en-route, and joined together in verses of *Willie Maley, Hail Hail*, and many other classic tunes. The locals were amazed at this vast green and white army on parade, and indeed many rushed for their cameras, many were given scarves, many cheered us on, and others simply wished us well for the game.

It was close to two months previously that several members of our club had decided to take a chance and obtain tickets through UEFA for the final, prior to the conclusion of the Liverpool tie, and subsequent semi-final. Stupidity? Tempting Fate? Optimists? You name it we were told it – but sure, if we don't make it Liverpool will, and well, the tickets can be sold on to their fans was our response. We didn't want to appear cocky, but deep down this had to be our year, we were fated to be in Seville – weren't we?

Liverpool came and went, then Boavista, and the almighty scramble for tickets and flights began. I was a little hasty in my travel arrangements, indeed the wheels were set in motion on the Tuesday prior to the second-leg of the Boavista game – I had decided irrespective of the result, I would be at the final. Dublin and Barcelona would be my stop-offs en-route to Seville, many others travelling through Portugal, Madrid, and Malaga.

Seville was the life – soaring temperatures, beautiful city, one big happy Celtic family, and no trouble! The afternoon spent in the Placa San Francisco will live with me 'til my dying day. So much craic, so many friends, so many memories! We had almost forgotten the reason we were in Seville – a game of football!

The march to the stadium drifted in quickly, and the butterflies suddenly

Memories of Seville

descended upon glimpsing the various entrance gates and backdrop of the Estadio Olimpico. As we bade good luck to the various members of our group, we made a hasty entrance into the stadium, and took up our respective seats to savour the build-up. Glorious!

Don't wish it away, we were constantly reminded, it'll come and go soon enough, – savour it! The players soon entered on to the pitch, warmed up and returned to the dressing rooms to leave us in the company of the internationally renowned Las Ketchup! C'mon, let's get this show on the road, I thought. I glanced around the stadium, said one final prayer, and rose to my feet to welcome the two sets of teams on to the pitch – *You'll Never Walk Alone!* – Never!

The game came and went quickly, with defeat inflicted by a killer 'silver goal' at the end of a great spectacle. The Bhoys had done us proud however, fought for every ball, and led by our 'King of Kings' had demonstrated that we are a match for any team. Deco had received the Man of the Match accolade, but in my mind Porto's Greg Louganis and our own Henrik Larsson were more worthy recipients.

The long and winding road back into the city centre was a subdued affair, and looking around I pondered the impeccable behaviour of these fans, and their loyalty. Surely these fans were deserving of as much credit as the team, and briefly pausing; I contemplated – what if …?

I suppose it is better to have loved and lost, than never loved at all!

FRANKIE McKAY, Lurgan.

HAVING been to Liverpool and Stuttgart, we knew we had to go to Seville. Me and a couple of mates decided it would be a great idea to dress up as Leprechauns to bring a bit of the luck 'o the Irish to our beloved Celtic.

On the day of the game, however, in 36 degree heat with serious hangovers it didn't seem so clever. There we stood outside our hotel complete with hats, jackets, beards etc. and of course our Hoops, laughing at how ridiculous we each looked and wondering how we would be received by the thousands of Hoops around the town and especially around Flaherty's bar.

We wandered down the town getting a few smiles and the odd photo as we went. Then we reached Flaherty's and all hell broke loose. We stood out like sore thumbs with our outfits and everyone wanted their picture taken with us, among Bhoys and flags from as far a field as New York, Bahamas, Sydney, Bahrain and Limerick. This was brilliant craic. We then decided to walk down towards the fountain to meet some mates, which was about 500 yds away. It took nearly an hour. Every five steps, and we were stopped for a photo. Excellent.

We eventually got to the stadium and were just chilling with a couple of brews as Leprechauns do in 36-degree heat when another load of Bhoys wanted to take pictures of us, and among them was the legend who is Tommy Burns. We even got our picture in the *Celtic View*. What happened in the stadium was not deserved by our wonderful fans. And people will look back on this match as the trophy that was stolen from Celtic, rather than won by Porto. This left a little sour taste in all of our mouths, but the memories of this trip and the craic in Seville for those few days will live with me till my dying day. Top o' the mornin to ya!

DON MOLONEY, Limerick
(The other two Leprechauns were: Pat Keating, Waterford and Pat Nagle, Dublin)

The Road to Seville

MY son had a ticket to the UEFA Cup final to cheer on his beloved Celtic. Not being the brightest, he had failed to book a flight to Seville, but he managed to organise something, flying from the Midlands to Malaga.

The phone rings … son wants mum to sort out how he is to get from Malaga to Seville. Forty-five minutes later, mum has succeeded in getting son booked on a train to Cordoba and then on to Seville. First problem … how near to Malaga Airport is the train station (mum allowed two hours). Second problem … mum didn't know time or date of return flight from Malaga. Being a bright mum, she guessed son would want to stay in Seville after the match, so booked him on the late afternoon train to Malaga the following day.

Day of the match – mum paces the floor. Had son's plane landed on time? Had enough time been allowed to get to the station for the train? Did he remember to change at Cordoba? Did he arrive in Seville in time for the match?

The match started – the phone rings. Son is in a queue outside the stadium. "What is happening?" he asks. Mum then has to commentate on the match. Mum isn't as bright as she thought. Apart from Larsson, she doesn't know the names of the players.

The commentary went: "Green man has the ball, passes to another green man … Now a blue man has it…" and so on. Ten minutes later son is in the stadium and strange commentary can cease. A thirsty, hungry son arrived home 6am on May 24, having had a fantastic time.

MRS MAUREEN O'NEIL, Colliers Wood, London

I HAVE been involved in sports travel since 1970 and have had the good fortune to have been involved in organising tours to almost every major sporting event, including Olympic Games, World Cup FInals and UEFA Cup Finals.

For this year's UEFA Cup final in Seville, our company organised two charters for the game, and I feel that everyone connected with Celtic Football Club must be complemented on the performance of your supporters in Seville.

The pride, behaviour and composure of the thousands of persons who made the journey to Seville was just incredible. This was more than a football final. I felt it was the coming together of one huge family, all of whom showed a respect for each other and the 'hosts' they were visiting. The created a party atmosphere which I personally have never seen before and am unlikely to ever see again.

The supporters must be shown to the world as the role model of how football should be watched and how supporters should be seen. It was an honour and privilege to be associated with the occasion and one that I shall treasure for the rest of my life.

DAVID DRYER, Product Development Manager, The Travel Studio, London

The Road to Seville

DRESSED TO IMPRESS: *traditionally dressed Spanish dancers were part of the UEFA Cup final build-up, which included a performance by local band, Las Ketchup*

PARTY BHOYS AND GHIRLS: *Seville became a sea of green and white as over 80,000 Celtic supporters, many of them wearing the new Hoops top, took over the Spanish city and enjoyed a week-long party, much to the delight of the locals*

IS IT A BIRD?...IS IT A PLANE?...NO, IT'S SUPERBHOY!
Never mind that the temperature in Seville in the 90s, this Celtic fan had already decided on his costume and he was going to wear it. What his pre-match weight was, we don't know, but it's a fair bet he flew back from Seville a fair bit lighter!

Memories of Seville

EVERYTHING'S GONE GREEN: *Seville Airport was overflowing with Hoops' fans, while, below, a piper leads the Celtic supporters in song in the centre of the city*

Chapter Two

FC Basel: One door closes...

by Paul Cuddihy

"If you start at the very beginning, it's a very good place to start."
MARY POPPINS

THE sense of anticipation that enveloped Celtic Park prior to the first leg of the Champions League qualifier against FC Basel was almost tangible. We were just 180 minutes away from another adventure into the most glamorous club tournament in the world. Soon, some of the biggest names in football would be making their way to the East End of Glasgow to be put to the sword by a side that maintained a 100 per cent home record in the competition the previous season.

The stadium packed to the gunwales, the floodlights shining down on the hallowed turf, the massive Champions League flag shimmering in the centre circle as a group of lucky local youngsters gripped it and waved it about. The orchestral strains of the tournament's theme tune – does anyone know what that's called – as the teams strode out of the tunnel and on to the park, sending a shiver down the spine that was only surpassed when the massed ranks of Celtic fans sang *'You'll Never Walk Alone'* before breaking into a roar of deafening capacity as the green and white hooped players huddled together in one, final pre-match ritual.

These were the memories of season 2001/02 which floated in the air on Wednesday, August 14, 2002, along with the self-belief that more of the same was on the way, perhaps with the added bonus of participation in the second group stages of the Champions League, and then.... Who knows?

Yet, the problem with raising the expectations of football supporters is that they expect more. It didn't matter that the pre-match pronunciations coming out of Celtic Park from manager and players were that of cautious respect for FC Basel. The fans knew better. We were Celtic and they were, well, they were just a team from Switzerland, a land famous for chocolate, cuckoo clocks and a secretive banking system. But football? We were as good as through already.

Whether people had conveniently forgotten the defeat against Neuchatel Xamax, back in 1991, or it had just been so traumatic that the memory banks had erased all trace of it, Celtic's last encounter against Swiss opposition, against FC Zurich in 1998, had ended abruptly and disastrously. Then again, it was a different Celtic now; better players, better manager, and infinitely better-run off the park. What could possibly go wrong?

The road to Seville had begun as the road to Manchester but was quickly re-routed after our encounter with FC Basel. It's important, even in celebrating a magnificent European campaign that saw Celtic reach their first European final for 33 years, to begin with disappointment and defeat. As supporters, we can only speculate – and often do – on what might have been and what could, or should have been.

You know that, even 20 years from now, the feeling, the conviction will remain that the UEFA Cup should have returned to Glasgow in 2003. If Bobo Balde hadn't been sent off. If the referee had been a stronger personality. If Porto hadn't play-acted, or time-wasted. If we had only gone in front when the game was tied at 2-2 and Porto looked as if they weren't capable of coming from behind. Ifs and buts and maybes…

On the road to Seville, similar conjecture would occasionally surface as each round was successfully negotiated. Was the defeat against FC Basel a blessing in disguise? Were the lessons learned from that tie more valuable than another crack at the Champions League? Was it the final piece in the jigsaw that completed the picture and made Martin O'Neill's side a formidable European outfit, capable of meeting and beating sides from the best leagues on the continent and, ultimately, make them worthy UEFA Cup finalists? As supporters, we don't know for sure, but our performances after defeat in Switzerland, especially away from home, suggest that something was gained from the setback.

One thing must be cleared up, however, before any analysis of the Champions League qualifier is conducted, and that is the proper pronunciation of our Swiss opponents. Is it 'Basel' or 'Basle'?

I have to inform you that it is Basel, though I realise there will be those who still choose to disagree with me. After all, why would a football team have a boy's name or be named after a herb; Basil Fawlty, Basil Brush, basil, but 'We'll support you evermore, FC Basel, FC Basel!' It doesn't seem right, but, hey, I don't make the rules.

Switzerland is a country with four distinct languages – French, German, Italian and Romansch. The city of Basel nestles in the German speaking part of the country, hence the harsher pronunciation of their city, and football team's name. I know this, not because of any geographical expertise on my part, but simply because I spoke to their supporters when I was there and, to a man, or woman, their pronunciation was 'Basel'.

More of Switzerland later, but I'm jumping the gun a little. There's the small matter of the first leg at Celtic Park and, as was previously alluded to, the relaxed complacency of the support was not reflected by the manager. In his programme notes prior to the home leg, Martin O'Neill sounded what was, with hindsight, a prophetic warning about our opponents.

"I can assure you that Basel will prove extremely difficult opponents," the Celtic manager wrote. "Having had them watched on a number of prior occasions, I myself took in their second-leg victory over Slovakian champions MSK Zilina in the last round of this competition, a victory they secured with an extremely convincing performance.

"A great deal has been said and written since the draw was made, much of it suggesting that we start this evening's match as massive favourites to progress. For us, however, complacency is not even an issue. Basel are, without doubt, a good side, with numerous players of genuine calibre within their ranks. They won the double in Switzerland last season, clinching the league championship by a comfortable margin, and our players are certainly under no illusions as to the kind of performance which will be required to see us through over the two legs."

And O'Neill's caution was echoed by Chris Sutton, although the big Englishman also touched on something that had been a glaring failure of Celtic's European campaigns over the past 23 years – that of remaining involved after the turn of the year.

"We've got to go into the game here tonight confident but Basel will be a very tough side for us," Sutton explained ahead of the first leg at Celtic Park. "They are champions of Switzerland and they'll be no mugs. They've had to get through a hard qualifying test to get this far and because we're seeded in some ways it makes it more difficult than last season.

"The pressure was off us when we played Ajax in Amsterdam and we played as though there was no pressure on us and got an excellent result out there. It would be nice to progress a stage further though. Last season we had some good nights and some memorable games but it would be good to go a little beyond that and still be playing in Europe after Christmas."

Whether any of the Celtic support heeded the warning from players or manager is doubtful, but O'Neill was shrewd enough to know it would be a difficult encounter and he was trying to rein in people's expectations. The disappointment when we exited the competition tended to suggest the ploy hadn't been an altogether successful achievement.

As was the norm in European matches, our opponents made a visit to Celtic Park the evening before the match. Ostensibly, it was for a final training session although it had as much to do with letting the players see first-hand the arena they would be performing in. Celtic Park is an imposing structure, the biggest and most enduring symbol of the Irish in Scotland, and a source of pride to every Celtic supporter, though it must still be difficult for players to imagine, as they train in the empty stadium, their own voices echoing round the ground what it will be like when nearly 60,000 people have taken the seats.

If Martin O'Neill and his players were uttering words of caution over FC Basel, then watching them train on the Tuesday night offered a further insight. Several Celtic Park colleagues who had stayed late to take a first look at our Swiss opponents, were all of the same opinion. This was a good team we were up against. Even then, it appeared obvious that their crisp passing and quick movement on and off the ball would pose a threat to the Scottish Champions and despite the absence of any big-name stars, they played together as a unit. All of this became obvious the following evening.

Yet, despite the inclination to praise FC Basel, and their subsequent progression to the second stages of the Champions League was an illustration of their quality, the game at Celtic Park was, at the time, a triumph.

To win 3-1 at home, even allowing for the away goal FC Basel procured, was a good result, and given the strength of our defence, we had every confidence for the return leg in Switzerland. That away goal, however, was to prove very costly.

It had come as early as the second minute of the match when Basel's Argentine striker, Christian Giminez, stole in behind Joos Valgaeren and Bobo Balde to prod the ball past Rab Douglas and into the Celtic net. It was a stunning start to the game but fans barely had time to register the shock of seeing their team go a goal behind before Celtic were back on level terms. Stilian Petrov was brought down in the box and Henrik Larsson stepped forward to fire the ball beyond the reach of Pascal Zuberbuhler in the Basel goal. Celtic fans have come to expect Henrik Larsson to be their knight in shining armour, riding to the rescue of the cause when all can appear lost, and he does so with such amazing regularity that he could even be excused a penalty miss in the second half.

The game was played at a furious pace from start to finish, and, even allowing for Basel's fluent and creative play, it was Celtic who ultimately came out on top with two second-half goals. Chris Sutton put the Bhoys ahead on 53 minutes when he flicked a Neil Lennon shot into the net, and Momo Sylla volleyed home a Steve Guppy cross with just two minutes remaining to give Celtic a decent lead for the second leg. Guppy's introduction early in the second half for Bobby Petta was a masterstroke by the Celtic manager. Guppy's direct running and penetrating crosses caused Basel many problems, culminating in the third goal.

Another player who caught the eye at Celtic Park was the Turkish-born Hakin Yakan. The midfielder, who had taken Swiss citizenship alongside his brother, Murat, the Basel captain, was the fulcrum of everything that Basel created. His passing, movement and all-round ability made him stand out and his name would continue to crop up throughout the season in the newspapers as a potential transfer target for Celtic, one of several candidates suggested as 'the new Lubo'. He was to remain with FC Basel until the end of the season.

In the two-week period between the first match and the return leg in Switzerland, events took a disturbing and disgusting turn for Neil Lennon. The Celtic midfielder was selected to captain Northern Ireland in a match against Cyprus at Windsor Park. In the days leading up to the game, Lennon, a Catholic, received a death threat from loyalist terrorists which saw him first withdraw from the game and subsequently announce his retirement from international football.

The reaction from most fair-minded football supporters was simultaneously that of disgust and support for Neil Lennon. It did not make him change his mind, however, nor did it stop the booing which accompanied him to every football ground in Scotland. Most importantly for Celtic, however, it did not stop him from producing a degree of consistency throughout the rest of the season which was instrumental in the team ending up in Seville.

Celtic travelled to Switzerland; wary of the opposition but still confident enough in their own ability to believe they would be taking their place in the Champions League

STRIKE FORCE:
Both Henrik Larsson and Momo Sylla were on target in the first leg of the Champions League qualifier against FC Basel as Celtic won 3-1 at home, with Sylla's late goal giving Hoops fans a sense of optimism for the return leg in Switzerland

SWISS MISS:
A 2-0 defeat in Switzerland meant Celtic would not be competing the Champions League and would instead take part in the UEFA Cup.

first group stages draw. The most striking thing about arriving at Basel Airport is the fact that it is situated in two countries – Switzerland and France. The city of Basel borders both Germany and France and the fact that its airport encroaches on French territory is enough to merit a French border checkpoint within the terminal building. Making sure not to take a left turn and end up in France, the Celtic travelling party made their way through the airport and on to their pre-match base – the Hilton Hotel in the centre of Basel.

Like many European cities, Basel is clean. Its inhabitants, as well as possessing enough civic pride to keep their city relatively litter-free, are also very courteous drivers, which makes driving on the right side of the road less of a stressful experience than in other countries on the continent.

The trip to Switzerland also afforded me the opportunity to meet an FC Basel fan who had e-mailed me following the first leg. Frank Geiger had travelled to Glasgow two weeks before and during his visit had purchased the match programme. On his flight home, flicking through the programme, he read an interview with former Celt Stevie Murray, who had scored the all-important extra-time winner when Celtic had last played FC Basel, in the European Cup back in 1974.

Murray explained that, while the goal had given him immense satisfaction, particularly since it put Celtic into the semi-final of the competition, he had never ever seen it again on TV. This was, after all, before video recorders and saturation coverage of the beautiful game.

"I haven't seen it on film, video or anything else, and it's something I would love to have on tape. So, if anyone out there can help, it would be a great keepsake for me." said the former Celt.

These words stayed with Frank Geiger after he had returned home. Prior to his departure for Glasgow, he had set his video recorder to tape the game, including all the pre-match build-up, and what should he see during that but black and white footage of the 1974 encounter, including Stevie Murray's goal. We had arranged to meet up in Basel, where Frank duly handed over a copy of the tape, along with a FC Basel scarf, to pass on to Stevie Murray. The tape was later forwarded to a surprised but delighted Stevie Murray, who was able to re-live one of his great Celtic nights, courtesy of some grainy black and white television footage.

The St-Jakob Park Stadium is an impressive structure, though with a capacity only half that of Celtic Park. It was a new home for FC Basel and represented, along with the reported £10million manager Christian Gross spent on strengthening his squad, a significant investment by the club. Gross was a stern-looking coach familiar to many Celtic supporters only because of his short-lived and unhappy spell as manager of Tottenham Hotspur. He had guided Basel to a league and cup double the previous season, their first title success in 22 years, and was intent on making his mark in Europe.

Indeed, one apocryphal tale which surfaced after the tie was done and dusted was of Gross, prior to the second leg, playing the Champions League theme tune as a way of galvanising his charges – allowing them to imagine what it would be like for real and then demanding of them how much did they want it? True or not, the first 23 minutes of the game at St-Jakob's Park tended to indicate that they wanted it very badly indeed.

Giminez conjured up another early goal, though he waited until the eighth minute before finding the Celtic net, latching on to a defence-splitting pass from Hakan Yakin and guiding it past Douglas.

Celtic had lined up with a back four instead of their usual three-man defence, and slotted Momo Sylla in behind the front two, but the early exchanges showed a side apparently ill at ease with the new formation and it was no surprise when Basel scored a second goal. This time it was Murat Yakin who stole the limelight from his talented younger brother, heading home a corner to cancel out Celtic's two-goal lead and put Basel in a commanding position; no further goals would see the Swiss side through on away goals.

For the small band of Celtic fans who had made the trip to Switzerland, along with the thousands of others watching the game on CelticTV, half time couldn't come quick enough. I was no different from anyone else, though my reasons were slightly different.

This European tie saw my debut as a commentator for the Celtic website. Our regular commentator, Tony Hamilton, has broken his leg in a game of football against the Scottish press during Celtic's pre-season tour of Austria and was unable to travel. I stepped into the breach and had been looking forward to the experience. All those years of commentating on Subbuteo games were about to pay off. How wrong I proved to be.

It was the fastest and most tortuous 45 minutes of my football life, and that was without thinking about the scoreline. I never realised how fast the game really was until I tried to describe it for the benefit of the tens of thousands listening across the globe. Quite what they would have made of it all, goodness only knows, but let me assure each and every one of them that those 45 minutes were not as disjointed and fragmented as was portrayed. The only saving grace, for them as well as me, was the presence of Jonathan Gould alongside me as summariser. The then Celtic goalkeeper was a beacon of calm amid my ocean of verbal chaos and I will be forever grateful for his help.

While Martin O'Neill attempted to resuscitate his breathless charges during the break, making two changes in the process and reverting to his tried and trusted back three, I was gulping copious amounts of cold water and telling myself over and over again, 'Take your time, take your time', and I believe both Celtic and I enjoyed a better second half.

Momo Sylla and Paul Lambert were replaced at half-time by Didier Agathe and Steve Guppy, and Celtic went looking for the away goal which would push them into the lucrative Champions League group stages. There had been signs, towards the end of the first half that Martin O'Neill's side were not quite dead and buried and so it proved to be. Chances came and went. Petrov went close with a low shot just by the post. Hartson went even closer with a header which Zuberbuhler saved and, as the dying seconds of injury time ticked by, Chris Sutton side-footed a shot that appeared bound for the net but at the last moment just trickled wide of the far post.

The referee's final whistle heralded wide scenes of jubilation from Basel's vocal support. It also signalled the end of Celtic's Champions League dream before it had really begun. Martin O'Neill could not hide his disappointment, nor did he ever attempt to.

"It was a low point for us all, there's no point in denying that," he admitted. "Basel are a good side, but I did expect us to score over there. What I will say in the lads' defence is that, poor though their first-half performance was, I thought they

were very unfortunate not to score in the second period. Basel's keeper pulled off a string of really top-class saves, and on another night we could have scored three or four. It wasn't to be, though, and the fact that we're now out of the Champions League is something everyone has to cope with. That goes for me too because, although I've been as down as anyone about what happened, life goes on. There is still plenty to play for this season."

The sense of disappointment felt by the manager was echoed by his players. They had enjoyed a taste of Champions League football the season before – Juventus, Porto, Rosenborg – and wanted more of the same. The 3-1 result from the home leg had raised hopes of another campaign in the top tournament, but the 2-0 defeat in Switzerland cruelly dashed those hopes. Martin O'Neill's decision to change his formation came under scrutiny but for Henrik Larsson, it was a case of united we stand, united we fall.

"You win with each other and you lose with each other," explained Larsson after the game. "There's no such thing as having a good game when you lose. People will always criticise you when you don't get the result that people expect but that's football and I'm certainly old enough to handle that.

"I think Basel played really well, against us here at Celtic Park as well. I think the media maybe thought it was going to be an easy game because it was a team from Switzerland but we were under no illusion that it was going to be an easy game. We knew it was going to be hard because they showed they had quality players.

"You do expect to go and score because we have a good side that can go and create chances. We only created chances through set pieces on Wednesday and you're going to have nights like that. That's the way it is. You just have to try to learn and get on with it."

A subdued Celtic squad made the trip back to Glasgow, with the UEFA Cup draw to look forward to. While FC Basel were to face Liverpool, Valencia and Spartak Moscow in the first group stages before going on to meet Man United, Juventus and Deportivo in the next phase…

Celtic were paired with the unknown Lithuanian side FK Suduva. At the time, it seemed like a stark illustration of what we so nearly had but lost, though as the campaign progressed, the name of Suduva became the first of the 'V' teams to fall against Celtic as Martin O'Neill's men continued on the road that seemed to lead inexorably to Seville.

TONY HAMILTON'S EUROPEAN DIARY
Part 1: Them's the breaks!

I wasn't there – it had nothing to do with me. I do, however, remember it vividly as I'm sure you do too, perhaps for different reasons than mine. Having had time to look back though, I've come to the conclusion that the final outcome was reasonably predictable considering half of our support were calling them Basel while the other half said Basle. Getting their name right still seems pretty fundamental. Potato, tomato, I suppose.

I was in plaster from my toe to my groin, recovering from a leg break and cruciate ligament damage while doing my bit for Celtic during a pre-season kick about on a horrible pitch in a horrible town in a horrible country called Austria.

If you ever get the chance to go – don't! Even if it's free and the person who is giving it to you is throwing in free fags, a year's supply of your favourite tipple and an autographed picture of Hank Williams – decline.

There wasn't even a kettle in my hotel room – I had to go and buy one. Can you believe it? Come to think about it there wasn't a phone there either, but I did manage to get through to The Samaritans on my mobile.

Anyway, what did I get for my troubles and for giving everything that my sweet left foot and I could possibly give for Celtic's backroom team?

I'll tell you – they dragged me off to the side of the pitch, shouted abuse and expletives at me for getting injured, eventually and with great reluctance gave me some morphine and a lit cigarette and carried on with the game (there was an hour still to play) while I was screaming ala Ned Beatty in 'Deliverance'.

Incidentally, I didn't even know I had a cruciate ligament at the time let alone a damaged one – though it wasn't long before I realised why the professionals go off in a bit of a huff when they snap one of theirs. Ouch!

Anyway, I digress, not for the first or last time. Not being fit to travel, I remained in Glasgow and produced a very successful CelticTV pay-per-view event for the viewing masses. (Incidentally, I don't mind saying so myself about the success of the production – no-one else is likely to now, are they?)

There was never any doubt in my mind that 3-1 was enough to take us through to the Champions League and I felt I had did well to be suitably diplomatic when I put it to Martin O'Neill after the home match at Celtic Park that "it was still in the balance."

My tongue was in my cheek but he wasn't fooled. Only I was the fool, but it would be two weeks later before I realised why those who can, do, and those who can't, write and make TV programmes about it.

Yet I still couldn't see it happening. I had asked Joe, my dad, to pray (he is the prayer-er in the family) that we got a Russian team in our group. Maybe I should have asked him to pray for a Celtic goal instead?

But there was no need in my mind – it would be a mere formality – Christian Gross would get his comeuppance for giving my colleague Margot McCuaig the custard pie treatment when she asked for a pre-match interview at Celtic Park.

No-one treats CelticTV like that, I told myself. We'll show this pub team who the boss is.

Before I knew what had happened I was asking questions like where exactly is Lithuania and did that pub team really get drawn in the same group as Spartak Moscow?

But as the so-called "diminished UEFA competition" (so-called only by those who had faced the mighty Viktoria Zizkov in the first round) developed, and Celtic progressed, I soon realised that this was more than just your common or garden blessing in disguise.

This would be the start of an adventure I'll be able to pass on (with plenty embellishments) as part of Hamilton folklore to many future generations.

More importantly, this would be a guaranteed way of not having to pay HM Treasury a fiver every time I wanted a packet of fags - for a whole season!

Here's two for you Gordon Brown. Nice one Basel/Basle...

Chapter Three

FK Suduva: Starter for 10

by Joe Sullivan

THE longest journey, as they say, begins with a single step and in the case of Celtic's long and winding road to Seville and the UEFA Cup final, that first step on the stairway to heaven was embossed with the words FK Suduva.

The unknowns from Lithuania were introduced to the Celtic vocabulary when UEFA Chief Executive Gerhard Aigner drew the teams together at the first round draw in Monaco at the end of August 2002.

Just another hurdle to be breached on the road to European glory but the limelight of that particular splendor had long since ceased to shine on Celtic Park, although the glare of midweek European floodlit matches at Paradise were increasingly becoming a little more familiar over the previous two seasons.

So it could be argued that the first single step on the road to Seville was taken in the summer of the year 2000 when the arrival of Martin O'Neill at Celtic Football Club heralded a steady shift in the club's European vision.

The aspirations had always been there, but in the unbalanced decline since the heady years of the late 1960s and early '70s, the manpower, talent and experience to match those dreams and ambitions have rarely fused together to live up to the gauntlet thrown down by the great teams constructed by the legendary Jock Stein.

O'Neill's objectives were clear and set in stone before he even put pen to paper on his contract in the East End of Glasgow – he was looking for stability on the domestic scene and any advances made in Europe would be a bonus, something to be built upon, something to be honed, something that could take years.

The new manager's first foray on the continent was indeed in the UEFA Cup of season 2000/01 and Celtic disposed of Luxembourg's Jeunesse Esch and HJK Helsinki of Finland before losing out 3-2 on aggregate to Le Championnat side Bordeaux. No embarrassment there then, French football was on a roll and elimination by a side such as Bordeaux was hardly a shock, but by then the Celtic support had long been accustomed to packing the passports away early.

However, any angst regarding the relatively short European run was lost amid the unrolling fervour of O'Neill's first historic season as his side steamrollered to the domestic Treble and another legend was borne unto a Celtic history littered with legends.

The homegrown success though upped the ante for our European expectations but when the Celts were drawn against Ajax in the Champions League qualifiers of season 2001/02, even the most optimistic of Celtic supporters knew this would be a tough nut to crack and the realism was there that another short Euro run was on the cards.

This year, though, the passports would be doing a little bit more than gathering dust in a drawer as eyebrows throughout the continent were lifted a little bit higher when goals from Bobby Petta, Didier Agathe and Chris Sutton gave Celtic an amazing 3-1 win in the Amsterdam ArenA and people started to sit up and take notice of what was going down at Celtic Park. The Dutch side recorded a 1-0 win in Glasgow but Celtic were through to the group stages of the Champions League for the first time ever.

Juventus, Porto and Rosenborg were the partners in Group E and despite winning all of their home matches, including a 4-3 thriller over Juventus, Celtic narrowly failed to qualify and another invaluable lesson had been learned – a lesson in away-match etiquette that would prove vital in the following season's nerve-wracking campaign.

There was the cushion of the UEFA Cup though, but again the draw was unkind and Spanish giants Valencia proved to be the undoing of Celtic but only after extra-time and a heart-breaking penalty shoot out. Again the bitter pill of European ill fortune was sweetened by the Bhoys lifting their second successive league title and Celtic would once more be entering the European arena through the door marked Champions League.

Switzerland's FC Basel were old foes of Celtic on the European front but a lot of water had flowed under the bridge since the Bhoys recorded a 10-1 aggregate win over them in the Cup-Winners' Cup of season 1963/64.

No-one was expecting anything like that to happen this time and Celtic were more than delighted with the 3-1 home win back on August 14, but the tables were turned over in Basel as the Swiss side managed the 2-0 win to take them through on the away goals rule.

Once more the door was opened to the UEFA Cup but this time the door wasn't slammed shut in our faces by a team of the calibre of Valencia … The draw had been kind and club officials, supporters and journalists throughout the land were trawling the Internet to find out just who the hell FK Suduva were.

The info was sketchy to say the least but most of it centred on two main points. They had recorded a shock win over Norway's SK Brann Bergen in the preliminary qualifying round and their star striker, Tomas Radzinevicius, was being touted as one of the hottest young properties in European football.

Even in back home in Lithuania they were something of an enigma and their

The Road to Seville

qualification for the UEFA Cup was pure *Roy of the Rovers* stuff as they went through more back doors than a cat burglar to reach the UEFA Cup.

To put it in a nutshell, try to imagine if you can, Albion Rovers not only competing in Europe a couple of years down the line, but qualifying through being second best twice and you will get the general picture – probably!

After gaining independence from the USSR in 1990, the Lithuanian leagues started in 1992 running from April through to September and until two seasons ago, Suduva were just another regional league club from the town of Marijampole. Season 2000 however saw them finish joint top of the regional table with Sveikarta Kybartai and they narrowly won the title play-off 3-2.

In their debut season in the second division they finished an excellent second, but 14 points behind top-placed Polonija Vilnius … However, as the first-placed club are a feeder team for Zalgiris Vilnius and could not be promoted, Suduva made the step up straight into the first division but they also capped a great season by reaching the final of the Lithuanian Cup.

They did lose the final 3-1 to the country's top club FBK Kaunas, but as Kaunas had already lifted the first division title and qualified for the Champions League, Suduva fell through another back door and found themselves in the 2002/03 UEFA Cup. That wasn't the final chapter of the fairytale though, drawn against SK Brann in the qualifying round, it was thought that the minnows' affair with European football would be short-lived as the Norwegian side were odds on favourites to go through.

Amazingly, in the first leg in Bergen, Suduva found themselves 3-0 up inside the first 20 minutes and just to add more drama and intrigue, SK Brann pulled two goals back AND missed a second-half penalty.

In Suduva's home tie, played in Kaunas because of the limited 2,500 capacity in Suduvos Stadione, again they were 3-0 up, this time featuring a hat-trick from Radzinevicius … However, once more the Norwegians pulled two goals back but 6-4 was the final aggregate score and Suduva really were now playing with the big Bhoys.

Algimantas Gabrys was the man who steered Suduva to the dizzy heights of UEFA Cup qualification and had sat in the manager's seat for nine seasons. After disposing of SK Brann he said: "We could have won by a much larger margin if it hadn't been for slack defending in both legs.

"We don't have any international experience but we gave it our best and it worked. We have a talented young team here and they will have learned a lot from these matches."

But would they have learned enough to cope with playing Celtic home and away? That was something for the immediate future but Gabrys certainly was correct about the youthfulness of his victorious squad.

Scorer of four goals over the two legs, Radzinevicius, was still only 21 and had been called up for the Lithuanian under-21 team. He tallied up a more than impressive 52 goals in the 48 games during Suduva's double promotion drive but life at the top was undoubtedly putting the hems on the runaway spirit of both the striker and the team.

Prior to meeting Celtic, they sat sixth in the nine-team league but with 27 points from 22 games they were well clear of any relegation worries, Sakalas (26 points from 22 games), Gelezinis (14 points from 25 games) and Nevezis (seven points from 24 games) all trailed below them. Although they were guaranteed first-division status for another season, the goals tally of Radzinevicius seemed to be drying up with just nine league goals.

His goals return in Europe though produced a much more healthy balance and the striker was looking forward to trying himself out against the defensive qualities of the Parkhead side. He said: "The UEFA Cup gives me the chance to test myself against some very good teams. We are all looking forward to playing in Glasgow in front of a big crowd. Celtic are a great team and the experience will be good for us.

"Obviously Celtic will be the favourites to reach the next round, but we showed against Brann that we are a good team. All we can do is try to play our best."

Radzinevicius wasn't by far the only youthful element in Gabrys' side. Only six of Suduva's squad were over the age of 25 with the veteran of the team being attacking midfielder Vidas Zitinskas, the 34-year-old who hit two of the crucial goals in Bergen against SK Brann.

The youthfulness of the Suduva team was mirrored by the relatively recent emergence of the Lithuanian league and cup set-up. Lithuania is the largest of the Baltic States and a healthy rivalry has developed between them, Estonia and Latvia. Still fresh in the memory of Lithuanian football fans is their 7-0 blitz over Estonia in 1995 and the country's most capped player is Romauldus Marcinkus who was selected 41 times for the national side between 1927 and 1938.

That was, however, as part of one of the old set-ups. Lithuania has spent the vast majority of the modern era as part of either the old Tsarist Russian Empire or the Communist Soviet Union. Independence arrived after the First World War but it wasn't until 1922 that the Lithuanian national football association started and a year later they joined FIFA. Political machinations took over though and in 1943 they were absorbed as part of the USSR and the football association obviously followed suit.

The age of Glasnost unfolded however and as Lithuania declared its independence in 1990, they rejoined FIFA and two years later a fully functional domestic scene was up and running once more. The new age of democracy wasn't just limited to the Baltic States though and elsewhere in Europe, particularly in the Balkan and Slavic homelands of Eastern Europe, the desire for freedom or separation through either democratic means or warfare delivered a whole batch of new countries, new football associations, new national teams and new UEFA members.

Some have obviously fared better than others, as the Scottish national team have found out to their cost on occasion, but Celtic's Bulgarian internationalist Stilian Petrov was taking nothing to chance. He said: "Football in Lithuania isn't a joke anymore, we will have to be very, very careful. All the old Soviet teams had problems at the start but they are getting better and better all the time.

"Most of the Lithuanian players play in their own league as well, so that means their domestic football is improving along with their national team. I played there with CSKA Sofia, against Kaunas I think, and although we won in the end, it was a very tough game. However, I must admit that I've never heard of Suduva. I think they have only come up in Lithuanian football recently, maybe a bit like Livingston, and it is always dangerous when your opponent is unknown.

The Road to Seville

"Not many of the Celtic players know much about Lithuania, but I've been there and it's a very nice place. It's quite like Bulgaria because there is still much development needed, but any of our fans who go across will like it, I'm sure of that. But we know that we have to win it. It will be a different environment for us to the one we are used to in Scotland, and that will make things difficult, but we need to show we are a team who can win anywhere."

The pairing of Celtic with Suduva wasn't the first time the Parkhead side had been penciled in for a trip to a former Soviet state, although three visits to the Ukraine to play Dinamo Kiev had been under the old USSR regime, as in season 1995/96 round one of the Cup-Winners' Cup threw up Dinamo Batumi in the old southern state of Georgia and former Celt Peter Grant echoed the opinions of Petrov when he reminisced on the 7-2 aggregate win and looked forward to the Suduva tie.

He said: "European nights at Celtic Park are always special and there'll be a great atmosphere. It's important to go out and get a decent lead but I can't imagine there will be any complacency on Celtic's part because no-one really knows what Suduva are like.

"You can't turn your noses up at anyone in European or international football these days because no-one has any right to believe they are a superior team. The so-called affluent West was a good bit behind Eastern Europe when it came to things like training facilities, technique and training kids and it is difficult to play against a team you know very little about."

Off the pitch though, flying into the unknown territories of European football can also throw up some unforeseen barriers and the former Celtic midfielder was well aware that you always have to expect the unexpected. He recalled of his trip to Batumi: "Georgia was a place and a half! We had a million things to deal with off the park because there was still a war going on there at the time.

"We were actually the first civilian plane to land in the country because it was usually all army planes that used the airport. I always remember that there was a dog on the runway as we were coming down to land! I think that was the first real indication we had of what we were going in to.

"The hotel was horrendous and we all slept with our clothes on because it was so filthy. The beds were damp and there were no curtains. It was the only trip I've been on where all the players were sitting round a TV at 3am – no-one wanted to go to bed! Brian Scott was about to give someone laser treatment when he realised there was no connecting electricity. It was a strange experience.

"Even after the match, the press phones went down after 10 minutes and on the way home we were stopped at the airport because someone hadn't paid a bill. There were cows in the street, washing hanging over the road and everywhere you looked there were people selling fags and booze. We talk about pampered footballers and it certainly made us a bit more appreciative of what we had.

"We should have slept in the changing rooms because, even although the pitch was a bit bumpy, the facilities were fantastic. The main thing though is that the players have to stay focused and remember what they need to do. It was a trip into the unknown and football-wise I'm sure it will be much the same for the team now when they travel for the return leg."

He added: "I'm sure everyone at the club was hugely disappointed that we never made it to the group stages of the Champions League but sometimes that's the way it goes. The second-half performance against Basel was brilliant. It was just one of those nights when the ball wouldn't go in. A decent run in the UEFA Cup would definitely do the club good and I'm sure everyone will be desperate to go as far as they can. Europe really improves you as a footballer and the experience of playing against some of the top teams can only be hugely beneficial."

So while FC Basel were looking forward to reaping the huge benefits of facing Liverpool (soon to be featured in another chapter), Valencia and Spartak Moscow in the next stages of the Champions League, Celtic knew they would have to sidestep FK Suduva if they were to pit their wits against any of the more notable teams on the continent.

Team captain Paul Lambert laid it on the line when he said: "Everyone would have loved to have gone into the Champions League, but that has gone now and we need to get on with it. The UEFA Cup was the safety net and we need to go out and do our best to make an impression on that.

"You know the calibre of teams that are in the competition and Europe is a hard place to conquer. Football owes you nothing, you need to grasp it and if you work hard then hopefully the rewards will come. You don't have a divine right to win every game. Football owes you nothing. I always want to win, and I have always felt the same demand to do so, whether I was the captain or not. You know that at Celtic you need to go out and try to win every single game and there's pressure with or without an armband."

The defeat to Basel was followed up by a 2-0 SPL home win over Livingston and manager Martin O'Neill, although upset at the Champions League exit, was delighted that the team bounced back just three days later. He said: "It was a low point for us all, there's no point in denying that. Basel are a good side, but I did expect us to score over there. What I will say in the lads' defence is that, poor though their first-half performance was, I thought they were very unfortunate not to score in the second period.

"Basel's keeper pulled off a string of really top-class saves, and on another night we could have scored three or four. It wasn't to be, though, and the fact that we're now out of the Champions League is something everyone has to cope with. That goes for me too because, although I've been as down as anyone about what happened, life goes on.

"There is still plenty to play for this season and, although it will take time to get over this disappointment, the best way to speed up the process is to win matches. That's why I thought the Livingston game was so important to us, particularly with an international week coming up. After what was a difficult week, our victory on Sunday went a long way to lifting the gloom around the place."

The previous season Feyenoord took a similar route to UEFA Cup glory after dropping out of the Champions League qualifiers and although O'Neill admitted that the consolation prize offered just a crumb of comfort, he was determined that his side made an impression on the tournament.

However, he had earlier warned against any over-optimistic predictions that Celtic could 'do a Feyenoord', and stated he'd be happy enough to progress beyond FK Suduva at that point. He said: "It goes without saying that we want to go as far as we possibly can in the UEFA Cup.

"What we have to appreciate, though, is that it could all depend on who we come up against in future rounds. The calibre, and sheer quantity, of teams involved in the UEFA Cup make it a very difficult competition to call. One thing you always know about European football is that it's about how you do on the night, and the lads will need to rise to the challenge when we meet Suduva."

True words of wisdom spoken on the night of the defeat in Switzerland and his tone and resolve hadn't altered on the Monday before the Thursday UEFA Cup clash with the Lithuanian side.

"I wouldn't want to start getting too far ahead of things," he warned. "We would like to enjoy a decent run in the competition but there'll be a few surprises in the UEFA Cup and I don't want us to be anywhere near that. We will be favourites to go through over the two legs and we need to approach it in the proper frame of mind, which we certainly will do.

"I've got some videos of them and Tom O'Neill (Celtic's Chief Scout) has gone out to see them play and we will have to be on our guard defensively. It would be ideal if we could score a couple of goals and keep a clean sheet and I'd be delighted with that. Even as a player I preferred playing the away leg first, but it's not to be so we have to make sure that over the two legs we are in the hat.

"I'm also hoping that by Thursday Rab [Douglas] will be fit. At the minute he is still feeling sore when he kicks the ball but it's easing each day and I'm confident he'll be okay for the Suduva game."

O'Neill was naturally playing it cautiously and rightly so, Celtic had been smacked to the floor by the sucker-punch from underdogs in European football before – specifically in season 1991/92 in the UEFA Cup when unknowns Neuchatel Xamax, another club who had journalists scouring through reference books in the pre-Internet days, rocked Celtic with a 5-1 defeat that had typesetters around the continent checking the facts to see if the scoreline was the wrong way round.

Infamous domestic cup upsets such as Berwick Rangers and Inverness Caley Thistle over the big guns of Scottish football are one thing and are generally only called to mind when rummaging through the yearly *Wee Red Book* ... But in the far more worldly realm of Europe heavyweight tomes such as *The Guinness Book of World Football* and have all the scores there in black and white – for the entire continent to see!

Amazingly, as the club officials waited in the departure lounge after that 5-1 shock-wave, the then chief executive Terry Cassidy turned on Andrew Smith who was reporting on the game for the *Celtic View* and, with finger waving, bellowed: "Don't you dare write anything negative about that." Yeah, right!

To be beaten on a tight scoreline by Xamax would have been bad enough for a club of Celtic's stature, as would being soundly beaten 5-1 by one of the Real Madrids of this world, but to be roundly embarrassed by a team we had never even heard of was surely the lowest point of Celtic's 40 years of involvement in European football.

The thought of anything like that happening to a Celtic team under the tutelage of O'Neill was surely unthinkable but if the Irishman was diplomatic, tactful and vigilant in not underestimating the opposition, the noises emanating from Suduva, and in particular O'Neill's opposite number Algimantas Gabrys, weren't quite so subtle or discreet.

True, Suduva had nothing to lose, as underdogs they were in a win-win

EIGHTSOME REEL:
John Hartson and Joos Valgaeren were on the scoresheet at Celtic Park as the Hoops hammered FK Suduva 8-1

TWO EASY:
Goals by *David Fernandez and Alan Thompson ensured Celtic's place in the next round in a comfortable 2-0 victory away to FK Suduva*

situation and they engaged themselves in an air of confidence that can only come to light in David and Goliath situations. It's also true that the media, especially considering the language difference, could have put a definite spin on Gabrys' quotes but the headlines were ready-made – Suduva were coming to Parkhead to beat Celtic and they were self-assured they could do so.

There was, of course, an element of gamesmanship and one-upmanship in the claims coming from the opposition but, considering the evidence – they were on the cusp of a fairytale rise to prominence, they had scored six against SK Brann and their striker was being touted as the next Henrik Larsson – could this team of unknowns from the uncharted waters of European football pull one over on Glasgow Celtic? We would soon find out.

The Suduva circus sideshow rolled into Glasgow amid undreamt of publicity for the Lithuanian side and they were all-but billed as the asylum seekers of European football with club officials decked out in denims rather than the accepted obligatory club suits and stories of sparse training gear being kept in bin liners. Their coffers didn't allow them an open choice of top hotel accommodation and then there was the hilarious Paradise photo shoot…

As usual on European trips, the opposition turns up at the stadium 24 hours before kick-off for a training session to acclimatise themselves to the conditions and surroundings and to give the press and TV ample images for the following day's round-up.

The difference this time though was that there were more cameras on the pitch than on the sidelines! The Suduva players seemed more interested in posing for snaps of themselves inside the famous Celtic Park and, like the archetypal gaggle of Japanese tourists, each player took it in turn to take photos of one of his team-mates in front of the gigantic North Stand.

Another comical footnote to the pre-match build-up was that earlier in the season the *Celtic View* produced a 32-page *Season Guide* which was given away free with the publication.

Following the club's prolonged run in the Champions League the previous season and in anticipation of another series of European nights when scores, sometimes hundreds, of foreign media people apply for press passes to add to already numbersome Scottish, Irish and English contingent who attend every game, the print run of the *Season Guide* was upped considerably so that it could be an invaluable addition to the press pack handed out to visiting journalists – FK Suduva brought ONE journalist with them!

Suduva were also keen to woo the not inconsiderable contingent of second and third generation Lithuanian immigrants based in Scotland, and specifically in old mining communities of Lanarkshire, to support them in their cause.

Among their number is none other than Celtic legend Billy McNeill and the background to his family lineage led to the oft-asked pub question: If modern-day criteria were around in the 1960s, which Celtic and Scotland star could have played for Russia?

The more politically correct question would have stated the USSR instead of Russia for the answer is indeed Billy McNeill but Caesar's 'Russian granny' was in fact Lithuanian.

But there was one major stumbling block in Suduva's hopeful plea to the

The Road to Seville

Lithuanian community in Scotland – Lithuania, historically, politically and geographically always had more in common with the neighbouring Catholic Poland than Communist Moscow so on arrival in Scotland, the West Coast being what it is, the footballing allegiances of the devoutly Catholic Lithuanian immigrants were more or less mapped out before they even reached Scottish soil.

Many a Lanarkshire Lithuanian Social Club is basically a Celtic Supporters' Club under an assumed name and although Suduva's appeal for Scotland's Lithuanian population to turn up at Parkhead was met – they were all wearing green and white scarves and were regular attendees at Paradise no matter who Celtic were playing.

And so to the game itself, this was to be Celtic's 51st in the UEFA Cup and of all the European competitions, Celtic's record in the UEFA is a lot poorer than in the others. In the 50 UEFA matches leading up to the Suduva game they had won just 23 and indeed, of the 12 home matches the Bhoys had lost in Europe, five were in this very competition.

But would this be the sixth, would this be another shock, would Suduva live up to their pre-match hyperbole, after all, they were an unknown quantity and Celtic, and their supporters, were basically walking into the dark – but not for the first time in European football.

Generally speaking, on the whole, the debacle in Neuchatel aside, Celtic more often than not took care of the un-fancied teams with goals to spare - the most prominent of these games coming from the European Cup in season 1970/71 when Finnish side KPV Kokkola visited Parkhead in the first round.

A crowd of 41,000 witnessed a goal feast of fulfilling proportions as a hat-trick from Harry Hood was added to by a brace from a young Paul Wilson and single counters from Billy McNeill, John Hughes, Vic Davidson and Jimmy Johnstone as the Celts ran riot over the champions of Finland.

The final score of 9-0 was Celtic's highest ever European win and Jock Stein made eight changes for the return leg in Karleby where a crowd of 4,500 turned up expecting more of the same from the Scottish champions.

Although not to the same extent, Celtic duly obliged on the goals front and this time a Willie Wallace double was garnished by goals from Tommy Callaghan, Vic Davidson and Bobby Lennox to give Celtic a 14-0 aggregate win – again their highest in a European campaign.

However, although there were no other shocks of Xamax proportions during any of Celtic's European runs, they didn't always have it exactly their own way when coming up against so-called 'lesser' opposition. One particular case in point was in the European Cup of 1979/80 when Irish side Dundalk were paired with Celtic in the second round.

Dundalk, of course, is a Celtic stronghold and much was made of the point that this would be a mutual love-in. The Pope had only recently visited Ireland and when the draw was made, a Scottish daily newspaper ran a cartoon with workmen in Dublin's Phoenix Park pulling down a massive crucifix as someone ran up to them waving a piece of paper and shouting: "Stop, stop, keep it up – Celtic are coming!"

And when the Dundalk manager was asked if there would be crowd segregation for their home leg he answered: "No, if we put in segregation the Dundalk people would all be in the Celtic end!"

Camaraderie reigned off the park but the mutual love-in never made it on to the pitch as Dundalk stubbornly refused to kowtow and show Celtic the respect the crowd were expecting. Celtic narrowly won 3-2 in Glasgow and the away tie in Ireland finished 0-0 as the Celtic fans in Dundalk ran the full gamut of emotions in the final minutes in the knowledge that one goal from the Irish would put Dundalk through on away goals.

In the year 2003, Celtic's recent close shaves in Europe had been against the likes of Juventus and Valencia so surely we wouldn't be taken to the wire by a side from Lithuania. After the aforementioned 2-0 win over Livingston, just two days later Celtic stumbled at Fir Park where Motherwell recorded a 2-1 win but Celtic hit back on the Saturday with 1-0 win over Hibernian just prior to the visit of Suduva...

And on the night of Thursday, September 19 in front of a crowd of 36,824, the following sides took to the field at Parkhead:

CELTIC (3-5-2): Douglas; Valgaeren, Balde, Laursen (Crainey 60); Sylla, Lambert, Lennon (Fernandez 60), Petrov, Guppy; Sutton, Larsson (Hartson 60).
Substitutes: Gould, McNamara, Thompson, Agathe.

FK SUDUVA (4-4-2): Padimanskas; Kunevieius, Sendzikas, Grigas, Devetinas; Zitinskas (Stankevivius 80), Suliauskas, Adomaitis (Kraipavicius 75), Sidlauskas (Haciulis 46); Slavickas, Radzinevicius.
Substitutes: Balyns, Klevinskas, Rukavicius, Larcenka.

If the truth be known, despite all the pre-match hype and the engineered wordplay of Gabrys, Suduva were so far out of their depth they should have been wearing diving suits, in fact some of their players did look as if they were wearing lead-lined boots.

Henrik Larsson hit Celtic's first in the 14th minute and the wonder is that it took Celtic so long to score at all. Had it not been for the heroics of Gytis Padimanskas who had a truly remarkable match in the visitors' goal, there's no knowing how many Celtic would have scored on the night. Never in recent memory has a team come to Celtic Park and capitulated so easily as the Celts rattled in eight goals.

Suduva kicked-off nine times during the match and it seemed as though Celtic took the ball back off them nine times before they even got it out of the centre-circle. Within 15 minutes of opening the scoring, Larsson got his hat-trick and equalled Ally McCoist's scoring record for playing in Europe with Scottish teams.

Between Larsson's second and third, Stilian Petrov scored a peach then Chris Sutton added to the tally before half time. After the turnaround, Paul Lambert, John Hartson and Joos Valgaeren all got in on the act by taking the score to eight on a night when Celtic really should have smashed the previous nine-goal record against Kokkola to smithereens.

But Padimanskas was in outstanding form and he was the difference between the eight goals scored and another 10 being added to the scoreline. Radzinevicius finally did get his name on the scoresheet in the 90th minute when he beat the limping Rab Douglas to the ball and stroked it into the net to the sound of good-natured cheers from the Celtic fans still left in the ground.

The Road to Seville

So at least Padimanskas and Radzinevicius left Celtic Park with some integrity still intact but Suduva also left with some training gear given to them by kit man John Clark. Celtic could now look forward to the away trip with no trepidation at all and back on the domestic scene they followed up the 8-1 trouncing of Suduva with 1-0 win at Dens Park where Martin O'Neill fielded the same 11 starters – the first time he had been able to do so for seven successive games.

The manager said: "More than anything, I thought that everybody, even the players who came on, had done very well against Suduva. From the way they had started the game, I could see that they were full of confidence, and I felt they would take that into Sunday's game.

"Picking the team is particularly difficult just now, though. I have a number of players, top-class players at that, who just need to play themselves into a bit of form. These lads have played a big part in proceedings over recent seasons, and they remain a massive part of my plans here. And although they need to find a bit of form, I've no doubt they will because they're too good not to.

"The reason I stuck with the side that played on Thursday was that, from the evidence of how they were playing in training, they were clearly buzzing – really full of confidence. They'd deserved the nod and, although the likes of Didier Agathe will soon be pushing for a place, the players in possession have earned the right to be there."

That same starting XI also took part in a 5-0 rout of Kilmarnock the following weekend at Celtic Park where Larsson also hit another hat-trick but it was his threesome against Suduva that made the headlines regarding McCoist's Euro record.

The Swedish internationalist said: "I have never been that interested in records, especially when I'm playing, these are the things that you look back on when you have finished your career but I am still playing. It is always nice when you get things like that, but I am still playing but I can't let things distract me and I still need to keep on performing."

There were a few grudging moans when Larsson was subbed during the home tie as punters wanted to see Larsson overtake McCoist's record but if and when he did manage to create his own record, it was increasingly unlikely that it would be in the away leg as Martin O'Neill announced that he was introducing a handful of youngsters to the travelling squad and resting some if his most influential players. He added under-21 trio Liam Miller, Simon Lynch and John Kennedy to a first-team squad which had also included youth goalkeeper David Marshall over the previous weeks.

He explained: "My basic plans for Suduva are that I'm going to take some of the senior players who could do with a game to keep up their match fitness, and also bring along one or two of the younger boys. I'll certainly leave some people behind, and I have a fair idea already who won't travel. It's a good position for us to be in, and it will be a good experience for some of the young lads to travel away with the team."

The game was to take place at the dilapidated Dariaus Ir Gireno Stadium in Kaunas, 60 miles from Marijampole despite the fact that the 1,200 people who did turn up for the game, and a fair number of them were uniformed soldiers, could easily have been accommodated in Suduva's 2,500-capacity ground.

There were, as expected, sweeping changes made to the team for the return leg as the Celts were obviously confident of protecting their seven-goal lead. Just as Larsson mirrored Harry Hood in Celtic 9-0 demolition job on Kokkola, O'Neill unknowingly imitated Jock Stein by making eight changes for the return leg in this latest high-scoring European tie. The teams on the night of Thursday, October 3 were:

FK SUDUVA (4-5-1): Padimanskas; Kunevicius, Grigas, Sendzikas (Kraipavicius 46), Devetinas; Slavickas, Adohairis (Haciulus 70), Suliauskas (Siplauskas,84) Litinskas, Larsenka, Radzinevicius. Substitutes: Balyns, Stankevieius, Rukavieius, Klevinskas.

CELTIC (3-5-2): Gould; McNamara (Miller 72), Kennedy (Smith 52), Crainey; Agathe, Healy, Maloney, Thompson, Petta (Lynch 78); Hartson, Fernandez.
Substitutes: Douglas, Sylla, Balde, Laursen.

First-half goals from David Fernandez and Alan Thompson kept Celtic's goalscoring streak on cue but this time there were to be no further additions to the total, mainly due to the woodwork and, again, the goalkeeping exploits of Padimanskas. The 2-0 win gave Celtic a 10-1 aggregate scoreline as 19-year-old John Kennedy, grandson of Hoops legend Jimmy Delaney, made his European debut by starting at the heart of Celtic's three-man defence.

The youngster said: "It was a good experience for me and for the other young lads that were included in the trip. I wasn't too nervous because of the result from the first-leg, it was more just looking forward to the game, but we still knew that we had to go out and do a job. The game wasn't up to much but at the same time it was another appearance for the first team and it was a good way to make my European debut for the club.

"I just want to do as well as I can at under-21 level and take it from there. It goes without saying that I want to try and make my way into the first-team squad and catch the manager's eye, but at the minute I'm concentrating on keeping my head down and working hard in training. It was a confidence boost to called up into the squad to go to Lithuania and I do hope that there are more opportunities like that as the season goes on, but as I say, I'll keep working hard in the under-21s and take things from there."

So Celtic had breached that first hurdle quite easily but there were bigger fish to fry and rather more worthy teams waiting in the draw for the next round. Who would it be? Which side from the many left in the competition would give Celtic a sterner test than that which had been offered by Suduva?

There were quite a few big names left including the likes of Blackburn Rovers and Boavista. Surely any one of these great teams could give Celtic a real lesson in football?

We would have to wait with bated breath for the draw but as we earlier quoted Martin O'Neill's words of wisdom following the FC Basel defeat, perhaps it would be quite apt to end this chapter dealing with Celtic's first step on the long and winding road to Seville with another gem from the man's crystal ball insight into taking each game as it comes while always keeping one eye looking forward to what could possibly come ahead.

The Road to Seville

From the manager's Pep Talk page in the Celtic matchday programme for the visit of Suduva he said: "Participating in European football is a wonderful experience. The Champions League is undoubtedly the Holy Grail but the UEFA Cup is still a major competition and like every other club taking part this evening we would like to remain in it for as long as possible."

TONY HAMILTON'S EUROPEAN DIARY
Part 1: Them's the breaks!

THE Road to Seville could have been the funniest and most exciting Crosby and Hope film that was never made – but neither played for Celtic.

Certainly for the Celtic media team it was an adventure which went further than any of us expected and was worth absolutely everything that we put in to it and everything we brought back.

All of the sleepless nights, the mental drivers, the high-speed police escorts, the hours of getting lost in foreign lands and the odd square-go along the road would be welcome again so long as we could get to revisit places like Lithuania.

I'll never know why I sighed with despondency when we were initially drawn to play there – it was a place of astounding beauty, great people and dirt-cheap fags – but more of that later.

Des O'Hara is the one person in my life that I spend the most time with. I spend more time with Des than I do with my wife and weans but it's not through choice - as anyone who has seen "Man at Oxfam" will confirm.

Apparently the producers of "What Not To Wear" are planning a whole series about him next spring – six entire episodes about the Maryhill fugitive, on the run from the fashion polis.

We have a love/hate relationship which seems to work well – Des thinks it goes dark when I sit down and I really have a problem with his Pedigree Chum dog-breath when we're holed up in a confined edit suite together for days on end.

I digress, again.

Des and I took a slightly different route to Kaunus, in Lithuania – temporary home town of FK Suduva – the team we had annihilated in the first leg back at Celtic Park and the place where we had meticulously planned that our first overseas live CelticTV programme of the season would take place.

It would be our last programme away from Paradise until May and it would be one which nearly caused my heart to stop on more than one occasion.

We went via Warsaw – another place, like Lithuania, where you SHOULD go if the opportunity ever presents itself.

The reason for the two-day visit to the Polish capital was simple: it was on the road (okay, I told Celtic's accountants it was – what do they know they only count beans, they don't do geography) and my Celtic idol, Dariusz Dziekanowski, had agreed to be interviewed on his 40th birthday – 30 September 2002.

We had a snag though and quite a major snag. KLM lost our equipment somewhere from the connection at Schipol, Amsterdam. No TV cameras, no TV interview – it wasn't Chinese algebra – it was and always will be a fact.

The irony here is that there's actually a convention that airlines should refer to and follow when they lose your luggage. Shrugging their shoulders and throwing a business card at you in Warsaw Airport without making eye contact isn't part of that convention – the WARSAW Convention!

The Road to Seville

Anyway, it was all my fault. I chose that airline and it would be my fault again, later in the campaign, when I would foolishly decide to give them a second chance.

The interview went well – eventually, after the cameras arrived - with the only down side being Des' ability (surely inability?) to take a still photograph of me with my hero. I look like 'David' in 'An American Werewolf in London' after three days of decay in that shot.

I'm glad it wasn't someone who I really wanted to be pictured with. Someone who I called number three son after or whose name I have tattooed on my arm...

But ultimately it was well worth it and the next day we got on the Ethiopian Airlines flight (genuinely) from Warsaw to Vilnius, picked up the hire car (after a dogged time trying to take our equipment into Lithuania), witnessed three accidents before we passed the airport's perimeter fence and then negotiated the 100-odd km to Kaunus.

When we arrived we met up with our engineer and good guy Bob Aitkenhead, who had been dispatched two days earlier to conduct the final reconnaissance ahead of what was proving to be a very difficult and ambitious Outside Broadcast to manage.

In the three weeks leading up to this I had been corresponding with a guy, let's call him Justinas, who had an OB facility in the city.

He spoke English with an American accent after watching cheap imported television for too long, and on our first day in the country he came to meet us at the ground where the game would be played in his BMW and with his daughter in his arms.

He could do anything we wanted. Absolutely anything. With dead US presidents stuffed in brown envelopes we could have the finest OB in all of the Baltic States.

More cameras? No problem. Satellite uplink? No problem. Fags at the equivalent of 45p a packet and a three-course meal for the entire CelticTV crew of 10 costing about £30, including drinks for the drinkers? No problem.

The bit about the fags and the scran was the only straightforward part of the trip. With half-an-hour to go before we went live we had two satellite trucks on-site – both of which were as useful as nearly coming out of the ballot for a UEFA Cup final ticket.

We had also been locked in the stadium the day before and had to grease a few palms to get the hire car and us out.

It wasn't going at all well, my job was on the line and I wanted my mammy.

I never actually got my mammy that day but I got the next best thing – a satellite uplink truck with the correct codes to transmit our pictures in time for me to hang on to my job.

And, on reflection, I have to say that there was something I admired about my new friend Justinas and his confidence as the programme went up into the air and back down again into living rooms everywhere from Seattle to Shettleston.

It was, after all the heart-stopping moments – "no problem" and I would (if I really had to) do it all again – for the fags if nothing else.

Chapter Four

Blackburn Rovers: 'Men against Bhoys'

by Jim Craig

"We dominated for long periods on Thursday and, to be honest, I think we can look forward to the second leg with confidence....our gaffer told us afterwards that it had been men against boys out there and that we should look forward to the return"

THOSE words after the first leg at Parkhead by Blackburn skipper Gary Flitcroft caused a 'stushie' and the Scottish press went to town. Graeme Souness was called, among other things, 'arrogant', 'big-headed', 'over-confident' and 'a disgrace'. Privately, Celtic fans used even more uncomplimentary terms which, frankly, have no place in a book of this nature.

Before any further attempts at condemnation of the Blackburn boss, two questions must be asked. The first is, did he actually say those words? Perhaps we should try to put ourselves into the shoes of a manager and analyse his feelings at a time like that. Without going into detail, Souness must have been pretty pleased with the performance of his team that night, although disappointed that they did not score.

After the match, in the dressing room, the players would have been a bit down. Surely, it was only natural that the manager should try to cheer them up, to raise their confidence for the return leg, to boost their egos. If, in doing so, he tended to belittle the opposition, then he would not have been the first boss in history to do so. Unwise, perhaps, bitter, almost certainly, but in no way surprising.

The second question concerns the fitness of Gary Flitcroft to be the mouthpiece of the team. Souness' comment was obviously directed solely towards the ears of his players and them alone. It was not meant to be aired outside the confines of the dressing room.

Having broken an obvious confidence, Flitcroft then decided to further deride the Celtic squad. When asked if there had been any Celtic players who had impressed him, he dismissively replied, "not really, no." Is it any wonder that the Hoops team came away from the match with a burning desire to shove those comments right down the throats of the English side in the return leg?

The Herald damned Flitcroft's press conference performance with faint praise: "Flitcroft could not be faulted for frankness but his comments suggest he is no great loss to the diplomatic corps." A Celtic supporter I bumped into the following day in George Square probably summed up the feelings of the support more accurately about Flitcroft's comments. "Dough-heid!" he sniffed.

Perhaps, at this early stage of the chapter, I should make an admission which might not prove too popular with the Celtic support. I have always liked the Blackburn manager and got on well with him.

As a part-timer with Celtic in 1966, earning my first wage of £8 a week, I had bought myself a car. Not exactly your latest sports model, or even all that new, but I was still very chuffed that the Morris 1100 outside the door belonged to me. It did have some 'minor' features of irritation. I sometimes had to put my hand outside the window and give the windscreen wipers a shove to get them going; and as the battery wasn't too clever, I would take the precaution of always parking on a hill, where, if necessary, I could employ what my mother used to call a 'bump start' to get it going!

At the training sessions on Tuesday and Thursday at Parkhead, we had been joined by a laddie from Edinburgh. He was in his very early teens, was unfortunately showing the acne of that age-group and, to be quite blunt, looked a little plump to be running round a football pitch. After the sessions, I would drive him into Queen Street Station where he boarded the Edinburgh train, his ears ringing, no doubt, with my not-too-subtle advice about the need for him to work harder and run more.

That was how I met Graeme Souness and, to be fair to the guy, he obviously appreciated the lift. When I was working with the BBC and he was manager at Ibrox, he was helpful and approachable; and just before this particular European night at Parkhead, he did an interview with one of the Scottish dailies and mentioned my running him into town.

So, like any other parent, when I occasionally feel obliged to offer my kids some advice, one particular piece of wisdom stems from that association with a future star. "Be nice to everyone," I tell them, "no matter the circumstances. You never know the benefits that might come back and help you in the future!"

When the UEFA Cup second round draw was made, a roar went up throughout Scotland and England as Celtic and Blackburn were paired. All the old clichés were trotted out. North of the Border v South, a clash with the Auld Enemy, a Battle of Britain. All of them emotive - and probably accurate.

Matches between teams from these two neighbouring countries have usually been exciting and are often accompanied by more than a touch of jingoism. Celtic had early experience of these encounters. In their first season of 1888/89, the club played friendlies against a number of English sides, like Mitchell's St George (7-1 H), Corinthians (6-2 H; 1-3 A); Newcastle West End (4-3 A); Bolton (0-2 A; 5-1 H);

Burnley (3-1 A) and Preston North End (2-1 H). In the following season, even though the Scottish League had started, Celtic still found room to play, obviously to please their fans, further cross-border friendlies. Sunderland, Everton, Bolton, Burnley, Preston, Wolves, Notts. County, Aston Villa and Blackburn all came to the first Celtic Park and return visits were paid.

All through the history of the club from that point on, there have been similar matches in various competitions.

When the first Ibrox Disaster occurred during the Scotland/England encounter of 1902, Rangers decided to put up for competition, the Glasgow Exhibition Cup which they had won in 1901. They invited Celtic and two English clubs to take part. Before beating the hosts in the final, Celtic comprehensively thrashed Sunderland 5-1 in the semi-final.

On the club's tour of Germany and Hungary in 1914, Celtic drew with Burnley in a specially arranged match for a specific trophy. The replay was arranged in September of that year at Turf Moor; Celtic won, but the trophy never arrived! The organising club, Ferencvaros, eventually handed one over in Celtic's Centenary Year of 1988.

After the successes of Celtic and Sunderland in their respective Championships in 1936, home and away matches were arranged for an unofficial 'British Championship'. The first leg at Roker Park was drawn 1-1; Celtic won the return by 3-2 to clinch the so-called 'title'. One year later, as respective cup holders, they met again for a British Cup. Celtic won 2-0 down in Sunderland but, again, no trophy ever appeared.

And then, of course, in 1938 came an official tournament for British teams, the Empire Exhibition Trophy, which Celtic won, beating Sunderland in the first round and Everton in the final. In a similar competition in 1953, for the Coronation Cup, again destined to end up at Parkhead, Celtic disposed of Arsenal and Manchester United along the way.

When European competition began in the mid-1950s, these matches took on a new importance. Since their first involvement in 1962, Celtic have been drawn against English opposition on four previous occasions, all of them receiving the same over-hyped treatment from the Scottish sporting press.

When it comes to reporting on matches played by the national team, it has been said the Scottish football writers are 'fans with typewriters'. And, of course, the Scotland/England encounter was just perfect for demonstrating that.

So, you could imagine their delight when European matches in the same vein came along. They could give abuse to the Auld Enemy, continue to demonstrate a fairly large chip on both shoulders and generally, give full throttle to a barely-concealed chauvinism.

And the papers were full of that for the double-headers against Liverpool in 1966 and 1997, Leeds United in 1970 and Nottingham Forest in 1983. Unusually, one goal in each of these games proved crucial.

In the first Liverpool clash, it was a disallowed goal. Celtic won the first leg 1-0 at Parkhead but with only a few minutes left of the return, were 1-2 down on aggregate. Then Bobby Lennox raced through on to a Joe McBride head-flick and stuck away what would have proved the winner, thanks to the away goals rule. However, not for the first time in his career, Bobby saw the linesman flag for offside. Referee

Hannet of Belgium later seemed to admit he had made a big mistake; in any event, Celtic were out.

Against Leeds in 1970, few commentators from south of the border gave Celtic much chance. So, when George Connelly struck after 45 seconds of the first leg at Elland Road, it not only gave Celtic a boost but more importantly, put Leeds on the back foot, a position from which they never recovered over the two games.

In 1983, a talented Celtic side gave a perfect example of how not to play in Europe. At a time when Aberdeen, with Miller and McLeish at central defence, and Dundee United, with Narey and Hegarty in the same role, were playing very much a continental game of containment and quick attacks, Celtic were still employing the 'cavalry-charge' mentality.

That proved suicidal in the second leg at Parkhead, when two quick breaks by Forest against a disorganised Celtic rearguard gave them two goals. The second, by Walsh after a great left-wing run by Davenport, was the clincher and Celtic were once again out of Europe before Christmas.

Liverpool were also the opponents in 1997, when a committed, disciplined performance gave the Hoops a 2-1 lead with only a few minutes left. Then Steve McManaman scored a fine individual goal, one to rank with any ever seen at Celtic Park. Receiving the ball just outside his own 18-yard line on the right wing, he avoided a challenge by Morten Wieghorst and ran diagonally towards the Celtic goal. As no defender came to challenge him, he continued his run, finishing with a fierce shot past Jonathan Gould for the equaliser. Since the return finished goal-less, those two away strikes by Liverpool were enough to take them through.

One success from four attempts. Not a great record for a team with Celtic's aspirations. Now, having been drawn against Blackburn Rovers, they had a chance to improve that tally.

As the day of the match approached, the excitement intensified. However, the UEFA Cup was not the only competition in which Celtic had an interest. On the Wednesday of the previous week, the team and its supporters received a fright from Inverness Caley Thistle in the third round of the CIS Insurance Cup. Their name always sends a shudder through every Hoops fan for obvious reasons and on this occasion, although Celtic eventually won 4-2 in front of a disappointing 34,592 crowd, the Highland side's close-passing game gave the home side a few problems.

Then, on the Saturday, Celtic travelled to East End Park for a league game with Dunfermline. The difference in class was immediately apparent and the 4-1 scoreline reflected it. On the following Monday, the headline in *The Herald* was rather sarcastic:

'DUNFERMLINE HELP CELTIC WITH THE PERFECT EUROPEAN WARM-UP'

But the comments following on from the headline explained it all. "Normally, a towsy, at times over-physical, match played at 100 miles an hour would hardly be considered as ideal preparation for a European tie. However, with Thursday's UEFA Cup opposition being provided by Graeme Souness' Blackburn Rovers, maybe this bruising encounter in Fife will prove to be the perfect tune-up for Martin O'Neill's side."

On that same weekend, Blackburn Rovers had gone down 1-2 at home to

Arsenal. This left the position of the two protagonists in their respective leagues as:

Celtic	P12	W10	D1	L1	F33	A8	Pts33	Pos. 2nd
Blackburn	P11	W5	D3	L3	F18	A13	Pts18	Pos. 7th

Unfortunately, as Celtic fans celebrated on the Sunday evening, they were unaware that one of their stars had been injured. In fact, it was not until the Tuesday morning that the story made the newspapers.

"Celtic suffered unexpected injury news yesterday when it emerged that the Bulgarian internationalist, Stilian Petrov, had broken a bone in his hand during the 4-1 win over Dunfermline at East End Park on Sunday ... the club's medical staff will be monitoring his progress."

The midfielder had complained of pain after the game and was taken to hospital, where it was confirmed that a small bone in his hand was indeed broken. However, it was unlikely to prevent him playing in the big match.

The same newspaper covered two other topics. Under the headline: 'Another chapter ready to be written in the epic career of Souness', the writer gave a brief resume of his managerial career, giving some space, naturally, to his sojourn at Rangers.

And our Old Firm rivals got a mention in another article, this time on Blackburn's goalkeeper, Brad Friedel. The USA internationalist recalled that he had very nearly signed for Celtic when Liam Brady was in charge but a transfer fee could not be agreed on. And he was also approached when Walter Smith was at Ibrox; however, as he had already agreed to sign for Liverpool, he did not want to go back on his word.

By Wednesday, as expected, the papers had good news for Celtic fans.

'PETROV FIT TO PRESSURE YOUNG ROVERS'

Stilian would apparently require only a strapping to take the field and apart from that both teams would be at full strength.

It was also pointed out that Souness had perhaps been a bit naughty in choosing Murray Park for his side's final match preparations but the Blackburn boss was quick to put his case forward: "If we had been drawn against Rangers, I would have asked Celtic to use their training ground. But this is Glasgow and I shouldn't be surprised."

And the managers were compared: "O'Neill is loved at Celtic and finds himself labelled 'St Martin' by adoring fans ... Souness has always been respected but never quite loved."

On the day of the first leg at Celtic Park, October 31, 2002, Celtic fans could feel reason to be aggrieved with the headline in *The Herald*.

'CLOUD OVER PETROV CONTRACT TALKS AS O'NEILL GEARS UP FOR BLACKBURN

The conspiracy theorists were once again in their element, claiming the press were trying to undermine their team's chances. Arguing over details like that kept the support happy all through the day, as they came in by plane, sea or overland. They thronged all over the City Centre, bedecked in the colours, all in good form.

On match days like this, I anchor the Internet broadcasts for Celtic. These have proved popular with fans all over the world. We go on air an hour-and-a-quarter before the start, during which time we provide both an audio and visual programme. This comprises excerpts from previous matches, interviews with the manager and players and team news, plus comment and discussion with my regular panel on the big issues of the day.

All this season, ex-players Bertie Auld, Frank McGarvey and Tosh McKinlay, along with our Web Administrator John Cole, have been in good form. They seldom agree with each other, which makes for good listening and viewing, and each has his own thoughts on football and the personalities involved.

On that particular night, they were cautiously optimistic. Bertie was only making a limited appearance, as he had to host a table in the Jock Stein Lounge, so I interviewed him outside the ground, on camera. Even at that time, around 6pm, the area from London Road up to the park itself was packed with cars and people, keen to savour the atmosphere of a big European occasion.

Bertie was mildly optimistic, as were the others but all of them pointed out that Blackburn had skill in midfield with Thomson and Tugay, plus good forwards in Cole, Yorke, Ostenstadt and Duff. However, just to show that you can hide little from an ex-player, all three of them were insistent that the ex-Man United pair, Cole and Yorke, were over the hill and now lacking pace.

But the whole panel agreed that this would be a big test for Celtic and that we would have to match them in midfield to find the control to win the game.

By the time the teams lined up for the kick-off, a crowd of 59,533 was packed into Celtic Park, the biggest attendance of the season so far. They were keen to give their guys a boost before the start; and equally ready to give the ex-Rangers boss a Celtic welcome. But they were in for a surprise, as Souness rather out-foxed them.

Entering the technical area 30 seconds after kick-off and striding towards Martin O'Neill, he shook hands with him before stepping forward to applaud the Blackburn fans. It was the hallmark of a showman milking a situation to full advantage.

The match itself proved to be as exciting as anticipated and Alison McConnell summarised it up well in the *Celtic View*. 'Henrik Larsson plundered a dramatic 85th-minute goal for Martin O'Neill's side as Celtic took first blood in the much-hyped 'Battle of Britain'. Not only did the strike give the Hoops a massive confidence boost ahead of the second leg but it afforded Larsson yet another opportunity to pen a footnote in the Scottish history books.

'The Swede's goal took his tally to 22 in European competition, outdoing the previous record held by Ally McCoist as the top Scottish Euro scorer. In truth, the fact that Celtic hadn't actually conceded any goals at that late stage in the match owed as much to a strong degree of fortitude as it did to a couple of timely saves from Rab Douglas, who was called upon on a number of occasions to stifle Blackburn attacks...

'However, despite the fact that they enjoyed the bulk of possession, Blackburn's failure to convert this territorial advantage into goals might well come back to haunt them in the return leg at Ewood Park.'

BATTLE OF THE BOSSES: *Martin O'Neill pitted his wits against Graeme Souness, and a Henrik Larsson goal, below, gave Celtic a 1-0 first-leg win over Blackburn Rovers*

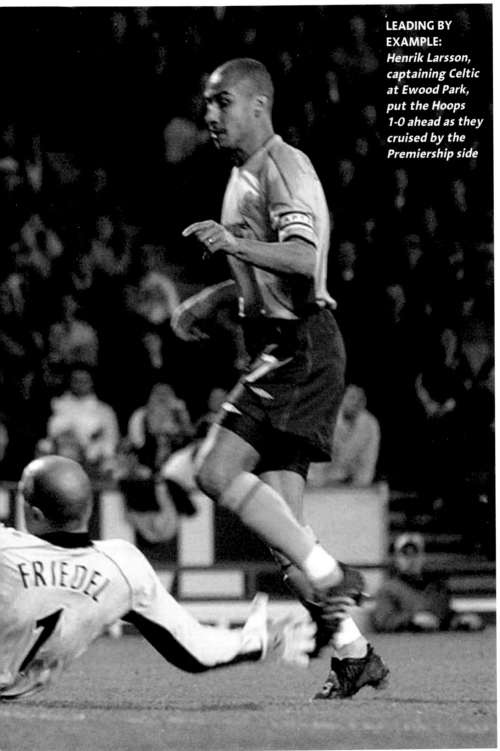

LEADING BY EXAMPLE: *Henrik Larsson, captaining Celtic at Ewood Park, put the Hoops 1-0 ahead as they cruised by the Premiership side*

TRIUMPHANT: *Rab Douglas and Neil Lennon celebrate victory over Blackburn Rovers*

In the event, prophetic words. At that stage, though, most neutral observers would have perhaps agreed that the English side deserved a share of the points. *The Herald* had a double headline to note that fact:

'HENRIK'S GRAND ACT OF LARCENY'
'Unlucky Blackburn thwarted by Swede's Euro record strike'

And then went on: 'This greatly anticipated UEFA Cup tie in Glasgow, from Celtic's point of view, very nearly proved a big disappointment. It is a while since Celtic were made to chase quite as many shadows as Blackburn produced at Parkhead last night, a fate which often left Martin O'Neill's team in a state of bewilderment. The only bewilderment Blackburn must have felt was over leaving Scotland a defeated side.'

In the *Celtic View*, the 'Legends' had conflicting ideas on the match. Ronnie Simpson: "The keeper was Man of the Match; way above anyone else." Bertie Auld: "We were turned over in the first half, when we wanted every pass to our feet and did not press the opposition enough." And Frank McGarvey: "Forwards need a plentiful supply of ball to do anything and they didn't get it."

The match stats read:

Celtic		Blackburn
1	Goals	0
6	Shots on Target	3
1	Shots off Target	4
1	Blocked shots	12
6	Corners	6
13	Fouls	21
3	Offsides	4
42%	Possession	58%

Celtic won the tie but Blackburn's play seemed to catch the eye of most watchers. In particular, the style of midfielder David Thomson, a close-season buy by Souness from Liverpool, the £1.5million fee exactly half what the Reds paid for him to Coventry two years previously.

Having read the above reports and checked the stats, any feelings of disappointment afterwards among the Blackburn players would not be unexpected. Like any good manager, Graeme Souness would have been keen to boost their morale and probably did use the 'men against boys' phrase as an ego-booster.

I expect, though, that he would have been astonished, if not mortified, to hear that his captain proclaim his private words to the media and I would have loved to have been present at their first confrontation after the outburst.

On the following Sunday, both teams were in league action. Celtic gave Aberdeen a thorough going-over on their way to a 7-0 victory at Parkhead; Aston Villa travelled to Ewood Park and held Blackburn to a 0-0 draw.

In the league match before the return leg, Celtic went up to Tannadice, where goals by Hartson and Sutton gave them a 2-0 win; Blackburn had a trip to the South Coast and another draw, this time with Southampton 1-1.

The Road to Seville

Now that they were out of the road, the build up could begin for the return leg. On the eve of the match, *The Herald* pointed out that 7,800 fans were heading for Lancashire:

'ALL SYSTEMS GO FOR THE CELTIC INVASION'

And there was another reference to the purchase of David Thomson.

'SOUNESS GAMBLE IS STILL PAYING DIVIDENDS'

In the *Celtic View*, an exclusive interview with Martin O'Neill started with a resume of events since the first leg: 'The Hoops claimed first blood from the UEFA Cup tie against Blackburn with a narrow 1-0 win last Thursday night and the manager has insisted that despite the reaction to the performance, he was delighted with the result ground out by his side. Furthermore, the Irishman not only knows that Celtic are capable of producing a better display but fully expects it to be on view at Ewood Park.

'Celtic were outplayed at times last week but the fact that they managed to stand firm in the face of some heavy first-half pressure and then ... snatch a late winner has given them a fantastic opportunity of progressing in the tournament.'

When asked for his views on the forthcoming return match, the Celtic manager seemed confident and upbeat: "I actually think we will have more of the ball at Ewood Park. If you had asked me beforehand if I would take a victory without conceding a goal then I most certainly would have. It concerns me little what people have to say about it because folk will put whatever kind of spin they want on things.

"We will go to Blackburn and try to win the game and I'm confident that we can do that. I thought we showed great determination to turn the fixture in our favour and we will need to show the same kind of willpower and more down there. I fancy us to score at Ewood Park and it's a game we are all looking forward to. The comments that have emanated from the Blackburn dressing-room give us further motivation to go there and do what we can to win the game."

From that last sentence, it seems fairly obvious that Gary Flitcroft's comments were not only heard but were also the subject of some discussion in the dressing room. I wonder if we will ever know Graeme Souness' thoughts on that particular situation. The job of a manager is difficult enough without his private comments being publicly aired by his captain?

From the comments in the letters sent to the *Celtic View*, the supporters seemed realistic about the match at Parkhead but confident over the return.

"Despite the performance, the Bhoys are still in the driving seat. They haven't lost an away goal yet." (a fan from Gateshead); "Yes, we did play below our best, yes, Blackburn had the majority of possession, but correct me if I'm wrong, did we not win?" (one from Co. Down); "I believe Blackburn are now under pressure and have increased that pressure through their own arrogant words." (fan from Glenrothes); "So don't be too hard on the Bhoys for not performing as well as they might. After all, they did win the first leg." (Airdrie).

There was a curious article in *The Herald* on the morning of the match. While one headline gave note of the Celtic manager's intention: 'O'Neill is going for the jugular', another, about the opposition manager, was sarcastic and chauvinistic. At a time like this, as I have said before, journalists would not be human if they did not let their feelings show. Before the first match of this tie, these writers needed Souness; their editors were pushing them to get previews of the tie from him and then his comments afterwards.

Even before the second leg, they would have attended his pre-match conferences, nodded at his sallies, taken down the relevant quotes. Now, however, as the 'away' manager, he would be expendable after the tie. So, this was the time to have a go and *The Herald* did. Under the offering: 'Fine language from man who scarred the beautiful game', one of their leading writers listed a series of incidents involving the Blackburn manager during his playing career, all of them contentious. Maybe a lot of Celtic fans thought it funny; my own reaction was of distaste. If they can do that to a guy they needed when he was in charge at Ibrox, who would bet on them passing up the opportunity to do the same to any Celtic manager after they have left the club?

On the day of the match, the M74 was flooded with Celtic fans heading for Lancashire. In Blackburn itself, in the hours before the match, there were stories about pubs running out of beer but in general, the local police were quite happy with the behaviour of the visiting fans.

Celtic's Brand Protection team was also enjoying itself. In conjunction with Blackburn Trading Standards and Lancashire Constabulary, they seized counterfeit hats, scarves, flags and badges worth an estimated £2,000 in the hours before kick-off.

By the time that arrived, on Thursday, November 14, 26,698 had squeezed into Ewood Park. Compared to Celtic Park, that does not seem much but the atmosphere was intense and the tension high. The main topic of all the chat was the team which Martin O'Neill would put out. He was certain to pick Larsson but who would play alongside him? Would it be the more mobile but deeper-lying Chris Sutton or the powerful John Hartson, more of a target-man figure.

When the team was read out, it contained a surprise! Both were in, Hartson to play right up alongside Henrik and Sutton to have more of a midfield role. Paul Lambert dropped out to accommodate him. As in the first leg, Didier Agathe would take the right wingback position but for this match but Alan Thompson dropped down to the bench and Steve Guppy took up the wide position.

At exactly 8.00pm, the start having been delayed to allow police to look for forged tickets, referee Cosimo Bolognino blew the whistle to start this crucial encounter. Just 15 minutes later, he may as well have blown it again for the finish as Henrik Larsson scored the opener to put Celtic 2-0 ahead on aggregate. Right from the off, the slippery surface caused problems for more than a few players.

After a quarter-of-an-hour, Sutton slipped a pass in to the path of John Hartson. He slipped going for it as did his Blackburn marker but Henrik was on to the loose ball in a flash, showing wonderful skill in lifting the ball over the diving Brad Friedel for a superb goal. Effectively, that finished the match but as the *Celtic View* report suggested, in the course of the 90 minutes, a few people deserved credit.

'Celtic achieved their passage in to the next round of the tournament with a classy showing in which they reproduced the kind of form that was evident last season against the likes of Ajax, Juventus and Valencia. While the players deserve plenty of credit for the aggressive way they went about exerting their control on the game, O'Neill too deserved praise.

'The Irishman took the plunge by going for a courageous line-up that fielded personnel fully intent on doing as much damage up front as they could. John Hartson and Henrik Larsson led from the front, while Chris Sutton was deployed in the middle of the park, just behind the front two. That meant Paul Lambert and Alan Thompson were left on the bench, with Stan Petrov and Neil Lennon also in midfield, while Steve Guppy and Didier Agathe were sent out to patrol the flanks.

'Sutton has already proven he is an astute and diligent performer as an attacker and has also been competent when asked to deputise at the back. Last week, he showed he is equally adept in the middle. The Englishman was immense, negating the effect Tugay had on the game and imposing himself all over the pitch. His header that sealed Celtic's passage into the next round was exquisite, as he lost his marker to meet Petrov's corner and bullet it into the net.

'That second goal, in the 68th minute, came as no surprise. From Larsson's strike onwards, Celtic were the team in command, restricting Blackburn's opportunities in front of goal yet threatening themselves when moving forward. They should perhaps have increased their tally: Celtic could even have underlined their superiority with further goals in the second period. Hartson was the main beneficiary after a neat one-two between Larsson and Guppy, allowing the former to supply him unmarked at the back post but the Welsh striker's attempt was wildly hit and soared wide of the mark. Sutton also offered an indication of what was to come when he headed a Guppy corner into the side netting.'

It was obviously an excellent result for Celtic; but it also gave Scottish football a massive boost. This is frequently denigrated South of the Border, the usual dismissive comment being 'there are only two teams up there'. From the list of winners of the Premier championship, which shows that only the Old Firm have won that trophy since Aberdeen's last victory in 1984/85, there could indeed be some relevance in that statement.

However, if English fans were to check the statistics of their own Premiership, they may note that, since the competition began in 1992/93, only Manchester United, Arsenal and Blackburn Rovers have won the trophy. Maybe those of us who live in Scotland are entitled to ask: 'are there only three teams in England?'

And yet, as often happens, the stats for the evening do not quite show Celtic's apparent domination.

Blackburn		Celtic
0	Goals	0
6	Shots on Target	8
6	Shots off Target	4
5	Blocked shots	8
7	Corners	4
14	Fouls	17
2	Offsides	1
56%	Possession	42%

On the following day, the headline writers were in their element;

'PREMIERSHIP HIGH-FLIERS SHOT DOWN IN BATTLE OF BRITAIN'

'O'NEILL'S STOCK SOARS TO NEW HEIGHTS AFTER PUTTING SOUNESS IN PLACE'

'MANAGER EXHAUSTS SUPERLATIVES IN PRAISE OF SUTTON & CO'

In the following week's *Celtic View*. The 'Legends' gave their comments on the game. Ronnie Simpson dealt with the defence: "I'm giving Rab Douglas the number one slot. He was the Man of the Match. In these games, he's been making good saves at the right time and that's exactly what the defence needs."

Bertie Auld dealt with the midfield: "I thought everything boiled down to workrate. We had that and stopped Blackburn playing...as we gained in confidence, they lost their way."

And Frank McGarvey covered the forwards: "Martin O'Neill's tactical switch in moving Sutton to mark Tugay was a master-stroke. After Larsson's wonderful touch for the first goal, Blackburn had no way back."

And from the letters they sent in, the fans were equally enthusiastic;

"That wonderful win over Blackburn will have given the Hoops a much-needed shot of confidence in terms of recent criticism over certain displays."

"Martin once again proved just what a brilliant man he is ... never once rising to the bait thrown down by Souness or the 'impartial' Scottish press."

"The most satisfying thing was seeing all the English guys who'd been cheering on Blackburn sitting in silence from the 15th minute."

"I think the Bhoys were absolutely immense on Thursday evening, they battled from the first whistle to the last. It was a joy to watch!"

"I was at the game and witnessed one of the great Celtic matches. A night I will never forget for its passion, commitment, skill and the fans' sense of humour."

"I think we're hitting form at the right time. The Blackburn game has given everyone a boost after the disappointment of the Champions League."

In the *Celtic View*, Martin O'Neill gave a less hysterical review of his team's recent performances.

"I think we have got more into our rhythm now. There was obviously great disappointment when we lost to Basel because everyone had been hoping for another crack at the Champions League. It hung over us for a little while but other than Motherwell which was a game we should have actually won given the amount of chances we created, I can't say that the players' attitude or application has been any different.

"We might have found our rhythm a bit more now but even in the early parts of the season I still thought that we were playing well. We got a great boost from winning the Blackburn game. It meant a great deal to the players, and I was pleased because even though we won the first leg, we took a lot of criticism and it was nice to come roaring back.

"I don't think the players have anything to prove to anyone but what was good to know was that when they really had to come through they weren't found wanting. I was surprised at some of the comments that emanated from the Blackburn dressing room after the first game because I have been a long time in it and I know that comments at what was effectively half-time can look empty if you don't follow through.

"If we needed further motivation, which to be honest I actually don't think that we did, then we got it"

Who says managers don't read the papers?

In the UEFA headquarters, on the day following the match, the draw was made for the next round. In the same group of five as Celtic were Porto, AEK Athens, Hertha Berlin and Celta Vigo …

TONY HAMILTON'S EUROPEAN DIARY
Part 3: Rovers and out

"Graeme Souness – are you watching?" The immortal words of our home match commentator and Newsroom Editor Paul Cuddihy, as Henrik Larsson sunk the Lancashire side at Celtic Park in the first leg.

A rhetorical question I feel – of course he was watching. He just couldn't believe what he was seeing.

Perhaps PC's description wasn't exactly up there with Kenneth Wolstenholme's *"they think it's all over…"* or Alan Hansen's *"you can't win anything with kids…""*but then again Paul *'it's-a-chance-it's-a-goal"'*Cuddihy has one up on the Englishman and the, eh, other Englishman – he's the love child of Arthur Montford.

Souness may be perceived as some dark force by our supporters but he did at least give the CelticTV team a personal audience before the first match at his club's training ground – dug out in the bottom of a valley in a setting befitting of a James Bond film, just off the A666! As if the conspiracy theorists needed more evidence.

Eileen Monaghan, Des and I drove down to the camp about a week before the Glasgow leg of the affair and he did his bit, allowed us to film his players in training and was at pains to stress that whatever happened in his birth country, he wouldn't be planting a flag in the centre circle of Celtic Park at the end of the match like he once did during his spell in Turkey.

A good decision, methinks.

He was, I have to say, overall very amenable at that point – not at all how I imagined him – although my opinion changed slightly as he strutted from the tunnel at Celtic Park on D-Day ala Chris Eubank in his prime, thriving in the boos and jeers from the majority of the crowd which were all for him.

As the final whistle went at the end of the second leg in Blackburn and the Bhoys were safely through to the next round I took a moment to think of George McCluskey, who Souness nearly halved in two on his Rangers debut while the ex-Celt was at Hibernian, and thought that what goes around, eventually comes around. Justice had been done.

Aside from the actual action, travel and my perpetual regret of dogging geography as a schoolboy in Glasgow's East End would come back to haunt all of the crew as we made our way to training at Ewood Park from the team hotel on the outskirts of Manchester, the night before the second leg.

The plan is that, where we can, I drive. I may not be the best driver in the world (although I think I am) but I'm certainly the worst passenger. So, you have to find a balance with getting there alive with me at the wheel or getting lost and not getting there at all – with me at the wheel.

Actually getting there on this particular occasion was not too much of an effort but getting back from the team's training session proved to be disastrous. The journey, which took about 40 minutes during rush hour, took more than three hours on a ring-road around Greater Manchester – an area I now know like the back of my hand.

The Road to Seville

Come to think about it, I don't know the back of my hand that well, not at all in fact. Try it out for yourself right now – close your eyes for a few seconds and leave your hand on a table with a load of strangers' hands and try and pick out your own...

Anyway, of all the places we were during this trip, the town of Blackburn was probably the least hospitable. Don't get me wrong – the people at the ground were very good with us before, during and after the match.

We had a look at Blackburn Rovers' very impressive TV operation at the stadium as they did with us before the first leg and the co-operation overall between the two clubs was excellent.

And the real Rovers supporters for their part seemed to accept defeat with a certain grace that others not a million miles from the stadium I'm sitting in right now sometimes find difficult.

There is however an element, a real nasty element, of their support who don't seem to tolerate non-white, Anglo Saxons so you could imagine that our all-inclusive supporters and that bad lot didn't always see eye to eye when they clashed.

Again, justice was done on the park thanks to an outstanding showing from the Hoops and the fascist element crawled back into their holes with their tails between their legs.

At the same time the Celtic entourage charged up the M6 in preparation for the draw which would pair us with Celta Vigo and take me to Spain for the first of four times during a truly remarkable UEFA Cup campaign.

As we look back on this season and this competition, the football is the one thing which deservedly has the most words written about it. As a Celtic supporter I've no argument with that and as you'll read throughout this book from the rest of the (real) writers, what the actual playing team achieved made us all prouder than we ever imagined we could be.

For me, however, I remember the supporters – the journeys they made, the places they slept and never slept, the money they spent, the songs that they sung, the hangovers they had and the smiles on their faces.

That's what it was all about. At Blackburn in mid-November and at Celtic Park on Halloween, when Souness came to the party dressed as Souness, very few of us were thinking about scoring goals on German soil, competing in Europe after Christmas or making it to another European final.

We were just happy to be part of it and happy to be Celtic supporters.

Chapter Five
Celta Vigo:
Away goals count double
by Alison McConnell

IT'S somewhat ironic that, as Maggie Thatcher's Tory party entered the embryonic stages of an 18-year hold over Britain, that Fern Kinney should top the charts with *'Together We Are Beautiful.'* At the same time Stanley Kubrick's *'The Shining'* was chilling spines throughout cinemas countrywide and Celtic were mixing it against the audacious skills of Real Madrid in the European Cup. John Hartson was barely out of nursery school; Shaun Maloney hadn't yet been born.

Had anyone consulted the nearest crystal ball and informed the 67,000 Hoops fans squeezed into Celtic Park for a breath-taking first leg against the Spaniards that it would be 23 long years before Celtic hosted another European match beyond Christmas, the fear would have been more unnerving than anything Jack Nicholson had to offer.

In between the desert of March 1980 and the celebrations of December 2002 were the frustrating agonies at the hands of Politechnica Timisoara, Rapid Vienna and Neuchatel Xamax, heart-breaking exits following the thrills of Partizan Belgrade and memorable nights against the likes of Real Sociedad, PSG and Borussia Dortmund. But no European football after the Yuletide festivities.

In another little quirk of fate, the team who went on to win the European Cup the last time Celtic lingered around beyond black bun and shortbread time were Brian Clough's unfashionable Nottingham Forest, with whom Martin O'Neill and John Robertson were intrinsic to the success. Real Madrid went all the way to the semi-final only to be dismissed by Hamburg, the finalists that Robertson would ensure left empty-handed after the current Hoops assistant netted a 21st minute winner. O'Neill's disappointment from 12 months earlier when he was left out of

The Road to Seville

Forest's first European Cup-winning squad was assuaged somewhat, Forest entered an elite by becoming one of a select few to win the competition in successive years and few would have guessed the intertwining fates of O'Neill and Celtic that would come in the years that lay ahead.

Fast forward 23 years and here's the story: Christmas time is fast approaching and the tension at Celtic Park is palpable given the precarious challenge of staying alive beyond a round that has repeatedly proved to be the unravelling of a dream.

Blackburn Rovers had already been put to the sword in a swashbuckling performance at Ewood Park that went someway to silencing Celtic's critics south of the border. Celta Vigo are the visitors in the first-leg and gust after gust of disorder follows pantomime villain Claude Colombo. The bungling French referee caused uproar among the natives with a string of incredulous decisions. After a hapless performance the bumbling whistler incurred the furious wrath of the Celtic Park crowd in the dying minutes when he ordered O'Neill to the stands with just three minutes remaining and the Irishman was forced to launch a UEFA appeal. The delay in the hearing of his appeal that he wished to present himself meant he was entitled to take his seat in the dug-out for the return leg in Spain. The round, however, will be remembered for its heroes, not its scoundrels.

Henrik Larsson has proved to be Celtic's talisman on too many occasions to count, and the Swedish internationalist continued his remarkable scoring prowess in the UEFA Cup campaign. Against Blackburn and Celta Vigo, the striker's goals on home soil were instrumental in easing Celtic over the hurdle and the manner of Larsson's performances in the competition silenced some of his dissenters who have repeatedly questioned his ambition for his decision to stay in Scotland.

Six minutes after the interval during the opening leg, Larsson showed his courage and tenacity when he beat three Vigo defenders to be first to the ball and bundle it into the net after John Hartson had jumped quite magnificently to head a Steve Guppy corner across the face of the goal. It was a slender lead and one that Celtic could have added to as the game went on, but for all their pressure and opportunities they had to be content with a narrow win to take to Vigo. Like those before and after them, Celta Vigo were silly enough to allow their mouths to take over when the game was finely poised at the half-way line with manager Miguel Angel Lotina quick to dismiss the significance of the first-leg result,

"I wasn't very impressed by Celtic," he had maintained after losing 1-0 at Celtic Park in the first leg. "They did not surprise me at all. The crowd did impress me very much, but the 60,000 fans will be staying in this country and will not be in Vigo for the next match." There may not have been 60,000 Celtic supporters in Vigo, but of those who did make the journey all got the Christmas present they so desperately wanted.

European football delivers a glamour unrivalled to anything the domestic game can offer and a decent run in any European competition garnishes as much prestige as it does cash.

Celtic's UEFA Cup run took them past teams of serious reputation on the European platform and perhaps the most satisfying aspect of these displays was the fact that O'Neill's side were capable of dismantling such salubrious opponents.

After so many disappointments, Celtic's triumphs were well received by a support that had been starved of significant progress on the European front. The season previously, O'Neill's side were unfortunate not to become the first Scottish club to make it into the second group phase of the Champions League after taking nine points from the first stage, but perhaps the foundations of such frustrations set the tone for the progress made 12 months later.

Certainly where Celtic's away form had cost them dear in their inaugural showing of the Champions League, by the time that they had recovered from the disappointment of going out to Basel – the only European team that O'Neill's side didn't score against away from home – some of their best displays were reserved for trips away from Celtic Park.

By the time that Celtic took a 1-0 lead, to Vigo they had amassed enough self-belief and confidence that even a trip to Spain on the back of a somewhat undeserved Old Firm defeat three days earlier couldn't dampen their fervour for the task in hand. Every family has its black sheep and of the six UEFA Cup rounds that Celtic negotiated before winning an invite to Seville only Celta Vigo was decided on away goals. It was, perhaps, Celtic's revenge for a Champions League qualifying exit at the hands of Basel who progressed because of the away goals rule.

Inside the Hoops' dressing room many are of the opinion that Celta Vigo provided the most telling test en-route to the final in Seville, but whether that is true or not, what is inarguable is that the La Liga side provided the most controversial meeting in the UEFA Cup campaign.

South African internationalist and Celta Vigo striker Benni McCarthy was fortunate not to end up dismissed in the second leg, or even worse, after an outrageous tackle on Hoops colossus Bobo Balde that left the defender writhing in agony on the deck. Peter Luccin was later disciplined by UEFA after TV evidence revealed him spitting at John Hartson, but the biggest controversy of the game came off the field when a jet carrying Celtic fans was diverted to Cardiff after allegations of trouble on board.

What was front-page fodder for every national newspaper later transpired to be a situation that was about as serious as Timothy Mallet hosting a special edition of *Question Time.* But more about that later.

John Hartson netted the goal that was the ultimate difference between the Hoops and Celta Vigo and the Welshman classified this tie as the most difficult of all the hurdles that Celtic had to negotiate to get to Seville. By then the striker was on his way to a magnificent season in a Hoops jersey after initially having a frustrating time at the beginning of the campaign. Chris Sutton and Henrik Larsson had been O'Neill's favoured strikers at the start of the season, but the Irishman's idea to deploy Sutton behind a front pairing of Hartson and Larsson was a tactic that would serve Celtic well throughout the season, particularly on the European arena. For Hartson, the UEFA Cup was where he really showed the class. Domestically the Welsh internationalist also showed his prowess with important and regular goals, but even now Hartson maintains that the goal in Vigo is one of his favourites of the entire season.

Hartson had arrived at Celtic in October 2001 with a heavy price tag hanging round his neck and the weight of expectation upon his shoulders. That he would have been a Rangers player a year earlier but for a failed medical was another source of pressure for the nomadic forward. Stints at Arsenal, Wimbledon, West Ham and

The Road to Seville

Coventry had showered the striker in controversy and adverse publicity regarding his right knee ensured he came to the club with a little unease. There was a queue of critics waiting to write off the striker as damaged goods with a disciplinary record that would clash immediately with O'Neill. Added to that, Hartson had the formidable task of interrupting a strike force that had proved to be the most successful in Scotland, with Sutton and Larsson forming a watertight understanding in their first season together. Nevertheless, the way the striker went about pushing himself into a regular starting slot was admirable.

His burly frame wouldn't look out of place in the midst of an international rugby scrum, the favoured game of many of his Welsh contemporaries, but as well as a 14-stone body, Hartson went on to prove to his dissenters that he can match brawn with quick feet and supple movement. Of all his goals this season, his stunning strike at Anfield is the one that wins the accolades, but the goal he scored in Vigo still goes down as one of his favourites of the entire season.

There is a good reason for that. When Hartson met Chris Sutton's clever flick from an Alan Thompson free-kick and spun on the edge of the box to sink a low shot into the bottom corner of the net, it wasn't only a goal that would take Celtic into the last 16 of a European competition for the first time in 23 years...

It was a goal that marked the arrival of John Hartson at Celtic. Indeed, the striker's goal might have proved a point to himself as much as it did to his critics. In a cruel twist of fate, Hartson would later miss the UEFA Cup final after losing his battle for fitness when it was revealed that he would require surgery on a back injury. By then the striker had become such a key part of Celtic's squad that the loss was bitterly lamented by O'Neill while the player himself was understandably gutted. Hartson had spent the weeks leading up to final trying to recover from the injury sustained in the Old Firm victory at Ibrox three days after the Boavista win, and the news on the Saturday afternoon before the game in Seville was inevitably gut-wrenching for the 28-year-old.

It was a measure of just far Hartson had come in the months between the start of the season and the end of the campaign. At the beginning of the season when Celtic's Championship status had given them a chance to qualify for the Champions League via a qualifying match against FC Basel, Hartson had delighted journalists with his unabashed honesty.

Speaking after a season in which he had started just one European game – the forgettable away defeat to Porto – he revealed his own lack of confidence by stating that both Larsson and Sutton might have been more suited to the finer points of European football.

"Maybe they are better equipped for the Champions League, maybe I will be left for the SPL," he had mused. "I don't know. I hear people say that and, fair enough, sometimes you have to take these things on board. Maybe that is what the manager might go with. I have not spoken to the manager about it. But if I am honest, I think we might well go into Europe with these two, leaving me to add to my goals in the SPL."

Hartson also offered a insight into the task he believed he had in forcing himself into contention for a regular starting slot at the forefront of Celtic's attack: "I thought Chris was absolutely unbelievable last year in the Champions League," Hartson had revealed at the start of the season. "I am not just saying that. Chris and

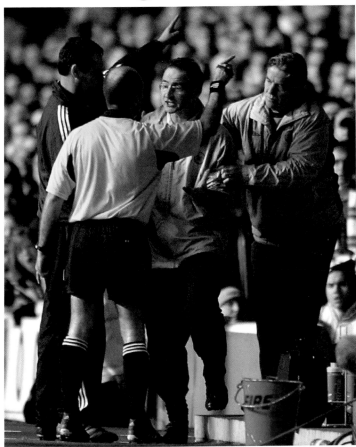

ENTENTE LESS THAN CORDIALE: *Martin O'Neill fell foul of French referee Claude Colombo, who sent him to the stand, as Celtic enjoyed another 1-0 victory, Larsson scoring the only goal against Celta Vigo*

DOUBLE DELIGHT: *John Hartson's goal in Vigo was enough to send the Celts through on away goals*

WE'LL BE BACK AFTER CHRISTMAS: *Martin O'Neill was delighted with the victory over Celta Vigo, which brought European football to Celtic Park for the first time after Christmas in 23 years*

Henrik, particularly in some of the home games, were as good as any pairing in the Champions League. If I am honest I will say that."

It, therefore, says much about Hartson's ability and character that not only did he go about his task quietly and effectively, but he did so by proving himself on the pitch with a series of clever performances. The Welshman used his frame to great effect to hold players off and carve open spaces for his team-mates to exploit and by eliminating Vigo from the competition, the most technically refined outfit that Celtic met en-route to the UEFA Cup final, the Hoops run started to increasingly gather momentum.

At that stage, those Celtic fans in Spain greeted the aggregate victory over Celta Vigo with almost the same unbridled enthusiasm that was on display when they later beat Boavista to secure a UEFA Cup final placing, simply because it represented a milestone, a place to be cherished in a European competition beyond Christmas. After so many years of failing to overcome the hoodoo, it was a symbolic win, a tangible representation that O'Neill's team were still making progress and had moulded into a fearsome unit.

The performance in Vigo against Lotina's side may not have generated quite as much hype as victories against Premiership opponents Blackburn and Liverpool, but to many observers it was a win against a quality side and an intelligent performance that won O'Neill plaudits throughout Europe for the manner of the progression. For Hartson, it was one of many memorable nights in the tournament and one that he looks back on with fondness.

"It was definitely one of my favourite goals of the season just because it proved to be so significant. Added to that, it was also a nice goal which I enjoyed scoring," smiled the 28-year-old.

"If you look back over the course of the season and look at the teams we beat in the UEFA Cup – the likes of Liverpool, Stuttgart and Boavista – then the result in Vigo was absolutely massive. There was also the whole thing of not being able to stay in Europe beyond Christmas and it was lovely to be able to put that to bed. There were a number of satisfying results in the UEFA Cup, but that is definitely up there with my best nights because I think it also kick-started some of the momentum in the competition. I still believe that was probably the toughest fixture we had throughout it.

"To get the goal which kept us in Europe after Christmas for the first time in 20-odd years was magnificent, a really great feeling. It was a great night," he continued.

"I remember Chris won a really good header just over the half-way line, and it was quite a wet pitch because we had trained on it the night before. The ball seemed to skim up and as the defender tried to get in front of me I shoved myself in the way. In many games on the continent that would be interpreted as a foul, but the referee did well and let play go on. I swivelled, hit it first time and I was delighted when it went in.

"They eventually went on and won the game and the significance of the goal was huge. It was the only round in which the away goal rule put us through so it was nice to get it but it was a really tough game for us. Celta Vigo were an exceptionally good side. They were a top team – as good as Liverpool and Stuttgart and any team that we played in the UEFA Cup.

The Road to Seville

"They came to Celtic Park and showed what they could do and although we won 1-0 here it was very tight. Henrik got the goal for us, and we knew that when we went over there that we would probably need to score. To get the goal was magnificent."

Luccin's spit at Hartson led to a four-game ban for the Vigo player, but Hartson was completely unaware of the incident during the game and had no idea about what had gone on until he got into the dressing room afterwards.

"I never saw it," he said. "The boys all asked me about it after the game, but at the time I never even saw it because my back was turned. The TV proved it and Luccin was banned, but it's just one of those things that sometimes raises its head in football. Sometimes I think that British players are a lot more honest. From a personal point of view I've learned a lot over the last three or four years because apart from playing with Celtic, with Wales we've come up against quite a lot of it as well.

"It's something I've had to learn to deal with because a few years ago I think that I'd have lost the head a bit more and got quite frustrated because it can be so annoying when you're playing against that kind of football."

Apart from the fact that the UEFA Cup run ultimately cemented Hartson's reputation in Scotland, for the player himself the picture was a bit bigger, "I think the UEFA Cup run was great for us because it got us recognition that I think we hadn't won by playing in Scotland," explained Hartson. "What I mean by that is that if we go out and beat a team 4-0 in a league match and play superbly then there will always be people who say that's exactly what we're expected to do. No-one looked at the pairings for the UEFA Cup and said that Celtic were expected to go to Anfield and win, or to go to places like Portugal and England and win and I think it says so much about the spirit and the quality within the squad. It was brilliant to play a part in it."

Hartson went on to pick up the Bank of Scotland Player of the Month for December, but a booking sustained in the second leg against Vigo, his third of the tournament, ruled him out of the next round against Stuttgart. It was a crushing blow for the player who had been so instrumental in taking Celtic into the last 16, but although he would spend the next round in the stands, his contribution was more than appreciated by O'Neill.

"It was a typical John Hartson goal with that ability to turn players and shoot very quickly and that gave us the spur again," said O'Neill. "It was a great goal. He has always scored goals, which is why we took him to the football club and he's rewarded us. The goal against Vigo was a very important one for us, but he's been pretty regular and the great thing about it is that Chris can adjust. We feel that there are plenty of goals in the team.

"It really was a terrific effort by the team to beat Celta Vigo over the two games. It was a really great achievement because they showed that they can definitely play a bit but it's not time to be praising the opposition, it's time to be praising our own players because they produced a great performance. We conceded a bad goal and then we got the equaliser which was what we had set out to do."

It was an anxious end to the game with Celtic knowing that one more goal would seal their progress, while another one lost at the back would open the exit door. Benni McCarthy caused further anger among the Hoops fans when he blatantly dived in the box in the dying minutes of the game in an attempt to win a penalty, but that aside it was a nail-biting finale to what was a demanding tie. Prior to the second 90 minutes of the round, a cheque was presented to the local community for 10,000 Euros on behalf of the Celtic fans after the Prestige tragedy on the Galician Coast.

The pollution wreaked havoc a few weeks before the game when the Prestige sank and the 60,000 tons of oil on board was spilled into the ocean. It was the kind of gesture from Celtic that has garnished an excellent reputation for throughout the football world, but it was a reputation and a gesture that would have little impact on the way the Spanish police over-reacted after the game.

That Celtic had never before ousted a Spanish side from any European competition in their history added to the significance of the occasion and the fact that Vigo were sitting in third position in the renowned La Liga at the time the teams went head-to-head offered further insight into the manner of the victory. Valencia, of course, were Celtic's first ever opponents in Europe back in 1962 when a somewhat cavalier performance left the Hoops 4-2 down after the first leg in Spain before going out of the competition following a 2-2 draw in the second leg. Celtic's previous meetings with Spanish oppositions had been fraught occasions, although by far the most controversial was the meeting with Atletico Madrid in April 1974. Still remembered for the sheer frustration of the evening, one of the few other games that could match it for unmitigated vitriol and blatant cheating was the encounter against Rapid Vienna in 1984.

However, if the first leg of Celtic's European Cup semi-final against Atletico Madrid can be looked upon with any magnanimity it would have to be for the sole reason that somehow a full-scale riot was avoided. Jimmy Johnstone suffered the most from the Spaniards' obvious thuggery, with the little midfielder bearing the brunt of some ferocious 'tackles'. From the onset, Atletico made it obvious that they had come to Glasgow with no intention of playing constructive football. They left no stone unturned as they fought, spat, hacked and kicked their opponents in a performance that proved too much for Turkish referee Dogan Babacan to deal with. Before the 90 minutes were out, seven of the visitors had been booked while three were sent off for violent conduct. In return, the very fact that Celtic had just two players go into the book suggests that the Hoops managed to retain a semblance of dignity and composure in the face of such outrageous provocation.

Disappointingly, although Celtic had plenty of possession and played the better football, they couldn't penetrate the Spaniards' goal and the first leg ended in an acrimonious 0-0 stalemate. The utter mayhem and intimidation deployed by the visitors resulted not only in ridiculous fouls committed repeatedly, but also ensured plenty of prolonged stoppages that Celtic were powerless to prevent.

Before the game, Jock Stein had apparently joked with the press that: "They've got half a dozen Argentineans in their pool, and the manager's one – so that means a riot for a start." It was a prophecy that proved correct but UEFA failed to take any significant action against the Spanish club, and they ducked out of the responsibility of playing the second leg at a neutral venue. Atletico Madrid's only punishment was a fine and the three players who had been red-carded were banned for the return leg. Only one of them was a first-team regular.

Great debate surrounded Celtic's decision to actually go to Madrid and play the second 90 minutes, but after some argument the Hoops made the decision to fulfil the requirements of the tie. It was a decision that the board effectively made, with the directors of the club fearful of the sanctions that would be imposed by UEFA had they failed to play the tie. Yet, throughout Europe there was genuine repugnance at the way in which Atletico had bullied their way through the opening leg.

By the time Celtic got to Madrid the atmosphere was already tense and a volatile Spanish media was avidly stoking the flames: 'Atletico versus Celtic and UEFA' ran a headline on a local newspaper. Players were confined to hotel rooms, surrounded by armed guards and policemen while riot trucks were parked around the stadium. Jimmy Johnstone received a death threat and there were no facilities for training or relaxation. It was no great surprise when Celtic went down to two late goals and lost out on a place in the European Cup final. Nevertheless, at the final whistle Stein's players stood in the centre circle and applauded the Spaniards. Atletico Madrid were beaten 4-0 by Bayern Munich in the replayed final.

When the Hoops played Atletico Madrid 11 years later in the Cup-Winners' Cup it was an equally dismal affair, although this time the bitter acrimony had been prevalent the season before when Celtic met Rapid Vienna. The second leg in Glasgow had turned into an ugly fiasco and although the Hoops thought they had eventually gone through the tie thanks to a 4-3 aggregate win, they were to be penalised. Rapid Vienna alleged that defender Weinhofer had been hit by a quarter bottle of vodka thrown from the Jungle, and although TV evidence was eminently dubious as to whether the player was even struck by the missile, he left Glasgow swathed in bandages, Rapid appealed and the teams were ordered to replay the game at least 150 kilometres from Glasgow.

Old Trafford was the venue and further sourness was to follow. In separate incidents two English-based Celtic fans attacked, first the Rapid goalkeeper and then goalscorer and the following season Celtic played Atletico Madrid behind closed doors at Celtic Park. The Spaniards took full advantage of the eerie atmosphere and the handicap of playing in their own empty stadium was too difficult for Celtic to overcome. After getting a respectful 1-1 draw in Madrid, the Hoops were eliminated from the competition after a 2-1 defeat at an empty Celtic Park.

More recently, Celtic were left heart-broken at the end of their first Champions League season. Pipped for a place in the lucrative second group stages, ironically by Porto, their consolation prize was a UEFA Cup meeting against Valencia. Chris Sutton missed the first leg in the Mestalla following worrying news from home that his infant son was seriously ill. The youngster had been born prematurely and although Sutton couldn't get a separate flight home and had to wait to return to Glasgow with the rest of the first-team, he was understandably too preoccupied to play against Valencia.

Nevertheless, Hartson stepped into his shoes and although Celtic lost 1-0, the manner of the performance was pleasing and O'Neill was confident his side had a real chance in the return leg. Larsson netted the goal, missed a penalty and as the game went to the lottery of extra time and penalties it was Valencia who triumphed 5-4 and Celtic were eliminated. It was a massive disappointment but the fact that the Spaniards later went on to win their own highly competitive league that season was testimony to the level of performance that Celtic had produced.

But back to Celta Vigo. Excusing some of the time-wasting tactics of the La Liga side and the nauseating spitting incident from Luccin, the biggest controversy of the game came off the field after the game. Reports of police brutality in dealing with Celtic fans after the match were prevalent, while an alleged 'serious incident' on board an aircraft bringing Hoops fans home from Vigo resulted in the flight being diverted to Cardiff.

Flying back to Glasgow on the Friday afternoon after the victory on Thursday evening, a complete over-reaction gave the media a field day with front-page headlines and national news bulletins screaming of an apparent riot on board the plane. At the airport itself in Spain there was widespread confusion and panic when only one narrow gateway was used to herd thousands of fans through to a departure lounge. Inevitably there were angry scenes and it was the turn of the Spanish police to over-react. Batons were wielded in the affray, fans were injured and the entire episode left a sour note after what had been a momentous victory.

Celtic View contributor Roddy Stewart is also an air steward with over 20 years of flight experience. He travelled to Vigo as a fan and was aboard the flight that was hauled into Cardiff because of 'rioting' and he was incredulous at the manner in which a non-story was translated.

"The headlines in the papers were ridiculous," said Roddy. "It seemed to me that the cabin crew totally over-reacted. There were misdemeanours – someone smoking and someone drinking their own duty free on what was an alcohol-free flight – but the whole thing could have been handled much better and to suggest that fans were abusing cabin crew is nonsense.

"I was unaware of any incident until the plane descended very quickly. We received no information and given the engine problems we had experienced in both Glasgow and Spain, there was a general panic among supporters who thought something had happened to the plane. I don't want to see Celtic vilified by headlines because it's just not true. Even the police seemed bemused when they were interviewing us in Cardiff."

The incident took a little gloss off the result and Celtic were forced to launch their own independent inquiry into the allegations. The club appealed to fans to come forward with their version of what had taken place and, in the aftermath of one of the greatest wins in their recent history, they were forced to spend the subsequent days embroiled into a controversial story rather than enjoying the chance to bask in the glory of the result.

Celtic put out an official statement that read: "The tremendous victory by Celtic in the third round of the UEFA Cup has been overshadowed by certain events involving Celtic supporters. Eyewitness accounts reported to the club have accused the Spanish police of using unnecessary force in their attempts at crowd management at both the Celta Vigo ground and the airport.

"We have received reports of a number of injuries to Celtic supporters as a result of police-baton wielding. In a separate incident, an aircraft, not chartered by Celtic or its official travel partner, was diverted from Glasgow to Cardiff en-route from Santiago de Compostela. The reason given for the diversion was an alleged 'serious incident' on board between passengers and crew. This matter is being handled by Cardiff Police, and Celtic Football Club has already indicated that it will assist the Welsh Police fully."

It was a frustrating story that distracted attention from the real achievement of the evening, but if O'Neill felt that his headaches had abated for the time being he had a turbulent few weeks still to come. After the delight of the result in Vigo, Celtic were brought back to earth with a disappointing 1-1 draw at Rugby Park, and within days the Hoops were back at the forefront of the Scottish media. The players Christmas night out in Newcastle ended with three Hoops stars in custody while the pictures of the apparent indiscretion were plastered over the tabloid press.

Joos Valgaeren, Bobby Petta and Johan Mjallby were alleged to have chased a *Daily Record* photographer, beaten him up and destroyed his equipment after they were 'captured' partying in a Newcastle cocktail bar that boasted bikini-clad waitresses. It was a story that appeared to have little foundation and certainly any evidence of an injured snapper was in short supply. It didn't stop the editor of the *Record*, Peter Cox, appearing on national television and labelling the three players in question 'thugs' before posting their faces on the front page of the newspaper under the headline 'thugs and thieves'.

The three players were held in a Gateshead prison for 18 hours before being released without charge, and at the time O'Neill spoke to each player individually before announcing that he had complete faith in the trio. It was a decision that vindicated some months later in March when, ahead of the UEFA Cup quarter-final against Liverpool, it was announced that no action would be taken against the three in question.

"I've listened to what has been said," said an ashen-faced O'Neill immediately after the incident. "I've listened to the players and I have total belief in them. Time will tell who is right and who is wrong and if I'm wrong that's another issue and the club will come down very, very heavily of any player found guilty if that's the case. I am fully confident that those players will be vindicated.

"The mood is very sombre as you could imagine. We have gone from an absolute high after knocking out Celta Vigo only to then find out a plane had been stopped in Cardiff and then to discover that an evening, remarkably and ironically, in Newcastle where the players went to get out of Glasgow and out of the glare of the spotlight ended with them well and truly in it.

"I've had easier times but it's part of the game. You have to accept it when you are manager of a football club and you get on with it. Things like this happen and you would prefer they didn't happen to be perfectly honest, but it's not too often matters as serious as this come into consideration.

"There were serious allegations made by the editor of the *Daily Record*. The most important issue is that those players who were photographed under the headline 'Thugs and Thieves' – not the nicest headline to wake up to – are protesting their innocence, I believe them and the law will eventually take its course."

When the law did take its course and there was no formal action taken against those concerned, O'Neill and his players were obviously satisfied at the chance to clear their name. "I am very pleased about that," said O'Neill. "The players who were on the front page of the *Daily Record* under the banner of 'Thugs and Thieves' were obviously very, very aggrieved to have that right in front of them.

"We asked them what was the case and they all said they were innocent. Not only did we go with that, but we believed them and I am delighted and they are especially pleased. The whole club is pleased and I would have to say that I am sure that the players will now look to see what they can do. I haven't had a chance to sit down and speak to any particular individual but I'm quite sure the club itself and the players will look to see what sort of redress can be sorted out because those were serious allegations and were obviously totally unfounded.'

Martin O'Neill's tenure at the helm of Celtic has resulted in a myriad of records broken and new ones established and there have been too many taboos put to rest to list them all. Prior to his arrival it had been 20 years since Celtic had last won back-to-back titles, it had been 32 years since the club had last celebrated a Treble, and many, many, years since the club succeeded in hanging on to a manager beyond the summer holidays. His time in charge has been characterised by an ability to motivate and draw out the best in the players he manages, and the club have reaped the success of that stability and commitment. This season's UEFA Cup run was the first time that Celtic have made a serious assault on any European competition for over 22 years, a frustrating failure that had long been a source of disappointment to those connected with the club.

O'Neill has since revealed himself that there was never any point in which he believed he would be asked to take up his place in the dug-out in Seville, and certainly in an era when money rules the game few would have expected a Scottish club of modest financial clout to make it into the final of a major European tournament. That he has, owes much to the faith he has in his players and his own talent for nurturing confidence in those he sends out onto the pitch.

If Celtic are to build on the achievements of this season O'Neill will need to reap some of the financial fruits that this season's run has created, but there can be little doubt that there is genuine optimism about the accomplishments of the season.

Back in December when the hordes of Hoops fans travelled to Vigo to see the La Liga outfit put to the sword, even the most optimistic would have assumed that if they were back in the country in the summer months it would be for little more reason that sun and sangria. Few would have envisaged the legacy of *'Y Viva Espana,'* sombreros and desperate pleas for gold dust tickets.

'Together we are beautiful...?' As far as Celtic fans are concerned, the marriage of O'Neill and Celtic has added glorious chapters to the history of the club.

TONY HAMILTON'S EUROPEAN DIARY
Part 4: Crash, bang, wallop!

Us Scots, and I suppose the Irish too, have an affinity with the Spanish and Spain in general. It's the first place abroad that many of us in my generation visited in the 1970s and 1980s and it's the place that we'll remember fondly for years to come after the excitement of May 21, 2003.

Back in mid-December however, as we went there defending a one-goal lead, things were mightily different.

Even in the aftermath as I predicted via the Celtic View that the local polis would be better for the final in Seville, I didn't really believe that either of those things would happen.

I didn't believe that the polis would be better and I didn't really believe that we would be in Seville. I'm glad to say I was wrong twice and that's a phrase you'll not read every day.

The local constabulary in and around the Vigo area seem to have a policy of 'no prisoners, only casualties'. And there were many, the majority of which were set upon for just being there.

The fans behaved no differently than they did in any other place – they just enjoyed themselves, tried to befriend the locals, went days without sleep, savoured every moment and tried to break the world record for sangria drinking.

Their efforts were rewarded at the end of the game with hard thumps on the back of the head from truncheon-wielding maniacs in unkempt polis uniforms with pistols at the ready – just in case the truncheon snapped on some poor soul's heid. (sic)

It wasn't for the faint-hearted and in a selfish sort of way I'm glad my only involvement in the unprovoked assaults was as an eye-witness to the proceedings.

We, however, the Celtic media team, had a slightly different dealing with the cops from those of our number who were attacked.

Part of the privilege of working for Celtic is the places we stay and the way we travel. I make no apology for it. Ordinarily I wouldn't make a song and dance about it but I still make no apology.

I'm not a snob - although I do find that there's nothing more humiliating than standing at a bus stop or using any form of public transport - but that's just me.

Looking back to how my wife Lynne and my two Bhoys roamed the streets of Seville the night of the final with nowhere to go and then thinking about the luxury of any team hotel I've ever slept in, I know what I prefer.

On these shores we tend to do our own thing as a small, happy and united media team. At Blackburn and Liverpool, for example, we would hire a vehicle big enough to take all of us, our gear and my talent and then we'd make our own way to and from training, the match and anywhere else we wanted to go.

Abroad however, we always bolt on behind the team bus when we're heading to training and take advantage of the police escort. The thinking in that is that we'll actually get there without the need to stop off for a shave and we'll be afforded the courtesy of proper parking when we arrive. That, of course, and the fact that I quite enjoy the excitement of chasing a police car!

The escort to training in Vigo was particularly interesting. Our base was about 40 minutes away from the city and obviously from the ground.

The route took us through one long stretch of motorway, which was topped and tailed with horrendous narrow single-track roads. Ironically it was on the motorway that we had trouble.

It was only Margot and I in the Iveco people carrier which I was driving – the others in the team were doing various things back at the hotel from trying to double her body weight by eating half a Mars Bar (Alison McConnell) to dreaming of lame donkeys (Des) to pretending to be able to speak Spanish (Sharon Gillespie) to forgetting what he was doing in Spain in the first place (Stephen Sullivan).

Anyway, the motorcade comprised a polis car, the team bus, us and another (unmarked) polis car with a really loud siren and a nice flashing blue light.

There's no speed limit on the road but it wouldn't have made any difference if there had been. Everything in our wake was swept aside save for these two Portuguese blokes in a clapped out 30-year-old Mercedes who decided it would be fun to nip between us and the bus.

It wasn't fun. It was a nightmare, and as the old Merc spun across the carriageway under the weight of our Iveco my immediate thought was that it could have been worse – I could have been on my own and not part of a polis escort.

I'd have been better off on my own – I wouldn't have been travelling at over 100 mph for a kick off or driving like Popeye Doyle in The French Connection.

The undercover cops behind us swerved to avoid the carnage and then filled the gap behind the bus as we took to the part of the motorway where the hard shoulder should have been (but wasn't – they hadn't got round to it) and then they carried on to Vigo with the team. I'm sure one of them even saluted us as they past.

We were left static in the middle of a real-life Scalectrix track with no pit stop where no-one could communicate because of the language problem. But luckily enough I found my Portuguese phrase book and managed to blurt out "I say old Bhoy, are your eyes painted on?" to the rather shaken but sober driver of the Merc.

We finally left the hell that was the motorway and made our own way into Vigo where a polyglot Spanish cop translated, mediated and completed the insurance forms for me and another (originally from East Ham in London) delivered us safely to the ground in exchange for a copious amount of Celtic lapel badges.

The Merc, as far as I know, is still lying in Vigo with its throat cut. Good enough.

Chapter Six

VfB Stuttgart: Vorsprung Durch Celtik

by Margot McCuaig

I HAVE a lingering childhood memory of a visit to the old underground in Glasgow. The expedition was taken with my aunt and as one who despises enclosed spaces the journey was trauma enough but to be honest the smell didn't help much either. The purpose of the visit was the quest to find a missing umbrella, an essential accessory in this city so I suppose the logic in trying to find it was fair enough. I vaguely remember that we went to the Lost and Found office but little did I understand then that symbolically the journey had relevance. I too was embarking in the search for lost property, a quest that would elongate over a significant period of time. Just one month short of 23 years to be exact.

Bizarrely, the lost object had never been mine in the first place, well not at a personal level anyway, and, fortunately, the majority of the searching wasn't spent within the confines of the Glasgow Underground, but rather more appreciatively on the terracing of Celtic Park. The first inkling I had that I may be nearing the end of my journey; that of discovering for myself the green brick road to European success, came about a year-and-a-half ago.

When Celtic hammered the giants of Italian football Juventus by 4-3 at Celtic Park something told me that I was on the brink of experiencing something special, finding my own European dream. Post Christmas European football was, surely, only a matter of time.

THE DRAW

Progressing to the next stage of the UEFA Cup, in the end thanks to a fabulous, if not a little unconventional strike from John Hartson against Celta Vigo was an incredible achievement. I'll never forget the look of terror, on the face of our cameraman Des 'Panic' O'Hara as we rode out the final minutes in what was to be the longest second half of a football match in the history of all football matches in the whole wide world.

Okay, so I was getting anxious, but we weren't the only ones. Des' wee face, bless him, embodied the emotions of thousands of Celts world-wide as we awaited the final whistle and the signal that this team, under the steady helm of O'Neill, Robertson and Walford had delivered a very precious gift. It was the first time Celtic had ousted a Spanish side, but that wasn't the only hurdle we had skied high over the top of.

At this particular juncture, December 12, the festive season was paramount in every Celtic fan's mind, not least, because this was to be the first time in 23 years that we would have the privilege of following our Bhoys on a European trail in the new year of a season. Post Christmas European football was a tantalising luxury few of the Media team had savoured, and for those of us that had, memories were for the best part entangled with that traumatic period in life – puberty! Like everything though, there are a couple of exceptions to that particular rule, but we shall come back to that later.

The final whistle reverberating throughout the stadium in Vigo was, as Joos Valgaeren would say, the cheese on the cake so far in our European journey. The sound of music had never, ever, been sweeter. Major events and stepping stones have a habit, regardless of their context, to spur us on trips down memory lane and, as the victory against Vigo signified, this was a journey after all.

The Celtic Media team was therefore; as to be expected, off and running before the draw for the next round had taken place when as they say, the balls were still cool inside the pot.

Indeed, awaiting the news on where to position our destination pin on our European map, we celebrated the wonderful news of post Christmas football with a "what were you doing when.." moment. The common question had, up until this point in all our lives, been "where were you when Celtic won the European Cup". I, like many of my colleagues, didn't exist in that era so what joy on the morning of December 13, 2002 when the question turned to March 1980 and Celtic's last post-festive adventure.

A period all (well, very nearly all of us) had an opinion on. However, very quickly events were taken away from us, as they tend to do when an excited rabble battle to contribute their ten bobs' worth all at once. A query became a quest for proof and the announcement that documentary evidence in the form of a portrait photograph from 1980 would be required to put all our stories into context. Just time for a frenzy of phone calls before the draw and a return to momentary calm. Well as DH Lawrence wrote 'there is no point in work unless it absorbs you like an absorbing game.' More on the memories and photographs later.

We're all terribly superstitious here at Celtic and we try to establish and maintain patterns that work. As such, as of previous rounds, we broadcast a live programme on the website throughout the draw and still on the theme of Christmas, well it makes sense to carry it through, we were like children gazing at the presents under the tree as the UEFA delegates put some heat, so speak, into those balls. Martin O'Neill has said that one if his proudest moments at Celtic had been when he was in attendance on behalf of the club for the Champions League group stages draw.

That experience was both wonderful and educational as well as tantalising. Indeed, it gave us a taste of where could go and for now reaching the next stage of the UEFA Cup was fantastic. So, to the draw, drum roll please.

The manager makes no secret about the fact that he prefers an away draw first. It makes sense, once the first leg is out of the way theoretically and logistically, you can approach the home leg knowing exactly where you are and what you have to do. You have to agree with him but removing the sensible head for a minute and replacing it with that mayhem of superstition, home and away had done us rightly so far.

The heat risen to unbearable temperatures and the drum roll over, we were going to Germany. Home first! (and then to Liverpool or Auxerre but one chapter at a time!) You can say a lot about our wee media team but you can't question the ability to throw stats in from nowhere, although personally I could have survived without the first one. The exclamation mark at the climax of Hail! Hail! was barely out of my lips at the end of the broadcast when the clanger was dropped. We had never scored on German soil.

That, even for our rabble, was a bit of a conversation stopper and in a room full of 'strong personalities' as the boss prefers to call us in order not to generate disdain, silence comes around every bit as often as European football after Christmas. Oh how good does it feel to be able to say that! A few deep breaths were in order all round as indeed was the necessitation to carry out some research on our opponents if only to steady some pre-match nerves. And given that this tie was to be played some two months into the bright and distant future of post Christmas European football (simply rolling off the tongue now!) initial concerns were that this going to be a long wait.

At the time of asking, VfB Stuttgart were sitting in fifth position in the Bundesliga, a very competitive league. They had endured an adventure-and-a-half to get where they were, having entered the competition via the Intertoto Cup and whilst we would love to have found salvation in the fact that they had entered into Europe through the back door, the reality was that they had played and won an additional four competitive games to afford themselves this privilege.

They were also familiar with the Scottish game, having ousted Hearts from the same competition some two seasons previously, on the away goals rule. That very phrase sends shivers down every Celtic supporter's spine. Who can forget the 'defeat' in the 5-4 victory against Partizan Belgrade, and of course, the FC Basel game…

We seemed to be, however, beginning to reverse the trend, the victory against Celta Vigo after all was won, in our favour, on the away goals rule. The trick was not to get too anxious as events were going our way. There was a distinctive pattern emerging. You play at home first, I record a pre-match interview for *Celtic Replay* with Alan Thompson as a matter of essential urgency and my newsroom buddy Tony Hamilton and I broadcast a programme from the scene of our visiting European team's pre-match training session. Well, allegedly.

Prior to the Blackburn game we couldn't see the players because of the thick fog. Actually, we blamed it on the fog at the time, but we later discovered they were simply hiding behind their 'men against boys' theory. Did they say boys?

How incredibly naïve. It was never going to be anything other than men against Bhoys! One final integral element to our superstitious build up. We play a team with a particular letter in their name, yet as this stage to be discovered. (but do stay with us, the theory is coming…!)

THE HOME LEG

When you've spent 23 years both agonisingly waiting and furtively searching for something you would think that another couple of months wouldn't be that much of a hardship but winter 2002/2003 has got to have been the longest ever. If you couple that with a winter break from the SPL and subsequently the total absence of competitive football for weeks, the build up to the Stuttgart match couldn't have come round quickly enough. Indeed, by the time February 20 arrived, Stuttgart had progressed from fifth to third in the Bundesliga. So, you wait forever, and then bang, it hits by exploding onto the scene in a catalogue of disasters.

Not that anyone needs reminding of this but by doing what he does best, and that's merely being the fantastically brave player that he is, Henrik Larsson suffered a double fracture of the jaw in a collision with Livingston's Bahokin and required emergency surgery on February 10.

A significant and indeed physical and painful blow to Henrik, but metaphorically speaking it blew us all away. The prognosis wasn't good as news quickly emerged that we were looking at a period of weeks for recovery. Enter the media frenzy, Celtic are a one-man team who cannot progress without Henrik Larsson.

If we're honest, life without Henrik fills every one of us with dread. He is everything and more to our team so his omission ensured a considerable period of anxiety. But, as much as we would miss him, the show had to go on. And besides, we still had Chris Sutton who put the icing on the cake at Blackburn and John Hartson, whose superb goal had allowed us to progress to this stage of the competition.

But, as you will be aware, bad luck tends to fall in wee groups of tragedies so of course it shouldn't have come as a surprise to any Celtic fan that John Hartson was set to miss the home leg due to a suspension. And of course, while we were on a depressing roll, we had to consider the impact the loss of our manager, due to suspension, to the stands for the duration of the match would have on our team. What is it they say in Glasgow, it never rains but it pours? Thankfully, that umbrella in the underground was awaiting an introduction to the fray, as indeed this was to be Shaun Maloney's day…

More of that in a minute. John Hartson, obviously extremely disappointed at having to miss out for the home stage of our European adventure took some time before the game to share his thoughts with us.

The big Welshman enthused: "Stuttgart are a very good side and we have to try and keep a clean sheet as we suffered the consequences of not being able to do that against Basel. There is a big lucrative tie waiting for us at the other end of this one but we have to make sure we get through this one first and they'll be a good side."

Paul Lambert due to his wealth of experience has an excellent football mind and he backed Hartson's early warnings, thus confirming our fears. "Stuttgart are no pushover. There are no easy games in football, I wish there were, but there aren't. This is going to be tough, they are a good side and we have to treat them with the respect they deserve."

Suggestions that Celtic Park had evolved in recent times as something of a European fortress after our recent Champions League success have absolutely no sway with the Celtic captain. Always a straight, no nonsense talker he retorted: "Nobody has a divine right to win a football match, no matter what you have done. We will have to play at our very best to take something from this game."

Lambert has a habit of making sure you keep your feet on the ground, even from the dizzy heights of post Christmas European football. And talking of feet on the ground, the Stuttgart side's boots look pretty sharp during their pre-match training session.

Tradition has dictated that we introduce our *Celtic Replay* show from the session as 'the build up to Celtic's biggest game of the season so far', obviously lapping it up with humour and pride as we progress further and further in the competition. But as Tony and I watched the Stuttgart training session there were no doubts in our minds that this was going to be a big, big game. They could play; there was no doubt about that. Still, I'm a fairly confident person when it comes to the Bhoys and never question their ability and capability of giving that little bit more.

Okay, so Larsson and Hartson would miss out but we had a little bit of magic in every player who would be involved. Neil Lennon, who was stretchered off with a hamstring injury against Celta Vigo had worked tirelessly throughout the winter break to ensure he would be fit, so with his intellectual and physical ability locked into midfield we were off to a flyer. When the team news broke I was happy enough that we could succeed. Douglas; Valgaeren, Balde, McNamara, Thompson, Lambert, Lennon, Petrov, Agathe; Sutton and Maloney. And on the bench; Marshall, Sylla, Fernandez, Healy and Guppy.

All we needed was a confident start and to try to ensure we kept a clean sheet. The break, we thought, came in the early stages of the game when Marcelo Bordon was shown red by celebrity referee Pierluigi Collina. The Brazilian's challenge thoroughly deserved the wrath of the ref after a ridiculous foul on Petrov who was impinging on goal after being sent through with a clever little pass from Maloney. Reduced to 10 men and forced to make an early tactical adjustment, Stuttgart must have felt under pressure.

Indeed, but for all of what seemed like 15 seconds! In the 27th minute, before we had managed to capitalise on the numerical advantage, Celtic media team's commentator Paul Cuddihy uttered the unthinkable. (Well, he didn't so much utter, Paul kind of shouts. Are the phrases 'it's a chance! It's a goal!' and 'he must score!' familiar coming at you at 50 zillion decibels? Yep, that's our Paul during CelticTV's highlights on the Big Screens. Bless!) "Ten men Stuttgart take the lead, this is a disaster for Celtic!"

It's hard to describe what that moment felt like except to say that for a

STAND AND DELIVER: *Martin O'Neill had to watch the 3-1 win over VfB Stuttgart from the stand, which included a superb Stilian Petrov strike for the third goal*

THE LONG AND SHORT OF IT: *Delight for Celtic as they saw off VfB Stuttgart, thanks to two away goals from Chris Sutton and Alan Thompson, previous page*

number of minutes time stood still as we felt the dream slip away. Then, with the resounding echo of "the away goal", "the away goal" ringing in my ears the Bhoys were suddenly back in town. I might have been momentarily worried, but never, ever in doubt that they couldn't dominate. After all this was their dream too, and they had the power to dictate the outcome.

Just eight minutes after Stuttgart had taken the lead; Celtic captain Paul Lambert was displaying some of the experience he had gained while winning the European Cup. After Maloney was brought down by Meissner, the subsequent clearance looked to be going nowhere until McNamara sent the ball back into Petrov who cleverly chested the ball down before delivering to Lambert outside the box who fired a simply stunning half-volley into the back of the net. 1-1 and a green and white eruption at Celtic Park, enveloped in the euphoria of relief.

With the Bhoys looking fluent and assertive, a goal before half time would have helped ease the old nerves a bit. So cue the Celt who had almost fired us into the lead in the second minute and had threaded an inch-perfect ball through to Petrov when Bordon saw red. Shaun Maloney was majestic, the pressure of the big match nowhere apparent as he capitalised on a mistake by Dangelmayr in the area.

When the Stuttgart substitute failed to clear from Thompson's seemingly harmless cross the youngster captured possession and squeezed the ball past Helderbrand. Maloney's reaction was a picture, as was that of his team-mates who scrambled to heap well-deserved praise on our star Bhoy. More praise would follow from the manager. 2-1. How good did that feel!

With confidence high and the Bhoys on form another goal seemed likely and when it came it was a peach. Lambert, who had benefited from a pass from Petrov to score in the first half, returned the favour when he knocked a ball through to the Bulgarian in the 68th minute and somehow, from the most acute angle at the by-line, Petrov squeezed the ball under the keeper to make it three on the night. So, first leg over, things were looking good at the halfway stage.

After the game I spoke to Martin O'Neill, reunited with his players after being banned to the stand. He was, as to be expected, "absolutely delighted" and said: "At half-time this is a terrific result. Especially for us to have come back from behind with Lambert's best goal ever. He struck it brilliantly and got us right back into it, it was the launching pad. And this was a great night for Shaun; he got us a great goal. He's only a kid but he will continue to get better and better, he is a multi-talented player. We have just beaten a side who are third in the Bundesliga and they are a terrific side so it's a terrific achievement."

Lambert added: "We're playing at a higher level now but we have given ourselves a chance. But we will have to play well to beat them. It's the German thing to sit back and hit on the break but the third goal was important, it's given us a wee cushion."

And Petrov enthused: "Critics say we are a one-man team and by saying this tried to put pressure on Maloney. But, we passed the ball about well and dominated the game and deserved to win. A score of 3-1 can be enough but we had the same result against Basel although we have learned from our mistakes and we will remain focussed and concentrate. To have scored three goals at this level of football and come back from a goal behind is really good."

There wasn't really much time to think about it as with only a week in between legs we had to squeeze in a cup-tie against St Johnstone and then head to Germany for the second leg, to be played on February 27. This day was significant in itself, as we would be flying back in the early hours of the morning of the 28th, the birthday of Ulrik Laursen and me! (and my lovely twin of course) On that basis we were hoping for the right result. What better way to celebrate than knowing you were heading for a UEFA Cup quarter final tie against Liverpool who were now favourites to win their tie against Auxerre!

THE AWAY LEG

Flying is a nightmare. It's the most unnatural thing you could do. Have you ever watched a plane from the ground as it flies across the sky? How on earth (excuse the unintentional pun) does it not just come crashing down? No, don't be writing in with technical answers, the less I know about the process the better. I'm not the only one who's not too good with the birds (the flying variety, here really isn't the place to discuss cameraman Des' love life).

There a quite a few of the media team, and the football team who can see it far enough which is quite ironic considering we have been greetin' about travelling far afield to play European football for the last 23 years. The price you have to pay for success!

The flight to Germany was as terrifying an ordeal as ever but it never fails to amaze me how our Alison McConnell is so completely unfazed by it all. For one so small she is very, very brave. You've got to hand it to her! Traumatic journey over the immediate priority on these trips, before we get a chance to get nervous about the football, is to find out the lay of the land in terms of equipment. Making sure we get frequent and exclusive content onto the website is imperative, as is being confident that our completely unashamedly Celtic-biased commentary reaches all our listeners in every corner of the globe.

So, all thoughts of the game were pushed to the side when it transpired my bag was missing. Disappeared off the face of the earth, along with about 70% of my broadcasting equipment. Panic; or think rationally in the belief that all will be fine? Panic of course, for the longest hour-and-a-half of my life before the gear turned up in the hotel dining room! Of course, I realise I should have looked there first...! And there was me thinking that with post Christmas European football I had found everything I had ever been looking for.

Anyway, during the panic, I hadn't managed to catch Alan Thompson to arrange my pre-match interview with him, an essential element of my superstitious ritual. So, I called him. After a few rings, that panic suddenly swept over me as I considered the possibility that he may be having an essential sleep before his pre-match training session.

But, no I wouldn't be so stupid as to wake up one of our star players when it was so important to sleep before the biggest and most important pre-match training session ever.

Of course I would! When I heard his sleep induced voice I could have died, prayed the ground would swallow me up and wondered where I could hide. But to be fair to Thommo, bless him, he understood the importance of my mission. Superstition dictated that we chat pre-match, so a time was arranged for after training at the stadium, which was ideal as it meant we could capture him as he viewed the field of play for the first time.

Seeing the opposition's stadium for the first time is really exciting and when you drive up to the ground the nerves really kick in. I don't know how the players get through a day I really don't. The Gottlieb-Daimler Stadium is pretty impressive, with selfishly speaking here, terrific press facilities.

For the supporters though the vantage point isn't fantastic with a huge running track circling the perimeter of the stadium creating a considerable distance between the area behind the goal where the 5,000 or so Celtic fans would be positioned and the field of play. But true to form, the green and white army turned all that to their advantage on the night, including the rather limited supply of tickets.

At the training session the players looked confident, as they always do. Tony and I recorded our show for *Celtic Replay* and then at last, to steady the nerves I did the piece with Thommo trackside. He wasn't impressed with the state of the pitch. The surface he explained was hard and bobbly and seriously lacked the kind of moisture on the top that our players relish to play on. The stadium manager explained to us that they hadn't watered the surface for fear it would have frozen over.

This, we were assured, would be rectified before the match. So, the pitch wasn't the best, but they had come up against worse. If the Bhoys can survive Fir Park, they can cope with anything. After what was sure to have been a restless night's sleep for many, the dawning of the day of the game finally arrived.

A few of our players went out to train in the morning, as they religiously do on the day of a match. It seems that the Bhoys too like to keep to a routine and if it works don't knock it. After all, this was the first time in 23 years we had a European game to look forward to at this stage of the season.

After selected training sessions the whole team goes out for a pre-match walk and on this occasion it was with immense pride that I watched them head for the door, along with several hundred high-spirited Celtic fans. The hotel that we staying at in the centre of Stuttgart was also resident to an entire regalia of Celtic fans who from the early hours, or should I say throughout the early hours, had been preparing for the game.

It's incredibly satisfying to look around and see so many happy faces. Caught up in the moment I briefly afforded myself the luxury of wondering what Seville, not Stuttgart would be like if the mighty Celtic were to conquer even further in Europe. Dangerous thoughts I know with such a crucial match looming but there was, and had been throughout the campaign, a certain level of confidence apparent in the team.

Nothing close to arrogance, they never emulate anything like that, but talking to the players, the extent to which they want success is wholly apparent, and more importantly so is how much they believe in their own ability. And rightly so, you only have to look at what had been achieved thus far. FK Suduva, Blackburn Rovers, Celta Vigo, are results that speak volumes.

With the players tucked up in bed in the afternoon for their final rest and our sidekick summariser Tosh McKinlay safely in the fold, we headed to the stadium for our own pre-match preparations and the 90 minutes we had been waiting 23 years for.

The Road to Seville

The Celtic fans began piling into the stadium really early and initial indications were that there would be a considerable higher number than 5,000 there to support the Bhoys. Indeed, some 10,000 or so commandeered the entire area behind the goal to the right hand side of the pitch and the atmosphere, even an hour before kick off was immense. The red ash running track behind the goal mouth area was soon quickly submerged in Celtic flags of every variety, largely thanks to the assistance of the staff at the stadium who were absolutely fantastic, and were in fine spirits too when the pre-match party began.

You could just tell that this was going to be a match that Celtic fans would talk about for years to come, whether they were there or not. Not quite Lisbon, but the emotion was there with the fans believing for the first time in a very long time that we had a chance to do something really positive in Europe.

Although, in every way we already had, overcoming a Spanish side in the last round, never achieved before, ensured that this wasn't so much a chance but an achievement.

And what an absolute star to kick-start the event. I don't think I have ever laughed so much when Tosh pointed out to me that the blonde singing her wee heart out down trackside was none other than *'It's a Heartache'* Bonnie Tyler! Like her or loathe her she had the stadium rocking and helped, along with a Celtic support in terrific singing voice, to create one of the best pre match environments I have ever experienced.

In danger of taking it just too far, Bonnie did her piece and left in time for the real stars to arrive on stage. Game on. Nervous? You bet, I was shaking like a leaf! At this juncture I was going to try and explain how I felt as the teams came out on to the pitch, but there's absolutely no need as it was an emotion that we all share. Swollen with pride, I along with tens of thousands of fellow Celts could only look on in admiration as Douglas; Valgaeren, Balde, Laursen, Agathe, Lennon, Sutton, Petrov, Thompson; Larsson, Hartson made their entrance.

As the proceedings began, preying on my mind, and our commentator Tony Hamilton's was the fact that we had never scored on German soil and as he repeated stats from our failed episodes in Germany I shivered anxiously before focussing on the game and praying for an early goal to settle the nerves. Obviously I wasn't the only one praying that night because there is no way I have the power to achieve what happened all on my own!

Just 13 minutes into the game Tony had the best possible new statistic and he can say it every working day for the rest of his life if he wants, as it'll never bore me! Didier Agathe, who was absolutely immense, broke free only to be hauled down. Big Joos Valgaeren took the free kick and sent the ball into John Hartson, back along with the manager from suspension, and controlling the ball with his chest, he gave possession to Speedy Gonzales Agathe.

With lightning pace Agathe sent the ball back into the box and Hartson headed it on for Tommo to fire it into the back of the net with a sensational header. Cue the words, "Celtic have scored for the first time on German soil with a diving header from Alan Thompson!" Wow, what an absolutely incredible feeling. The stadium erupted.

There were Celtic fans everywhere in this stadium bedecked in our glorious colours, and they were partying like only the Celtic fans can. This is what I had been searching for, this feeling of absolute euphoria, which at that moment I believed could never be surpassed. Cue Chris Sutton, and of course Didier Agathe.

Once again Agathe flew down the wing leaving everything shaken behind him before sending an inch-perfect pass on to Sutton, who made it 2-0 just two minutes after the opener. Destiny, fairytales, dreams - they were all there. We were edging closer and closer to that prestigious quarter final UEFA Cup slot! Not before a few anxious moments but I don't suppose it would be a game of football if you weren't on tenterhooks at some point or another.

With 38 minutes gone, Tiffert offered the Germans a lifeline. With Alan Thompson off the pitch receiving treatment, the German exploited the opportunity and pulled one back. At half time though, an aggregate scoreline of 5-2 wasn't just respectable it was incredible and indeed more than enough to see us through. The next 45 minutes are a haze of palpitations, anxious screams and excitement. 76minutes into the fray Hleb got an equaliser that momentarily generated a bit of self-belief into the home side.

At this point, I'm sure I wasn't the only irrational Celtic fan panicking about Partizan Belgrade, and I'm definitely sure I wasn't when Mutzel buried a confident shot past Douglas in the 87th minute. I know it was never really in doubt and as Tosh pointed out they had to score two in two minutes, so suggested I shouldn't panic (although not as politely as that). Don't panic? Had we not scored two in that very timeframe in the first half?

But, I always knew they would do it and when the final whistle sounded and the home side pumped *'You'll Never Walk Alone'* through the p.a. system I, like several thousands of my fellow Celts, was in tears. This was it; this was what being a Celtic fan was all about. My Bhoys were in the quarter final of the UEFA Cup. The quarter final! Forget my allegiance to my favourite saying of the minute, 'post Christmas European football', UEFA Cup quarter-finalists sounded far better!

For the minute I was enraptured in the euphoria of the achievement and the momentary lapse of concentration meant I hadn't given any consideration as to the final confirmation of our opponents. That was of course until a message on the big screen in the stadium flashed 'Good luck at Anfield Glasgow Celtics!' How beautifully humbling.

This was a team who had just missed out on the opportunity to go into the quarters and they had time to wish us well. That type of consideration is something I hope football never loses.

So, 5-4 the result, although this time the advantage was in our favour in what had been one of the most tremendous nights for Celtic. Stuttgart, as we had been warned prior to the tie were a good side and had already reached two European finals, most recently in 1998 when they runners up in the Cup-Winners' Cup final to Chelsea.

Quite bizarrely, we were to be criticised in the minutes and days to come for losing 3-2 on the night, but so what? If we had been 3-0 down and Tommo and Sutton had scored two in the final two minutes of the game we would have been labelled the conquerors of Europe for reaching the next round in such a dramatic fashion.

But we didn't need that mantle; we had achieved what had seemed the impossible against Celta Vigo and then surpassed it! How good did that feel? We had swept aside FK Suduva, Blackburn Rovers, Celta Vigo and now VfB Stuttgart and now had a prestigious tie against Liverpool to look forward to. No, you're not dreaming, this is actually happening...

Elated and exhausted we packed up for the journey home on the official team flight. Celtic legend Murdo MacLeod was as chirpy as we were after the night's events and we agreed to give him a lift to the airport. As is absolutely standard on any European trip we got lost but fortunately for us Murdo is a fluent German speaker and with his exemplary use of the lingo he claimed he would be able to get us to the airport in no time. ...

An hour later, trapped in an underground tunnel in a big scary mountain, somewhere in Germany, I remembered where this story had been set in motion. 23 years ago I was looking for something I had never lost but knew I had to find. Now I hadn't so much as lost anything but wanted to find something very special indeed, success, and longevity in European competition.

I wasn't the only one who wanted it, and certainly not the only one who believed we were capable of achieving it, but I was the only one in the office who had put a few quid, in the aftermath of the Basel game, on Celtic reaching the UEFA Cup final! I always believed we could progress. On the flight home from Basel the immense disappointment was so apparent and the players' determination to overcome that and achieve what they knew they were capable of achieving was so intense you could almost touch it.

It was only a matter of time, as the pivotal element of the structure was already in place. You only had to look at the players and the management to see that the desire was there.

And look where that journey took us – to the quarter final of the UEFA Cup! Maybe that bet wasn't such a bad idea after all...

EPILOGUE

Before the home leg the plan had been to include pictures of 'the Media team', from 1980, along with a little piece on where we were, and what we had been doing the last time Celtic had played European football so far on in the season and publish it in the *Celtic View*.

Jim Craig was the first to produce the goods and if you have a good imagination you should see a kind of cross between Rikki Fulton and Clint Eastwood. Yes, our resident legend was sporting a full-grown beard in 1980! And believe it or not, he looked 50 years older 23 years ago. Thank goodness for Gillette. Sharon Gillespie and Eileen Monaghan produced pictures of little sweet innocent girls in bunches. I suspect they were forgeries.

John Cole and Beccy Nightingale's efforts appeared to be more genuine, but that was until I noticed the magazine print on the back. Alison McConnell's was absolutely genuine because Tony said she was the same height in the photograph as she is now. Talking of Tony, does he really expect us to believe he ever had hair? Paul Cuddihy's photograph couldn't possibly have been for real. If it was genuine, there is no chance he could be married with three children right now. Love is never that blind.

Joe Sullivan. Goodness, are you really that old mate? You disguise it very, very, well. Stephen Sullivan's photograph for me was the most genuine. He brought a picture of his parents' wedding photograph from March 1990. Apparently he was born nine months later, making him13 at the minute. Have you seen our Small Bhoy? This one is definitely for real.

You probably won't be too surprised to learn that the piece was pulled, with only moments to spare before it went to press….

TONY HAMILTON'S EUROPEAN DIARY
Part 5: Good old German efficiency

I mentioned it once but I think I got away with it…

The German people were the nicest bunch I've ever come across in any foreign land and their English (unlike this) was just magic. While I've learned to say "no mushrooms or butter please, or anything that looks like mushrooms or butter" in 14 different languages, other everyday things such as asking for directions are a bit more difficult.

So for that reason alone I was happy to be in Germany and, more to the point, happy that my team were still in the competition at this stage.

It was in Stuttgart that Des confessed the secret of our success of the competition. Here was me thinking that Big Bad John Hartson's goal in Vigo had taken us through to this level but it was in fact another John – Des' late da – John O'Hara.

Des coughed the truth the night before the match – he had been wearing his da's gold watch on every away trip and he had been secretly rubbing it on all of us for luck and that's how we were still competing.

It was only now that he felt he wanted to take the credit for our best European run in 23 years – I can't blame him – I would have done the exact same thing had it been me.

Naturally we believed him and, along with checking that Stephen had his passport with him and had permission from his mum to come with us, we ensured that the lucky watch was hanging in its rightful place before we set off on every future trip.

The build-up to the home game should have been easier for me but wasn't. BBC Scotland were the host broadcaster and we would take their pictures for the stadium, our archive and for Celtic Replay.

I also took their pictures for our PPV event outside Scotland and as we went a goal behind in that match I had visions that I would look like Dougie Donnelly did at half time the day Scotland were getting it tight from the Faroe Islands.

Thankfully it never came to that – at half-time in our match, Billy Stark, Derek Whyte, Margot and I were all Smiley-Happy-Baby-Jesus and not one of us even gave Dougie a second thought.

Anyway, the taking and giving the BBC pictures thing is a system that I knew well and if it had just been the BBC it would have been straightforward.

The problem was, though, that in addition to my friends from the Broken Biscuit Company there was also a German broadcaster and, as much as I'm loathe to use the phrase 'German Efficiency', they were efficient to the point where I thought there was going to be an unfortunate accident – with no witnesses.

I was exhausted from running after them for days leading up to the match. They wanted everything and with jam on it, and they wanted it yesterday. I can't say I was sorry to see them go but I looked forward at least to reciprocal treatment when we went over for the second leg.

When we arrived and I realised that it was a different broadcaster from the one who had been in Glasgow I cried, aloud and in public.

It did, however, all work out in the end. The people sitting in front of us, initially a bit miffed when Tosh McKinlay and I screamed and hugged each other during commentary as Celtic scored twice early in the match, came to us at the end and congratulated us on our performance.

At first I thought they meant the commentary and summary but then I realised it was the team's performance they were talking about.

Imagine being congratulated for something you had absolutely nothing to do with – except of course being a close friend of the guy who wore the lucky watch which made the whole thing happen in the first place.

But they weren't to know that. Unless Des told them. Tosh still thinks they meant the commentary but I don't have the heart to tell him.

Like everywhere we had been the atmosphere was electric in the Gottlieb-Daimler Stadium. It sounds a bit weak to one who doesn't know about Celtic but the good Bhoys and Ghirls who follow the Celts really are something else when they put their mind to it and on this trip they were no different.

It was as if they were the only support there – they were certainly the only support you could hear. Even Bonnie Tyler (the world's worst mimic) was drowned out as she was 'singing' live before the game.

Even the team hotel in the centre of town was filled to the brim with our number. Such places are normally sacrosanct to the fans, but for some reason about there being no space in the city there were a couple of hundred good-humoured supporters of the thousands who made the journey, living with us for a couple of days.

Even my dentist, Gerry Boyle, took those couple of days away from legally torturing his patients to stay in the hotel. And, apart from electric shocks from everything we touched and nightmares about Dr Boyle drilling his way into my room while I slept, it was spot on.

Efficient in fact.

Chapter Seven

Liverpool: Walk On

by John Cole

SUPERSTITION plays a big part in the building of the lore of a football club. The Irish in the West of Scotland, from whose minds sprung the Celtic ideal, have long been renowned for their superstition. My great grandmother instilled a reflex in her children (and children's children) to save a spider under any kind of human threat, malicious or accidental. Shoes were never placed upon a table (under pain of death), and time stood still if you put an umbrella in the house. Celtic's own club emblem is testimony to that superstition, implicit in the construct is the belief that the four-leaf clover will bring luck to its bearers.

Footballers themselves go to ridiculous lengths to recreate the events that lead up to successful outcomes. Lucky suits are worn down to the last thread; some scutter unselfconsciously down the tunnels of the world's top grounds bereft of various items of clothing, barely concealing baits-that-should-be-concealed, because 'that's the way I always get dressed for a match'.

Fate and coincidence too, play a part in football. Time after time, cup draws throw one team up against another for the umpteenth time, championships are decided at the same venue, the same individuals or families play major roles in a club's history.

There is, therefore, a school of thought that the 2002/03 UEFA Cup campaign was influenced by the 'V' factor. Celtic had, by the time the Liverpool tie was a reality, disposed of FK Suduva, Blackburn Rovers, Celta Vigo, & VfB Stuttgart. Celtic fans, consequently, believed that as long as each opponent's name contained a letter 'V', our cup run would continue.

It seemed inevitable then, that the name Liverpool would pop out of the hat immediately after that of Celtic to set up the old adversaries in the quarter final. But, the significance of Liverpool had more to do with numeric than alphabetic considerations. Celtic had twice before been drawn against Liverpool in European competition; first in the Cup-Winners' Cup in 1965, when both clubs were on the brink of a decade of domestic dominance, and again in 1997 in the UEFA Cup when both were emerging from periods in the shadow.

On both occasions, Liverpool won through narrowly, so it was 2-0 to them – and a bit of redressing of ancient balances was called for. Celtic and Liverpool are divided, to paraphrase Churchill, by a common anthem. Celtic fans will tell you that they were singing *You'll Never Walk Alone* when the stage show *Carousel*, from whence the song came, was playing in Glasgow in the '50s.

Liverpool fans would have you believe that they started singing it first, in 1963, when Gerry and the Pacemakers made it a Merseybeat classic. They are in error, of course. Whoever you believe, there are few among those at Celtic Park in 1997 when the sides met in the UEFA Cup who will deny that the joint rendition of song the moved them in a very special way. And of course we had a re-run of that famous piece of community singing to look forward to when this match eventually came around.

Celtic and Liverpool are also joined at the hip so to speak in other ways. Both cities of Liverpool and Glasgow rose to prominence during the industrial revolution on the back of Irish immigrant labour. The increased trade which took place during industrialisation in the 19th century projected both cities as the twin beating hearts of the nation. As ports, they were vital hubs for trade and that maritime status made them suitable for the construction of the ships that carried the trade.

The people of Liverpool in the mid 19th century spoke with a Lancashire accent not unlike that of Manchester before the so-called famine and mass emigration from across the water, so it is arguable that the Irish have left even more of a mark on Liverpool than in Glasgow (I'd be appalled to think that we EVER spoke like Edinburghers).

Glasgow and Liverpool were targeted for the exodus to some extent because the poorest and weakest victims of food shortages could not afford the trip to the Americas; and the proximity of the growing cities on the west coast of mainland Britain must have been tempting. Even the term 'Scouser' is testament to the poverty of the Liverpool's immigrant population, deriving from the Norwegian 'Lobkaus' – poor man's stew. Norwegians were then regular trade visitors to Liverpool – another coincidence because Norwegians are currently the biggest foreign presence in Glasgow through strong educational ties with the city.

There is a strong radical, working class tradition in both cities. During the 1926 General Strike, the Royal Navy allegedly had guns trained on Liverpool docks for fear of revolution, whilst the army were locked in Maryhill barracks in Glasgow for fear of mutiny, and the soldiers siding with workers. Some will wryly reflect that the de-industrialisation which took place in the 1980s again united Liverpool and Glasgow in the misery of unemployment giving rise yet again to that political radicalism which has helped shape the nature of 21st century politics.

It is probably a cliché, but the cities of Glasgow and Liverpool are commonly referred to as being spookily similar. Given the history, that is no coincidence, but it remains a perception amongst people who travel to either city, that the people are among the warmest in the world.

The Road to Seville

Taking coincidence to the nth degree, Liverpool Football Club was also founded (like Celtic) by an Irish Scot; John McKenna. And the team that McKenna built was composed almost entirely of Scottish players, and were known as 'the Macs'. The one Englishman in that team? His name was Bill MacOwen! And who doesn't know that the man who had more influence on the club than any other, Bill Shankly, hailed from Glenbuck in darkest Ayrshire. Shankly, like his friend Jock Stein (Celtic's most influential individual), was a coalminer before football allowed him to expand his horizons.

So it would be odd if there was an absence of affinity between the two cities, but the bond between Celtic and Liverpool is even deeper than that. Celtic tradition is based on triumph out of adversity, not only in a football sense, but in terms of the emergence of Glasgow's Irish community, who not only helped to found the club, but emerged from impoverished conditions to become a vital part of Scotland's prosperity. The club became the personification of the folk who gave birth to it. Its triumphs were theirs; its tragedies felt by all.

Perhaps the most poignant moment in Celtic history is the death, on the playing field, of goalkeeper John Thomson. Maybe more than anything else, his death fused the spirit of the Celtic family in a way that up to then was not possible. Celtic fans were united in horror and disbelief that a young, talented man, career ahead of him, should be struck down so cruelly. Similarly, the tragic deaths of Peter Scarff in 1932 and John Doyle in 1981 again united the Celtic family in grief. It is an unfortunate lesson perhaps that the bonds of grief are stronger and longer lasting than any other.

For Liverpool, the death of 96 fans at Hillsborough in 1989 was a blow almost too terrible to bear for the city and football club. This needless loss of life, the impact on the families of victims and survivors alike, sent the city and nation into a period of morning. In a community as proud and familial as Liverpool's, they may never recover from the blow. It is probably no surprise to most then, that in the aftermath of that terrible tragedy, Liverpool turned northwards to Celtic when they played their first game after Hillsborough – in a benefit match for the victims and their families – at Celtic Park on April 30, 1989.

Liverpool won the match comfortably, adding to their tally of wins over Celtic, but in the context of the match, a bond in tragedy was created which will perhaps never be broken.

Thinking back to 1965 and the Cup-Winners' Cup semi final tie between the two sides, it is hard to forget just how gutted we were when Bobby Lennox's goal was disallowed at Anfield with minutes to go. Had that goal stood, it would have been Celtic and not Liverpool who lined up against Borussia Dortmund at Hampden in the final of that year's European Cup-Winners' Cup.

Of course the best medicine we could possibly have had was dispensed in huge doses in Lisbon two years later, but on a personal level, that particular Celtic – Liverpool tie was my first taste of a really HUGE European night at Celtic Park. Nine of the team who would go on to win the European Cup in Lisbon faced Liverpool on April 14, 1966 at Celtic Park. Only Jim Craig and Willie Wallace were missing from Celtic's most famous XI, their berths being filled by Ian Young and Joe McBride respectively.

The match was played on a Friday evening, and was an 80,000 sell-out. Media interest in British terms was also high, and a BBC outside broadcast team was sent up from London to cover the match live. I am sure that the people at Queen Margaret Drive in Glasgow (BBC Scotland HQ) would have been miffed to know that they could not be trusted to handle such a momentous event – and indeed they still were not trusted to handle the same tie almost 40 years later. Maybe the BBC regard Scottish broadcasting prowess with the same disdain they reserve for our football abilities.

Even then, we all felt we had something to prove to the English. Celtic were at that time embarking on a journey that would take them to the most fantastic success in the club's history. In a little over a year, Jock Stein had transformed Celtic fans into a mini-nation of optimists. Such was the belief in our side; the top team in England were not seen as an impossible hurdle to overcome. In international terms, even although Scotland were the perennial underachievers, Scotland were nobody's mugs, and on any given day, were capable of beating the best there was. Celtic had already been in a Cup-Winners' Cup semi final, and Rangers had been in the final of the same tournament. Still the English media wrote off our chances of doing anything against the might of the old First Division.

As it happened on the evening, Celtic did Scotland proud, and at the same time gave the English commentators plenty to talk about on the arduous journey back to civilisation the following day. Celtic played fantastically well that evening, outplaying Liverpool throughout, and pushing them back into defence from the off. For all their exciting, attacking efforts, though, we had only a one-goal advantage to take to Anfield, thanks to a Bobby Lennox strike in the 51st minute after Bobby Murdoch's advance on the right wing.

After the match, Celtic Manager Jock Stein said: "It was suggested that we weren't good enough to be in the same tournament as Liverpool. This result has proved we are."

That comment is an indication that the smug, patronising tones of the English media were resented then as much as now. The return leg at Anfield took place only five days later on April 19. Just as Celtic had dominated the first match, Liverpool did likewise on this occasion. The conditions were very heavy after torrential rain, and consequently Celtic were denied the pace of Lennox and Chalmers. Kerrydale in the *Celtic View* of April 27 told it like this; "The greatest 'break' that Liverpool got – and remember that their superiority in the second match is not in doubt – was the refereeing. The official in charge, a Belgian, was what is popularly known as a 'homer'. He awarded a free kick to Liverpool just after an hour had been played, and this enabled them to score the goal that they so badly needed.

"The penalised tackle by John Hughes in the centre of the field and 25 yards from goal was 100 per cent fair. He challenged an opponent from the side and clearly played the ball away from him. However the referee gave a foul. This was taken by Smith, the Liverpool player who wears the number 10 shirt but who plays as deep lying wing-half. His far from powerful ground shot was deflected by the Celtic line-up into the corner of the net as Ronnie Simpson imagined the ball was going past.

"Then as the final minutes of the second half approached, with Liverpool leading 2-0, but on aggregate by only a single goal, the referee disallowed what appeared to many of the spectators who were not Celtic supporters to be a perfectly legitimate goal by Bobby Lennox ... Lennox strode past a defender, who actually tried to pull him down, for a pass headed into his tracks by Joe McBride, and shot past Lawrence (Liverpool keeper), who with his attempt to save gave no indication that he thought offside entered into anyone's calculations. But the referee was pointing for an infringement and the linesman seemed to me to raise his flag only when he saw the referee's gesticulation."

If Lennox had not been adjudged offside, then Celtic would have progressed due to the away goals rule, but through an evening of relentless rain, Liverpool had scored twice in the second half, Lennox's goal was chalked off, and Dortmund eventually won the cup in Glasgow. I think from that moment on, we had a need to get our own back on Liverpool. It would take another 32 years before we got the chance.

The next time Celtic met Liverpool in competition, Wim Jansen was in charge at Celtic Park. Celtic's main mission that season (1997/98) was to preserve the nine-in-a-row record of Jock Stein's 1966-1974 side. Rangers had already equalled the nine the previous year. To allow our greatest rivals to make it 10 would have been football Armageddon in Glasgow, and all of our hopes were really pinned on that.

On September 16, 1997, a welcome diversion to the rigours of stopping the 10 came in the shape of Liverpool and the first round of the UEFA Cup. Again the southern TV juggernaut ventured north to the provinces to capture what they imagined would be the humbling of a mediocre Celtic by Liverpool. However Roy Evans' side were also emerging from a period in the doldrums themselves.

Their great rivals Manchester United had established themselves as the main players in the English Premiership, and Liverpool were without a trophy since their FA Cup win in 1992, and the last time they had won the league (a trophy they had begun to think of as their own in the '60s, '70s and '80s) was in 1990. The truly inspiring thing about this meeting of the two teams was the camaraderie amongst the opposing sets of fans. Liverpool fans were welcomed to Celtic Park like old friends. Beer was drunk, jokes were told and songs were sung – including THAT song.

The provenance of the origins of *You'll Never Walk Alone* may never be possible, but nobody was claiming it for themselves on the night of the Celtic Park leg of the tie. Before the match, 48,526 highly vocal fans of Celtic and Liverpool conjoined in a rendition of that song which moved even the coldest cynic to tears. Few who were there will ever forget the passion and fervour with which the fans rendered the anthem. Even John Motson of the BBC paused in his opening remarks to allow BBC viewers to see and hear how opposing fans at a football match CAN behave towards one another. Such was the emotion that everyone present knew they were witnessing something a bit special. The match would prove to be not so ordinary either.

The sides which lined up on that evening were as follows;
CELTIC (3-5-3): Gould; Boyd, Stubbs, Mahe; McNamara, Burley, Hannah, Wieghorst, Blinker; Donnelly, Larsson.
Substitutes: Marshall, McKinlay, MacKay, Thom, Annoni, Gray, O'Donnell
LIVERPOOL (4-4-2): James; Bjornebye, Wright, Kvarme, Jones; McManaman, Thomas, Ince, Matteo; Reidle, Owen
Substitutes: Berger, Warner, Babb, Kennedy, Carragher, Murphy, McAteer

Andrew Smith of the *Celtic View* saw the match like this; "No-one gave Celtic

THOU SHALT NOT PASS: *Bobo Balde was in outstanding form against Michael Owen on an emotional night at Celtic Park, which saw a double pre-match huddle, next page*

PARTING THE RED SEA: *Henrik Larsson took less than two minutes to put Celtic ahead at home, and Alan Thompson provided the first of two magnificent second-leg goals at Anfield, with a blistering free-kick just before half-time*

UNSTOPPABLE: *John Hartson's strike against Liverpool at Anfield was one of the great Celtic goals of the season, and the big Welshman couldn't hide his delight*

a snowball's chance in hell of doing anything against the supposed mighty Liverpool. And after five minutes of what was to prove a rip-snorting UEFA Cup tie, you thought those who had predicted walkovers for the Anfield men in both legs of the latest Battle of Britain European pairing were going to be proved right. The fact that Wim Jansen's side didn't simply emerge from an epic encounter at Celtic Park with a chance – albeit a remote one – of progressing to the second round but were only denied a deserved victory by a glorious individual effort in the last minute, speaks volumes about the spirit and ever-growing belief of the men in green and white.

"The pity of it is that Celts gradually woke up to the realisation that Liverpool were beatable only after they'd dug themselves into a gaping hole. It was how they scrambled out of it that was so thrilling and once again proved a tribute to the resilience of Jansen's side. In the second period it was Celts who ran the show, and Jackie McNamara's glorious volleyed equaliser and Simon Donnelly's confident spot-kick conversion aside, the chances presented themselves.

"Almost immediately, Jansen's men were stretched afar from an assured looking Liverpool backline with Mark Wright exposed on several occasions. Six minutes from the interval Regi Blinker wriggled clear but hesitated before shooting and three minutes later the same player threaded the ball through to Burley only for the midfielder to hit Dominic Matteo with his shot on the turn.

"However, not until Gould had produced a superb reflex stop from a Reidle header two minutes after the restart did the Celts come alive. For half-an-hour they put Liverpool through the wringer and got the two goals that looked like they might open the door to one of the club's great European victories of recent times. McNamara set the ball rolling in the 53rd minute, sprinting down the right and playing a one-two with Burley before connecting with a volley that ripped into the top corner. Thereafter Celts were on fire, but it must be said it took a soft penalty award in the 74th minute for them to get their noses in front.

"Larsson fastened on to a fine through pass from Wieghorst and slipped the ball round James before losing his balance, with minimal contact appearing to have been made. Donnelly blasted the subsequent spot-kick high beyond the Liverpool keeper. Larsson twice came close to selling a win for Celtic on the night in the last 10 and with the Anfield men seeming to have run out of steam it all looked so good … but you can never rest easy against opposition containing internationalists who can turn games upside down in an instant – and that is what, agonisingly, McManaman did in the 89th minute.

"Picking up the ball on the halfway line the England star drove forward, showing superb balance to ride tackle after tackle before supplying the perfect finish by curling a shot beyond Gould from the edge of the box."

Celtic had exceeded expectations, but they were to rue the lapse that cost them the opportunity to take a lead to Anfield. In the return leg on September 30, in front of 38,205 fans, the teams lined up as follows.

CELTIC (3-5-3): Gould; Annoni, Stubbs, Mahe; McNamara, Burley, Hannah, Wieghorst, McKinlay; Donnelly, Larsson.
Substitutes: Kerr, MacKay, Gray, McLaughlin, McBride
LIVERPOOL (4-4-2): James; Jones, Wright, Kvarme, Bjornebye; McManaman, Carragher, Berger, Ince; Fowler, Owen
Substitutes: Reidle, Nielsen, Harkness, Kennedy, Thomas, Murphy, McAteer

The Road to Seville

Andrew Smith of the *Celtic View* again: "In the past 20 years of European competition, rarely has a Celtic side turned in such a supremely disciplined performance, as was the case as Anfield on Tuesday evening. The fact that it wasn't enough for Wim Jansen's men to force their way past Liverpool and into the second round of the UEFA Cup has everything to do with the events of two weeks ago and little to do with what happened two days ago.

"No-one expected a Celtic side in its very early stages of transformation to even test a star studded Liverpool outfit. But over the course of this 'Battle of Britain' UEFA Cup first-round clash, Celtic didn't simply remain unbeaten, they stretched to breaking point a team that in the past has time and again come up with the goods on an international stage.

"Of course, the outcome leaves Celtic to rue what might have been, but they played the Anfield clash almost to perfection and this should never be forgotten, limiting their opponents to only a couple of glimpses at goal thanks, in the main, to an unlikely three-man backline of Rico Annoni, Stephane Mahe and Alan Stubbs.

"In terms of Celtic's approach and their defensive resilience, there was little more that could have been asked of the men in green and white and, on reflection, Celts' hopes of causing a major upset against Liverpool and posting what would have been their finest win in Europe for 15 years, were undone by a 2-2 draw in Glasgow. More pointedly it was a last-minute strike from Steve McManaman that tied the first leg when a home win appeared the most appropriate outcome.

"In the 20th minute, Tosh McKinlay threw a high ball into the box that caused panic in the Liverpool defence with David James and Stig Bjornebye getting themselves into a fankle as they attempted to cut out the danger. The ball broke to Donnelly but, with the keeper stranded, he lofted a delicate lob over the bar.

"Fatigue set into Celtic's play as the second half wore on without the all-important goal arriving but it wasn't until four minutes from time that Liverpool got the better of Jonathan Gould with a Karlheinz Riedle header stopped on the line by Donnelly. And there's no doubt that the confidence Celtic will take from what genuinely represents a heroic failure will have much to do with their ability to snuff out the threat of Robbie Fowler and Michael Owen despite missing key defenders – Tom Boyd, absent through suspension and ineligible Marc Rieper."

Again, it was all so close, and the old Celtic moral victory brigade was sounding the klaxons once more. It seemed our friends from Liverpool would forever have the Indian sign over us. After all, what chance would there be that we would ever meet them again in European competition?

It is with all this historic baggage in mind that you have to place the context of that UEFA Cup pairing. A common bond is one thing of course, but the business of winning a football match still has to be addressed. For reasons already stated, there is no antipathy between the clubs, but a bit of needle is no bad thing in the run-up to football match.

Martin O'Neill and Gerard Houllier were both sensibly and courteously saying nice things about each other's teams ALL the time. In stark contrast to the amateur psychology played by (and which backfired on) Graeme Souness in the Blackburn Rovers tie, the absence of psycho-absurdity was a blessing. However it is possible to be TOO nice. For the fans, some straighter talking is required, so just exactly who ARE these people?

On the plus side, you have to give them John Lennon and Paul McCartney, but don't forget Ringo. It is said that Liverpool people are not afraid to laugh at themselves; but they also laugh at Ken Dodd and Les Dennis, both famous Scousers, and both about as funny as a fire in a wigwam. On the football side the city gave us Alan Stubbs of course. Make your own mind up on that one.

We also pilfered reserve goalkeeper, Tony Warner, who played about two games for Celtic, one of which was the 5-1 match at Celtic Park on November 21, 1998 which became famously known throughout the Celtic world as 'The Humping' However, they did, unforgivably and unforgettably nick Kenny Dalglish from us. When I want to feel antipathy towards Liverpool, I think of that quite a lot.

There were the Liverpool players we liked, Kevin Keegan, Ian Rush, Steve McManaman, Michael Owen, Grobbelaar, Heighway, Dalglish, Jimmy Case, Tommy Smith … and the ones we didn't like very much; Souness, Emlyn Hughes, Ian St John, Souness, Dalglish, Sammy Lee, Souness, Alan Hansen, Souness.

Seriously though, we in the media side of things at Celtic Park were looking at all of the angles, the frivolous and the not so frivolous; like what prospect we had of beating Liverpool for the first time over two legs in competition. At the time of qualification Liverpool had been having a bad time. Their league challenge had faltered and they had been attracting a lot of criticism. In fact rumour had it that Martin O'Neill had been lined up to replace Gerard Houllier as manager at Anfield. Not a pleasant read for the O'Neill fans in the Celtic camp, but an indication if just how critical the media had become of Liverpool.

However within three days of both sides qualifying, Liverpool had performed splendidly to overcome the great rivals Manchester United, by two goals to nil in the final of the Worthington Cup. A week later, they also beat Bolton Wanderers at Anfield by the same score. The media talk of discontent in the Kop evaporated in the reflected glare of the new silverware on the Anfield sideboard. Suddenly Liverpool were performing as their fans expected.

For my own part, I felt that Celtic had already made their mark in Europe this term. Had we gone out at that point, I felt we had put ourselves back on the European discussion agenda. After over 20 years in the post-Christmas European wilderness, we had announced our intention to re-commence serious competition.

Martin O'Neill is a difficult man to read, and gives little way when questioned, but I still think that his real goal in European terms was to get past the psychological Christmas barrier at which so many talented Celtic sides had fallen over the last two decades. That was my own hope for Celtic anyway; and anything else would be a bonus Brian – over the moon and all that. For many of us the prospect of Liverpool, and the opportunity to redress the historic balance was as important as progressing to the next round. We may be like kin, us and the 'Pool, but we were fed up being the poor relations in the family get-togethers.

The media circus which attaches itself to Celtic on a day-to-day basis is a self-sustaining thing in the main. The vast majority of the interest and column inches devoted to Celtic and Rangers – in the parochial environment of the Scottish game – is more about the self promotion of the peddlers of the tripe that gets written than it is about a genuine excitement over the football or a genuine interest in the clubs themselves. Every day, the same old, same old gets trotted out in the press.

The Road to Seville

For this UEFA Cup tie however, there was a genuine and sincere thirst for information from all parts of Europe about Celtic, and about football. E-mails and telephone calls poured into the media department, as did requests for press accreditation. National radio stations talked of little else from the day both teams progressed – and the demand for tickets for the Glasgow leg of the tie was a Tsunami.

Liverpool, like Celtic, has a big Internet presence. Unlike Celtic however, they had never broadcast a live away match over the net, but were desperate to show this match to their online subscribers. So the celticfc.net team put together a system whereby the Liverpool fans could see the game live on the Celtic website. Of course the match was live on TV in over 30 countries, but the Internet helps to plug the gaps for those who have no access to either satellite, terrestrial or closed circuit feeds.

When the Celtic Matchday Live show started that evening on the web, Jim Craig, Frank McGarvey and I sat in the studio along with assorted media-people-without-tickets anxiously awaiting the kick off as Paul Cuddihy, Margot McCuaig and Tosh McKinlay soaked up the atmosphere in the stadium. Frank was confident that Celtic would give a good account of themselves, particularly since we knew that Henrik Larsson was fit.

Jim is a wise old bird (I'm sure he'll forgive me for saying) and usually keeps his counsel about predictions, but he too was fairly confident that we would do it. I remained the pessimist, with Margot ever optimistic, her correct-score predictions as always in the stratosphere. Paddy Power too had the benefit to the extent to which we all backed out judgement.

The emails coming into the studio were of a nervous bent. They fell into two major types; the call to arms/date with destiny, and the 'they've already done us proud this year' obituaries. Being firmly in the latter camp, I was comforted to some extent by my miserable track record in predicting Doom-That-Never-Happens during the campaign.

Within a couple of minutes of the start of the match, all hell had broken loose in the studio. Just before kick off, everyone expect for myself had gone outside to hear and see Gerry Marsden doing his impersonation of, er, Gerry Marsden singing *'You'll Never Walk Alone'*, before pledging undying love to all 60,000 souls in attendance, and stepping slickly into his Dick Fosbury (he of the Flop fame) routine, miraculously high-jumping his way over trailing microphone and camera cables. "We paid for a singer – and we got an acrobat!" "A MerseyBat!" quipped Peter VanDal, resident Rangers' supporter whose Native American name, 'Sooks On A Lemon' pays testimony to the last three seasons.

The match then kicked off and within ten seconds, John Hartson blasted the ball off the Reds' crossbar. A minute later the ball was in the back of the Liverpool net, despatched there by the returned-from-injury Larsson.

"AND CELTIC HAVE SCORED ALREADY! HE'S BACK!" screamed Paul Cuddihy in the commentary position. Small dogs in the back streets of Bogota are now known to have pricked up their ears at this point. Since I had my headphones on, I immediately assumed the posture one assumes when one bites into a prickly pear thinking it's an apple.

As cups and media-people-without-tickets flew across the room colliding with a homeless Radio 5 reporter who had lapped up all he could of the atmosphere without needing a seat, the phone in the studio rang. It's the guy from the Liverpool website;

Panic. "Our *"f$%6 connection isn't working!" he said.

Calm down now. "CELTIC, CELTIC!" I reply, remembering that episode of *Cracker* when Robbie Coltrane sings that in a Liverpool fan's face. "I've done you a favour anyway. We've scored. Are you sure you still want to see it?"

The connection, which had fallen over due to the surge in demand for the Internet version of the game was hurriedly restored. Soon after, Liverpool got an equaliser, and sanity was restored to Paradise for the moment anyway. If I had a quid for everyone who walked into that studio that night and said: "I've never seen/heard/felt anything like that out there in my life!" I'd be living in Jersey.

The gladiators chosen to do battle that evening were as follows;

CELTIC (3-5-2): Douglas; Valgaeren, Balde, Mjallby; Thompson (Guppy 26), Petrov, Sutton, Lennon, Smith; Larsson (Lambert 76), Hartson.
Substitutes: Marshall, McNamara, Sylla, Maloney, Crainey.
LIVERPOOL (4-4-2): Dudek; Carragher, Traore, Hyypia, Riise; Diouf (Biscan 90), Hamann, Gerrard, Murphy; Heskey, Owen.
Substitutes: Arphexad, Baros, Smicer, Diao, Cheyrou, Mellor.

Relentlessly, the fans urged on their teams to greater efforts. Liverpool looked to be in control and Larsson perhaps a bit rusty (which seems a bit churlish since he scored in the second minute).

In terms of the play on the evening, Liverpool probably looked the better side as the match progressed. Certainly Heskey sinned when he missed a golden opportunity to put Liverpool ahead, but Celtic too had their moments. Stan Petrov went close in the second half, and we were denied what appeared to be a clear penalty when Hyypia handled in the box.

The monumental thing that the Celtic side achieved that night – just as they had earlier in the tournament against Blackburn, was their refusal to give in. Their opponents were in the middle of an excellent run of form, and were showing the Glasgow public that they were a quality football side, but Celtic hung on to them, competed all over the pitch, and in the end a draw was probably a fair result.

One rather disappointing aspect of the evening was the incident where Diouf fell into the crowd, got up and spat on the very people who had broken his fall. Fortunately the incident, which could have spilled over into crowd trouble on another occasion, was dealt with quickly by the Liverpool bench, who withdrew the player from the field immediately after.

It is worth mentioning here that the e-mails received at Celtic Park from Liverpool fans deploring Diouf's actions went a long way to healing any wounds that might otherwise have festered. As it turned out, Liverpool, who appeared to be in pole position with an away goal and a draw, had cause to rue the in-form Diouf's actions, since he was suspended by UEFA for the return match.

At the end of the match as I said, it looked as though Liverpool had the upper hand. I then took comfort again in the knowledge that we had indeed had a good UEFA Cup, but the ex-pros, Craig, McGarvey and McKinlay were all optimistic. In fact the broad consensus was that Celtic had done it every time at away grounds when the chips were down – and there was no reason why we couldn't do it again.

In the weekend before Celtic's trip south seven days later, Liverpool had beaten Spurs 3-2 away from home, continuing their run of good form, whilst Celtic had been beaten 1-2 in the League Cup final at Hampden by Rangers. The big story emerging from the match was that Celtic had the chance to level in the last minute when Amoruso clattered Balde in the box and the referee awarded a penalty. John Hartson, whose goals had made such a huge contribution to the season, missed the kick, and a trophy was lost in the process.

Not the best preparation for Celtic or Hartson one might expect, as the green and white hordes invaded Liverpool for the third time in expectation of the first hooped triumph. The equation was pretty simple. A 0-0 draw would put Liverpool through on away goals as it had in 1997. Celtic simply HAD to score. We all believed they could do that, but the question was; could we stop Liverpool from scoring at home?

For me, Jim Craig, Frank McGarvey and Bertie Auld, we would miss out on the fun in the field. Instead our job was to once again tell the story of the match, its build-up and aftermath, to the Internet fans around the world. Again we were showing live pictures of the match to those who fell between the BBC broadcast and satellite stools.

It has become, over the course of the couple of seasons we have doing this, quite a vibrant community. We are regularly contacted by people from all over the planet. Regular contributors such as Camillo Santana in Boston, Chris Melville in Busan, South Korea, Tommy Toal in Venice and many, many more add spice to the debate and argument.

The theme on the evening of March 20 was whether Celtic's priority should be the league or the UEFA Cup. Again it was easy to pick out the optimists from the pessimists. Still firmly in the latter camp, I believed that our main priority had to be the league. A view that was shared by almost everyone was this. Even if we failed to progress beyond Liverpool, we had put our own special stamp on the competition this year. In particular, the travelling Celtic roadshow, the colourful, cheerful, singing, dancing and partying Celtic fans had spread good things about Celtic from Lithuania to Germany to Spain and England. Once again, the name Celtic was bringing a smile to the lips of football people all over Europe.

The managers picked the following sides to make progress to the UEFA Cup semi-final;

CELTIC (3-5-2): Douglas; Mjallby, Balde, Valgaeren; Thompson, Lennon, Lambert (McNamara 73), Petrov, Sylla (Smith 86); Hartson, Larsson.
Substitutes: Marshall, McNamara, Laursen, Maloney, Guppy, Crainey.
LIVERPOOL (4-4-2): Dudek; Carragher, Hyypia, Traore, Riise; Smicer (Baros 56), Hamann, Gerrard, Murphy; Owen, Heskey.
Substitutes: Arphexad, Berger, Diao, Biscan, Cheyrou, Mellor.

Again, nails were bitten to the quick in the studio. Frank agitated when nervous, was all over the place. Jim Craig, who generally makes Perry Como look like a fidget, was all ants in his pants as well. Over the course of the TV spectacular, Bertie was to disappear from time to time, unable to watch as the tension mounted. Not until we were in the last minute of added time, did the tension lift.

For the second time in seven days, the Celtic and Liverpool fans teamed up for their by now regular joint rendition of *'You'll Never Walk Alone'*. Then it was down to battle. Liverpool started well, and nerves were extremely frayed amongst the Celtic people when Michael Owen turned John Mjallby before being turned over himself by the big Swede who got booked. It was to be the last mistake Johan would make on the night, as he, Bobo Balde, Joos Valgaeren and Neil Lennon denied Liverpool any space with which to exploit the possession they would have.

Mjallby was in action again soon after, clearing as Owen waited to score. Then Celtic began to show that they were fully intending to get the goal they required. First, when Thompson shot over from long range, then when a Larsson free kick was pushed away desperately by Dudek. Almost immediately thereafter, Robert Douglas again showed how valuable he has been to Martin O'Neill's side in Europe with a quite unbelievable save from a wonderful volley from Gerrard.

Liverpool though went close halfway through the first half when Heskey shot wide after good work by Owen, and the same player had a header cleared first by Douglas and then Lennon. Celtic though, were having a better time of it than they had at Celtic Park – and not for the first time in this campaign either. Larsson went close with a back-post header and Sylla, who was emerging as an outstanding contributor to the Celtic cause, played a one-two with Larsson before shooting, forcing Dudek to concede a corner.

With a minute to go to half time, pandemonium! Celtic were awarded a free-kick outside the box for a challenge on Larsson by Traore. Alan Thompson took the kick and sent it low and hard under the wall past Dudek. When I emerged from the pile of bodies in the studio, it was half time. The tension was only beginning.

Early in the second half Larsson might have put us two-up. Sylla crossed from deep right, and Traore and Dudek seemed to leave it to each other. Henrik was almost on to the loose ball, but Carragher intervened to block the Swede's lob.

Tension mounted as the half wore on with Celtic still in front. Liverpool, with little to lose, piled forward. The red threat increased with Baros' introduction, but as the minutes ticked away, John Hartson, the man who had missed the cup final penalty, strode forward, played a wall pass with Larsson, side-stepped Traore, and crashed an unstoppable shot past Dudek. Nine minutes left and we were through.

Incredibly, Bertie had managed to see both goals, those arriving with happy coincidence at a time when he was not silently walking the corridor, too feart to look.

It is east to use superlatives in football. In fact the game itself arouses passions which often preclude objectivity. But this was a genuinely superlative performance by Celtic. Once again the critics were confounded by a performance which had us swelling up with so much pride, we feared we might burst. It was a great night for Hartson, who had overcome his cup final setback to strike the decisive blow which allowed Celtic at last, to best their Merseyside rivals - not JUST beat them. We had done it with style, and with something to spare. Not even the biggest die-hard in the Kop that evening would have disagreed with the proposition that Celtic were the better side by some distance. This Celtic was the real deal, and I felt guilty I had doubted them. I vowed not to do that again.

One hundred and sixteen years after its inception, the old Celtic story was again being told; John Hartson's personal triumph over adversity reflecting that of old.

And the really wonderful thing is that after the affray, and despite the obvious disappointment they must have felt, the Liverpool fans, like the Celtic fans in 1997, accepted defeat with a grace and honour which is in the best traditions of those cities which are so alike, and which over the course of this UEFA Cup, became a little bit closer still.

As we looked forward to the draw for the semi-final, we looked with a conviction that we need not fear anyone. Would Liverpool have feared any of the three teams left?

Of course there was one with a 'V' in the name…

TONY HAMILTON'S EUROPEAN DIARY
Part 6: With hope in our hearts ...

I never did it at the time, mainly because my modesty knows no end, but I feel it's time to put the record straight.

Having Gerry Marsden perform 'You'll Never Walk Alone' live at Celtic Park was all my own doing.

Having asked him to appear three or four times before, always with the promise that he would as soon as he hadn't something on, was beginning to make me wonder how much, if at all, he wanted to perform in front of the biggest and best audience of his long and distinguished career.

At one point in the past few years when I called, his wife told me that he wasn't in – he had a concert in Denmark! Not even Danish people go to Denmark. Who was she kidding?

Anyway, the first call I made at the final whistle in the Gottlieb-Daimler Stadium was to dear old Gerry and he told me there and then he'd be with us – F.O.C. – and he wouldn't be doing Anfield for the return leg.

It was the best call I ever made in my entire life (apart from the time I called my Rangers-supporting mate Gary Chambers in the middle of the night and asked him to remember and tape The Bill for me while I was in Seville.)

Getting Gerry was a double result I thought, but I was wrong. Des and I have since discovered that it's more than that – it's a triple result. The footage we got of him singing and the live audio can be used for anything.

All you have to do is have him at the start and the end and replace the footage in between with whatever it is you're trying to do to induce emotion – it works a treat.

Channel 5 produced the match at home and it was a real pleasure to work with them. I couldn't, however, keep my face straight when an (anonymous) member of their production team said to me before kick-off: "So, Gerry Marsden, wrote that song himself, didn't he?"

I felt obliged to agree – he had already made his mind up – who was I to disappoint him?

Being paired with Liverpool was a legitimate reason (in my mind) to travel to Madrid and interview Steve McManaman, get him to say that Celtic would go through and make him apologise for scoring that goal against us the last time we played the English club in European competition, back in 1997.

I failed on both accounts but Madrid was magnificent (although KLM cancelled our flights AND lost our luggage AGAIN on the way back) so all was not lost – we had broadened our minds and got a bit of sun and some more cheap fags to boot.

When I say 'we' I actually mean me. You see, Des is, how can I put it, a bit tight. So tight in fact he only breathes in. So tight he squeaks when he walks. So tight that he can't ever see the point of spending more than a fiver in one transaction – not without a lie down and two paracetamol tablets at any rate.

You get what I'm saying – he never bought any fags. In fact, he never bought anything – just a pair of scissors to cut off the bobbles from his fleece that he wears everyday in all temperatures and that he's been wearing for the past three years. I think it's attached to his body.

But, back in less pleasant climes we had to travel to Anfield with a 1-1 draw from the first leg. We had the opportunity to fly with the team but as I (and I'm not at all proud of this) wasn't overly confident of how it would pan out we decided, after consultation in the media team, that I would drive us there instead.

My thinking was that if it didn't go well it would be better to leave the team with a bit of privacy on the flight back home but I made sure we were all included on the plane to and from Inverness for the Scottish Cup match…

Still, Liverpool for me holds a special place in my heart as it does I'm sure for many others who love the Celts. I suppose it goes back to Kenny Dalglish and all that went on in August 1977 and, aside from the time Graeme Souness was there, I always wanted them to do well. Incidentally, the spell checker on my Mac offers Sourness as an alternative to Souness. Funny that.

But let's get back to the point. My slight affinity with Liverpool through Dalglish and them stealing 'You'll Never Walk Alone' from us and pretending it was theirs and all of that was never going to interfere with the job at hand.

I wanted us to win and I wanted the whole of these islands to know that Scottish football (okay, Celtic) can't be ignored any longer and that there's no legitimate reason why people in Scotland have to get the results from the Vauxhall Conference and the Doc Martin's league or whatever they are called before results from the SPL.

I wanted all of those smug English commentators to see that we weren't an easy passage for Liverpool to the last four of the UEFA Cup and I wasn't disappointed. In fact, it was probably the proudest moment of the campaign away from the team's efforts in Seville.

And just as I was wanting all of those thing to happen, up stepped BBJ Hartson. Only a few hours earlier he had produced a ticket for my young brother, his namesake John (another fool who declined the Away European Registration Scheme) and here he was at Anfield, in front of the team he supported as a kid, producing the goal of the season for Celtic and the one which meant more cheap fags in Portugal.

Fagtastic!

147

SEVILLE SIGHTS: *The massive green and white army turned the southern Spanish city into one giant Celtic party, and the new Hoops strip, already a best seller was everywhere to be seen*

149

CLIMB EVERY FOUNTAIN: *This Hoops fan was obviously feeling the heat and decided to cool off, while three leprechauns, below, were turning on the charm for the Hoops fans*

GIVE IT UP FOR THE BHOYS: *Celtic Park MC, Michael Hamilton, was at the Estadio Olimpico to help get the Bhoys and Ghirls in the mood before the game*

FAMOUS FANS: *Celebrity Celts Billy Connolly, above, and Rod Stewart in Seville*

Chapter Eight

Boavista: One giant leap ...
by Stephen Sullivan

"The last thing we wanted to do was go out with a whimper."

MARTIN O'NEILL

AFTER Anfield, anything seemed possible.

Whereas, before, Celtic fans had followed their team across Europe in hope rather than expectation, now they truly dared to dream. As one BBC reporter enthusiastically proclaimed, Martin O'Neill's Celtic stood perched 'on the cusp of greatness.'

Yet, for all that they had already achieved so much, the players knew that the margin for error was now more minuscule than ever, and that one below-par performance could ensure that they were not remembered as the club's most celebrated XI since Lisbon – but rather as a team which promised much, but delivered little.

It's worth remembering, after all, that at the time of the quarter-final draw, some of the club's fans had been bullishly discussing the prospect of a 'quadruple'.

Now, thanks to an unfortunate defeat at the hands of Rangers and a decidedly more ignominious one against old foes Inverness Caledonian Thistle, the UEFA Cup had taken on even greater significance as the trophy many adjudged to be the more attainable of the two Celtic had left to pursue. It was an awkward, nervous time for the Hoops players, who no doubt appreciated that, impressive though their progress had been, history tends to quickly forget beaten semi-finalists.

And the omens did not bode well. Of their six previous European semi-finals,

The Road to Seville

Celtic had won just two, and at least two of the competition's three remaining teams would have been supremely confident of further denting that record had they come out of the draw alongside the little-fancied Scots. The first of these, runaway Portuguese league leaders Porto, had already succeeded in humiliating Celtic once before, something no other team had managed in European competition during O'Neill's tenure. The other, Lazio, had yet to taste defeat at home in any competition during season 2002/03.

There was, thankfully, one runt in the litter. Little Boavista, languishing a full 35 points behind their Oporto rivals in the Portuguese league table, entered the draw boasting a miserable record of just seven victories from their previous 25 matches and with a reputation considerably less imposing than any of their fellow quarter-finalists. It was difficult to feign astonishment, therefore, when the press and football public concluded that Celtic had succeeded in pulling the proverbial rabbit from the hat by drawing Jaime Pacheco's team.

Further investigation yielded yet more encouraging tidings. Boavista were, in fact, the first side Celtic had met in Europe who were not from one of the continent's major leagues or challenging for their domestic title, or both, and it appeared their route to the semi-finals had been more than a little fortuitous. Put simply, the team nicknamed 'the Chequereds' because of their distinctive black-and-white checked shirt had led a charmed life in the competition thus far, having relied on penalties to dismiss Malaga and the away goals rule to see off both Paris-St Germain and Hertha Berlin. Furthermore, their UEFA Cup campaign had seen them avoid defeat just once on foreign soil, and their solitary victory had come against Cypriot minnows Anorthosis Famagusta.

This, it appeared, was as favourable a draw as Celtic could possibly have wished for. Yet, publicly at least, Martin O'Neill insisted upon contending that Boavista were the equal of any side remaining in the competition, accompanying it with a barbed jibe that the press were underestimating them simply "because Boavista is more difficult to spell than Porto". His argument was that Pacheco's side's indifferent league form made them all the more dangerous, given that they had little else to play for besides the UEFA Cup, and their elimination of highly-rated teams from Spain, France and Germany did add some weight to his argument.

Looking back now, it's possible that O'Neill's cautious words were aimed as much at his players as much as they were the media. Some observers were, after all, already drawing parallels with the Celtic of 1970, who, as many of you will no doubt remember, allowed complacency to creep in when faced with considerably less glamorous and fancied opposition to the high-profile English outfit they had dumped out in the previous round.

In any case, having revelled in the role of underdog thus far, O'Neill wasn't for allowing his side to be declared favourites now. "You know how we thought Porto and Lazio were the two big sides to avoid in the draw?" he said ahead of Boavista's arrival at Celtic Park. "Well, I have it on good authority that Boavista let out a big whoop of delight when they were drawn against us. I find that interesting."

Ricardo – the Oporto club's inspirational keeper and the hero of their quarter-final shoot-out victory over Malaga – may not have 'whooped' exactly, but he certainly made it clear that he and his team-mates expected to see off the challenge of their 'predictable' semi-final opponents. Such confident pre-match talk was nothing new to Celtic, however, and barely merited a yawn, never mind a mention, within the dressing room as the first leg approached. The players appeared completely focussed on the job in hand and, having already studied numerous videos of Boavista's impressive European exploits, it had become clear to them that they were about to be set a challenge very different to any they had faced thus far.

Certainly, those expecting a team akin in style to Celta Vigo or Porto could hardly have been more mistaken. Pacheco, the man who had guided Boavista to their first ever title in 2001 and the second group stage of the Champions League the following year, evidently prized commitment, strength and energy – traditionally 'British' virtues - above the qualities which mark out most of their Latin contemporaries. Dick van Burik, part of a Hertha Berlin side eliminated by Pacheco's side earlier in the tournament, summed up their approach. "They wear you down," he warned, "they don't let you breathe, and they are very, very tough."

An additional factor was Boavista's apparently institutional persecution complex, one which made Celtic's legendary 'paranoia' appear entirely reasonable in comparison. In Portugal, we were assured, there existed a long tradition of this little Oporto club being wronged by an establishment that had always favoured the country's 'holy trinity' of Benfica, Sporting Lisbon and Porto. And we soon found that the club's wrath was not reserved merely for the domestic authorities.

Indeed, in the run-up to the first leg at Celtic Park, it was UEFA who found themselves subject to allegations of bias after they rejected Boavista's plea that their playmaker, Edwin Sanchez, be allowed to play despite his ineligibility. "The poor people of football always have the most hardship," moaned Pacheco later. "When a big team and a small team meet, the small team is not usually favoured."

All this barely caused an eyebrow to be raised inside Celtic, where there was a growing realisation that defeat to the Portuguese would represent a truly devastating conclusion to the club's most notable European campaign in a generation. For all that the Celtic players recognised that their opponents possessed certain admirable qualities, the universally-held opinion was that better teams than Boavista had already been seen off en-route to the last four.

Paul Lambert merely articulated the determination of the dressing room when he told the *Celtic View*: "It would be a huge disappointment if we were to fail at this stage. After all the hard work we've put in we don't want things to come undone now. What's the point in getting to the semi-final and congratulating yourself? We have won absolutely nothing but, now that we are so close to it, I want it; I'm desperate for it."

Elsewhere, the mood was even more bullish. I can recall being assured, off the record, by one member of the club's backroom staff – not Martin O'Neill, I hasten to add - that Pacheco's team would be beaten home and away if Celtic reached anything close to their full potential. Less than 48 hours later, however, such optimism lay confounded as Boavista emerged from Celtic Park strong favourites to reach the final.

They had arrived at Celtic Park almost unheralded, and certainly without the feverish hype which had preceded the visit of Liverpool. Yet still their manager succeeded in stealing all the pre-match headlines with his decision to leave out Brazilian striker Epido Silva, widely considered to be the one Boavista player capable of disturbing the Celtic defence. Of course, after an hour-and-a-half of frustration – and despite Pacheco's post-match claim that the decision had been made to protect Silva, who was just one booking short of a suspension – it had become evident to everyone inside Celtic Park that attacking concerns had, in fact, been the last thing on the Boavista manager's mind.

Rather, he and his team had come to Glasgow merely to stifle, suffocate and suppress their hosts, something which, much to the disappointment of the home support, they succeeded in achieving for the best part of an exasperating match. There had, in fact, been a tangible sense of anti-climax to an occasion which had been eagerly anticipated ever since that memorable March evening on Merseyside.

Perhaps it was the earlier-than-usual kick-off time of 7.05pm, but there simply wasn't the same spine-tingling atmosphere that we have grown so accustomed to on countless magical nights beneath the floodlights at Celtic Park. On and off the field, it was a night of decidedly mixed emotions and, in the end, frustration was the one that prevailed for the supporters who had arrived at Paradise with high hopes of seeing their side establish a commanding advantage ahead of the trip to Oporto.

By this point in their European journey, however, O'Neill's side's predilection for leaving themselves with the proverbial mountain to climb on foreign soil was already firmly established, something alluded to in the following day's *Scotsman* by Glen Gibbons, who wrote that the 1-1 draw with Boavista had "emitted the upsetting stench of pre-ordination."

Celtic had utterly dominated the opening quarter-of-an-hour, and yet the tone for a frustrating evening was quickly set by Larsson squandering a string of half-chances and, more contentiously, the referee denying Celtic what appeared to be a indisputable penalty. Just eight minutes had been played when Filipe Anunciacao – under pressure from Didier Agathe – blatantly handled inside the area and yet, unmoved by the universal claim of 60,000 Celts, Frank de Bleekere waved for play to continue. Martin O'Neill was incensed and, having watched the Belgian match official repeat the mistake midway through the first half, he made his feelings clear at the post-match press conference.

"I said before the game that we would need a bit of luck, but it deserted us tonight," he complained. "The referee missed a couple of clear-cut penalty decisions, and that's really disappointing because he was in great positions to see what happened. Those are major decisions in big matches and you have to get them right."

It certainly wasn't a night on which fortune favoured Celtic; indeed their bid to reach the final began to look positively cursed when, just two minutes into the second half, they conceded the lead in the most calamitous of circumstances.

Ironically, it was Anuciacao – the very Boavista player who had escaped punishment in the first half - who broke away down the right flank and drilled in a right-foot cross which Joos Valgaeren, in an attempt to slide the ball behind, instead diverted past the stranded figure of Robert Douglas. It capped a miserable night for the Belgian, who had earlier broken a finger, and he was honest enough to admit the following day that he should have allowed the ball to run through to his goalkeeper.

"It wasn't the best cross," he recalled, "but it was in an awkward area and I felt that I had to get in to clear it behind. I did hear a shout from Rab, but it came just too late for me to stop. I had already made up my mind that I was going for the ball, and my momentum was taking me towards it. Rab shouted after that, and the rest, well…"

It was a genuinely heart-stopping moment and, as Valgaeren held his head in his hands, a collective gasp emanated from the stunned Celtic support. Those same fans rallied quickly, though, roaring their team back to the centre-circle, where began a passage of play which led to a leveller little over a minute later. And an extremely well-worked goal it was too, fashioned by Stilian Petrov trapping a Neil Lennon cross and cushioning a through pass for Henrik Larsson, whose side-foot shot low to Ricardo's right was executed in almost casual fashion. Larsson, it appeared, had once again saved Celtic's UEFA Cup campaign – and his team-mate's blushes.

There was, however, one final twist in the tale which had yet to unfold. It arrived with 15 minutes remaining when de Bleekere – perhaps attempting to prove that two wrongs can sometimes make a right – pointed decisively to the spot after Eder accidentally struck the ball with his hand in a clumsy attempt to boot clear, leaving Celtic's talismanic striker with the task of delivering justice.

It's an unfortunate and unfathomable fact, however, the Swede's ability from the spot is nowhere near as impressive of his overall prowess inside the penalty area and, though he struck his kick firmly, it was at the perfect height for Ricardo to leap across goal and palm it to safety.

"It wasn't as if he hit it poorly, just predictably," was the verdict of Kenny Dalglish in his newspaper column the following day, and Larsson himself was candid enough to admit that the end result is everything in such situations. "I thought I struck it well," he said afterwards, "but the bottom line is that it didn't go in, and I suppose that makes it a bad penalty."

Nevertheless, there remained time enough in the match for Celtic to establish a lead with which to travel to Portugal and, four minutes from the end, John Hartson – the outstanding performer on the night - would have obliged had it not been for the timely goal-line intervention of Paolo Turra. It seemed fitting that it was Turra who should have stuck out a boot to clear the Welshman's net-bound effort because he, more than any other player, had encapsulated what was good and bad about his team. We had been told before the match of Boavista's club motto: 'God loves you if you are on our side; but if you are against us, God help you.'

It was a dictum which Pacheco's players took with them on to the field and, having incurred two red cards and an incredible 26 yellows prior to facing Celtic, Turra duly earned the 27th booking of their season to nudge himself over the points threshold and disqualify him from the return leg.

Yet the big centre-half, who sported a protective mask to protect a broken cheekbone sustained during training, had typified his team's resolute work ethic, labouring tirelessly – and, for the most part, successfully – to grind Celtic down in midfield. A symptom of this was the below-par performance, and subsequent heckling, of Neil Lennon, who midway through the second half found himself booed after choosing to return the ball to Rab Douglas when the fans, from their elevated vantage points, could see a more offensive option available to him.

"I wasn't happy about it," Lennon complained a few days later. "I thought it was uncalled for and unjustified and, although I will forgive in time, it's hard to forget. I was very disappointed with it."

In truth, no-one with Celtic's interests at heart left the match on April 10 without some disappointment and yet, with there being little question that Boavista were of an inferior standard to each of the teams eliminated by the Hoops in the previous three rounds, most remained genuinely hopeful that O'Neill's side could once again triumph on their travels.

Not everyone was so sanguine, though. Kenny Dalglish, for one, criticised Celtic for once again "failing to live up to their fans' expectations at Parkhead," and signed off with the less-than-optimistic remark: "nothing lasts forever." There was defiance, however, from Martin O'Neill, who insisted at the post-match press conference: "The boys are disappointed in the dressing room for a number of reasons - but there's nothing to be disappointed with. We're not finished yet. There's a big prize at stake in Portugal in two weeks and we'll go for it with everything."

The most critical post-match coverage centred not on Celtic's performance, in fact, but on Boavista's negative, unsporting and, at times, downright dishonest approach to the game. "You have to try and play fairly," O'Neill said in response to questions on the issue. "But unfortunately rolling around, staying down and feigning injuries is a major part of the game, and it's very disappointing. They came here to do a job and that's what they did. They tried to kill the game at every opportunity and, had the ref signalled over 13 minutes of injury time, I wouldn't have been surprised."

In fact, de Bleekere signalled for just three and, for many inside Celtic Park, the most frustrating aspect of the match had not been Boavista's tactics – but rather the referee's utter failure to clamp down on them. This was certainly John Hartson's principal complaint, and the big Welshman made no attempt to disguise his contempt for the manner in which the game had been handled.

"You need a strong referee," he said afterwards, "When the ref isn't strong, it can ruin the game and it can all become a bit of a farce... I thought the three minutes made a mockery of the extra-time rule. I'd like to watch the game again and count it for myself because it seemed to me that there were at least half-a-dozen times in the second half when they had players down for a couple of minutes."

There were indeed times when the situation became genuinely ludicrous as player after player completed miraculously quick recoveries on the touchline just seconds after the more naïve among us might have been led to believe that their very careers were in jeopardy. Following the match, Pacheco pleaded his case for the defence with an attempt at flattery, claiming that, in Celtic, Boavista were up against a 'great' club. However, as Kevin McCarra observed the following day's *The Times*: "It would have been more candid to say that he doubted Celtic's creativity."

For Pacheco, a 1-1 draw represented mission accomplished and, though he struggled manfully to suppress a smug smile of self-satisfaction spreading across his lips as he left Celtic Park, it was apparent that he believed that the hard work had been done in the tie. And yet the Boavista boss didn't depart Glasgow without one more obsequious tribute to Celtic or, more accurately, the club's fans.

"I am glad to have experienced the Celtic support," he said. "It was amazing, the most emotional I have felt at a football match. When we scored our goal, I could not believe the way those fans reacted. They made a huge noise immediately in support of their team and it helped the players respond. It was fantastic."

Many a cynical head was shaken on hearing of this particular tribute and yet, by the time the second leg came around, it began to look increasingly like it might just have been genuine. It was certainly a sad indictment on Pacheco's own supporters that, as their team contested a European semi-final in a stadium with a capacity reduced to just over 15,000 due to extensive pre-Euro 2004 refurbishment, there were numerous empty seats visible in their areas of the ground. Not only sad, but highly frustrating for the thousands of ticketless Celtic fans who had spent the day in Oporto dodging countless counterfeit briefs to seek out the nearest genuine tout.

Initially, these supporters – all of whom were desperate to be able to say that they had been there the night that the club reached its first European final in over three decades – had been given just 750 tickets between them. However, deals were struck, concessions secured and, by the time kick-off arrived on April 24, there were in excess of 3,000 Hoops fans inside the Estadio do Bessa, all of whom arrived in need of some solace.

It had, after all, been a trying week. Only Celtic, it was concluded, could prepare for their biggest match in recent memory by losing to Hearts, a result which all but ended any lingering hopes of retaining the title, and losing their Chief Executive – all within 48 hours! It certainly served a painful remainder of the bad old days when internal strife and domestic disappointment were the norm at Celtic Park, and it didn't auger well for the meeting with a Boavista side which was convinced that destiny was on their side.

The semi-final second leg was, you see, Boavista's 100th European match in their 100th year of existence and, having never before reached a European final, they intended celebrating their centenary in style. They were also wary and well prepared, knowing only too well what had transpired on Celtic's last European trip. Indeed, it was said that, immediately after returning to the away dressing room at Celtic Park in the first leg, Boavista discussed within themselves the events at Anfield – and made a pact that they wouldn't fall victim to the same fate.

Martin O'Neill, meanwhile, and for all that he continued to protest otherwise, had slowly been coming to terms with the fact that, after their defeat at Tynecastle, Celtic's season was now all but certain to be defined by events in the Estadio do Bessa. And yet, on the eve of the match, he could hardly have appeared more relaxed. The Celtic boss had chosen Santa Tirso, a sleepy little town around half-an-hour's drive from Oporto, as the base for his side's preparations and, without a photographer or fan in sight, it proved to be perfect setting in which to unwind.

Throughout the evening, O'Neill sat surrounded by his backroom staff, joking, chatting and taking the occasional sip of red wine as we all sat down to watch the second leg of Real Madrid and Manchester United's Champions League quarter-final. It was a great game, United crashing out in a blaze of glory with a gallant 6-5 aggregate defeat, although O'Neill – so often tipped to succeed Alex Ferguson at Old Trafford – appeared more taken with the array of sublime talent Vicente del Bosque had at his disposal.

Later, a quiz game brought to the fore another side to the Celtic manager's character, namely his legendary will to win. With John Robertson the irritable quizmaster, O'Neill won the award for most competitive contestant by some distance and, at one stage, was even moved to heatedly accuse both Alan Thompson and Neil Lennon of cheating. All things considered, you would never have guessed that this was a manager with considerably more important matters weighing on his mind.

Looking back, it's possible that O'Neill's relaxed demeanour was due to a team meeting which had taken place on the Monday following Celtic's 2-1 defeat at Tynecastle, a meeting which, by all accounts, had witnessed the most frank of discussions over the perilous position the team now found themselves in. Whatever it was, it had left the Celtic manager and his players in a determined and positive frame of mind.

"The mood is very upbeat," said O'Neill the eve of the match. "I mean, here we are on a glorious April evening preparing for the semi-final of the UEFA Cup. The lads are looking forward to the game – they're bound to be – and they're as upbeat as you could want. We have to score, and in all probability we will have to win the game. From that aspect, it simplifies the equation for us, and the lads know exactly what is required of them if we are to go through to the final."

There seemed little doubting, too, that O'Neill had been stressing to his squad in no uncertain terms that they were about to take their one shot at reaching a European final. The Irishman would subsequently speak about rebuilding the nucleus of this squad – which remains based around 30-somethings such as Paul Lambert, Johan Mjallby and Henrik Larsson – and he left them under no illusions that, as a group, they would never be presented with such an opportunity again.

It led Neil Lennon, one of the Hoops players on the wrong side of 30, to label the game with Boavista as "the biggest of my career," and it was clear that he was far from alone in holding this belief. Indeed, O'Neill was adamant that, regardless of what stage of their respective careers they were at, every one of his players had to treat this opportunity to reach a European final as if it was their last.

"This is generally a once-in-a-lifetime opportunity," he told the *Celtic View,* "and, no matter what age you are, it's one you have to seize with both hands. So, regardless of whether it's young Shaun Maloney or one of our elder statesmen, my advice to them will be that games like this one don't come around too often.

"The likes of Shaun and David Marshall might well think that this sort of thing will come around regularly and, if they don't make the most of this opportunity, well, there will always be others. And hopefully there will be. But ask any of the Celtic supporters who remember the Lisbon Lions and they will tell you that, having enjoyed a plethora of success over a number of years, you can sometimes be left asking where it has all gone. That's why I'll be saying to the players to give it everything and more. If there's such a thing as more than 100 per cent, then that's what I want them to put into the game tomorrow night."

There were no surprises in the side O'Neill put out to give him this at the Estadio do Bessa. The line-up was identical to the one fielded at Celtic Park and, depending on whether you're a fan of fielding Chris Sutton in midfield, it was easy to conclude that it was also O'Neill's strongest.

However, while we knew exactly what to expect from the away team, we awaited with interest to discover how Boavista would approach the match. Joos Valgaeren articulated the expectations of many when he said: "At home, they will have to give their supporters something, and that's where we can maybe take advantage. I think it will be a more open game in Portugal."

The noises from within Pacheco's dressing room also suggested that Boavista

DEADLOCK: *the first leg of the semi-final against Boavista at Celtic Park ended 1-1*

GENIUS: *Henrik Larsson's late goal put Celtic into the UEFA Cup final, sparking off great celebrations*

would emerge from the defensive shell they had inhabited from the first minute till the last at Celtic Park. "We are not going to play for a 0-0 draw with 10 men in defence," insisted Ricardo, their goalkeeper, ahead of the match. "We will defend our 'lead' by going for goal."

Whether this was a deliberate attempt to mislead, we may never know. However, 'going for goal' rarely appeared to figure in the thinking of a Boavista team whose gameplan, if anything, was even more infuriatingly negative than it had been at Celtic Park. Graham Spiers summed it up neatly in the following day's *Herald,* likening the men in chequered strips to chessmen and justifiably suggesting that they had been sent out by their manager to "suck the life out of Celtic."

Indeed, while O'Neill's side's domination of the opening stages suggested that Pacheco had been justified in claiming pre-match that Celtic were a side better suited to playing away from Glasgow, further analysis brought the inescapable conclusion that the Hoops were, in fact, being forced to played as if they, rather than Boavista, were the home team. The result? A truly dreadful match.

Play was ragged throughout, and it was difficult at times to avoid reflecting on how starkly it contrasted with the pictures we had seen beamed from Old Trafford the night before. Indeed, for 79 minutes, it appeared that Pacheco – who had sent out a side tactically identical to Celtic's to help guarantee that the teams would cancel each other out – would be rewarded for having shown no hint of attacking adventure during the tie with a place in the final.

The Boavista boss lamented afterwards that Celtic didn't look as if they believed they could score and, for large chunks of a dire encounter, this was probably true. Larsson was presented with a chance in nine minutes that was perhaps more straightforward than the one he would later convert, but, after latching on to a John Hartson knock-down, he sclaffed his right-foot shot wide of Ricardo's right-hand post.

Celtic's cause was further damaged by the premature withdrawal through injury of Paul Lambert, replaced midway through the first half by Chris Sutton, who O'Neill later admitted had only played in a couple of five-a-side matches since returning from a broken wrist. There were also a couple of isolated moments in which Hoops' hearts were in mouths, the first of which arrived in 42 minutes when an uncharacteristically sloppy touch from Joos Valgaeren, playing what was quite possibly his worst ever game for the club, allowed Santos to race in on goal. The Boavista midfielder then drew and nutmegged Bobo Balde before delivering a tantalising cross which Rab Douglas only prevented being diverted home by emerging positively from his goal to push to safety Silva's header.

However, if the big keeper had saved his defence on this occasion, the favour was certainly returned just a few minutes into the second half when, having flapped at a speculative Duda cross, he was left to look on gratefully as Mjallby saved his blushes by blocking Silva's net-bound header on the goal-line.

The signs appeared foreboding for Celtic at this stage and, for all their huffing and puffing, opportunities to score – already scarce – had all but dried up. It appeared to everyone inside the do Bessa that their efforts were likely to prove to be in vain, and that the dream was coming to an unsatisfactory end.

However, as Henrik Larsson later enthused: "We kept at them and we never gave it up. That is our strength – we do not believe it is finished until it is finished."

The Road to Seville

With time running out, O'Neill threw on Smith for Valgaeren in a bold attacking move and, 11 minutes before the end, received his reward. Here, I'll allow to Henrik to take up the story. "When I tried to thread the ball through to John (Hartson), I thought he was in," recalled the Swede. "Then I saw the guy coming in with the sliding tackle, so I thought to myself that I'd take a position where the ball might end up and it came straight to my feet.

"I took a touch, then over my shoulder I saw their right-back closing in on me so I tried to concentrate on getting something on the ball. There wasn't very much pace on the shot, but I got enough to get it into the net."

That it took an agonising eternity to reach there mattered not a jot. Celtic had the goal they so desperately required, one later described by the Swede as "the most important of my career – so far" and, though it was the signal for Boavista to finally begin applying pressure to Douglas' goal, Pacheco's side didn't appear to have a 'Plan B' of any real merit to fall back upon.

And yet, while Larsson's 39th goal of the season always appeared to have an air of decisiveness about it, there were one or two nervy moments as the clock ticked down, most notably when Jocivalter went down theatrically as he and Didier Agathe jostled for possession inside the penalty area. "It was a worrying few seconds," Agathe later admitted. "I definitely didn't touch him, but he went down and I thought: 'What if the ref gives a penalty'. But he didn't and now it's not important."

Agathe was right. At the end, everything else – the quality of the match included - was forgotten. Victory really was the be all and end all and, predictably, Larsson had been the man to provide it.

His strike partner led the tributes. "It was different class," said Hartson, beaming from ear to ear. "Henrik has come up trumps for us again. It was a superb goal, he's a hero for us once again and I am absolutely delighted for him. I'm also really pleased for the fans and for the players and the manager because this is where we should be."

Hartson was, however, candid enough to admit that "at one stage, I thought we were never going to do it," and it was evident that there was as much relief as there was joy in Celtic's post-match celebrations.

The fans, both in the Estadio do Bessa and back home in Glasgow, were simply delirious. Time brought with it more incredible stories, tales of Sauchiehall Street being closed off to accommodate an impromptu celebration and an account of a group of fans refusing to leave the blazing Oporto pub in which they were watching the game only to change their minds when burning debris began falling on their heads!

Among the more bizarre sights inside the stadium was *Chewin' the Fat's* Greg Hemphill stumbling joyfully down the stairs, singing and dancing with his fellow supporters. It was also there, inside the do Bessa, that the now legendary chant of "They'll be watching *The Bill* while we're in Seville!" first took life, and it wasn't long before variations involving *Take the High Road* and *EastEnders* were being given an airing.

It truly was a scene to behold, and it was entirely fitting that Neil Lennon should be the Celtic player to dedicate the victory to the supporters who had gone to such great efforts, and expense, to follow the team throughout Europe: "This is for them," he said, "those supporters who have been great. It's for them and the whole club."

Lennon wasn't alone in acknowledging the fans' contribution, however. In the following week's *Celtic View*, Martin O'Neill – so often critical of the club's notoriously difficult-to-please home support – paid a warm tribute to the club's green-and-white army of travelling fans, which had, he claimed, proved itself once again to be without equal.

"The team have given the fans some great nights this season," he said, "but I don't think there's any doubt that they've been given a lot back in return. When it comes to matches away from home, there does appear to be a camaraderie between the fans and the players, and I think that probably comes from a knowledge that, in Europe at least, we're battling against the odds and that everyone is 'in it together,' if you like.

"The support which has followed us in the UEFA Cup this season has been immense both in numbers and in volume, and I doubt that I'll ever forget the scenes at Oporto Airport following the Boavista game. These supporters have spent a lot of money to come and cheer us on, behaving impeccably throughout, and I can assure you it has not gone unappreciated in the dressing room."

O'Neill himself spent the hours following the victory in Oporto struggling to comprehend the enormity of the achievement. I was with his two daughters, Alana and Aisling, when they first met their father following the match and, though clearly delighted, he did not possess the air of a man who knows what he has achieved, something extremely evident in his demeanour following Celtic's 2-0 victory at Anfield. This was also borne out by his subdued performance at the post-match press conference.

"It's obviously a terrific feeling, but I think I might have a better description for it tomorrow or the next day," he told the assembled hacks. "It genuinely has not sunk in yet. I always felt that we could get goals, but obviously time was running out and they were dropping back in numbers. Over the two legs, though, I don't think there's any question we thoroughly merited a place in the final."

This was merely a statement of fact, and yet not everyone agreed. Pacheco, who ultimately paid for elimination with his job, came out fighting with the predictable and decidedly dubious assertion that Celtic had been 'lucky'. "This the hardest day of my life," he mourned. "We tried everything and had the best chances, but luck was not on our side."

Fortune had, in fact, merely favoured the brave. Celtic deserved to win, if only because they had shown themselves to possess all of Boavista's best qualities – their workrate, their passion, their defensive solidity – and none of their worst. Pacheco's team would be remembered for having spent the tie play-acting, feigning injury and spoiling, and the lack of sympathy for their plight came across clearly in the hours following the final whistle.

"Boavista only came forward in the last 10 minutes – they got exactly what they deserved," contributed Rab Douglas. "I've no idea how much time they killed by lying down injured, but they will be spewing now."

This reporter, like many Celtic fans, had spent much of the match contemplating elimination, and I recall pleading with the heavens: "Please - not like this. Not after such a terrible game, and definitely not to a team like Boavista."

O'Neill, it transpired, had been thinking along similar lines. "I know what people mean when they say that it would have been somewhat anti-climactic had we not managed to beat Boavista," he told the *Celtic View*. "It's been a long road for us, and I would have hated to see that road come to an end in Oporto last week because, on reflection, Boavista were perhaps not as formidable opponents as Celta Vigo, Liverpool or Stuttgart. But getting to the final was always the most important thing, and we did that."

And, in ensuring that their seven-month long UEFA Cup adventure would continue in the Spanish city of Seville, O'Neill and his Celtic team inadvertently sparked the biggest frenzy for flights and tickets Scotland has ever witnessed.

There had been chuckles all round when *Sportscene* presenter Dougie Donnelly, having attempted to make sense of Scottish football's most momentous evening in decades, signed off with some shrewd advice. "If you work in a Glasgow travel agency," he counselled, "get an early night. Tomorrow's going to be a busy day."

In fact, no one could have predicted the incredible reality which unfolded over the days and weeks following Celtic's victory in Oporto. Everyone, it seemed, wanted to be in Seville, and the larger the magical date of May 21 loomed, the more feverish became the scramble to find a way – any way – of making the pilgrimage to the city which was rapidly becoming Celtic's very own Mecca.

This was nowhere better illustrated than on Saturday, April 26 when *The Sun* ran with the front page headline 'HENRIK... 1 SADDAM... 0,' ahead of a story which reported that Celtic had saved the Scottish travel industry from being brought to its knees by the war in the Iraq. It even prompted Martin O'Neill to observe with a chuckle that: "... in the nicest possible sense, I don't think Seville has any idea what's about to hit it."

For Celtic, these were indeed the best of times. As UEFA's own website put it, this famous old club was now 'back on the grand stage,' after many long years spent roaming, often aimlessly, through the football wilderness.

Now all that remained was the final, and the small matter of FC Porto.

TONY HAMILTON'S EUROPEAN DIARY
Part 7: Language barriers

Language, as we've established, can sometimes be a barrier on foreign shores. Even if you shout in English really loud at a foreigner the chances are they still won't get what you're saying. Funny that, I think.

Anyway, the city of Oporto was no different from anywhere else we had been during this campaign – including Merseyside.

Sharon Gillespie, our very own cameraman and Shania Twain stunt double, has a command of the English language only one who hails from Hamiltonhill (Possil to you and me) has.

And then there's Barry Davies – BBC commentator with a mouth full of toffee and a man who obviously isn't as accustomed to the home town of Boavista as we are.

With about half an hour to go before kick-off and in an accustomed bout of nervousness, I was making my umpteenth trip to the gents, behind the press or 'tribune' area in one of the steepest stadiums I've ever been in.

Davies was there too, ogling me as I stood at the urinal. I thought at first that he was going to ask me for some tips on commentating but I was wrong.

As I made for the wash-hand basin I could feel his eyes burning in the back of my neck.

"DO-YOU-SPEAK-ENGLISH?" he asked me in long, pronounced tones. As I stood there with my Celtic suit, lapel pin and tie on (a big clue in my mind) I made a gesture that, yes, I could speak a little English.

"Is it," he continued slowly, "Es-ta-dio do Bessa or Es-tha-dio do Bessa?"

"Nae idea, mate," I said and hurriedly made my way back to join the rest of the crew who, by this time, were becoming just that tiny bit ratty with each other. It often happens when we spend too much time together and always happens when we're nervous about the game.

All of this a far cry from the previous evening when Sharon and some of our team had arrived in town and were picked up by a Portuguese chauffeur at the airport.

By all accounts it was a slow and peaceful journey back to the team base to meet the rest of us until Shaz, out of the blue, shouted from the front passenger seat "Plane – sky – bumpy-bumpy" to the bemused driver.

That, however, compared to the guy we pulled up alongside the night before the game on the way back from training, was nothing.

I've already made the point about being no good as a passenger so I insist on driving everywhere we go and I always get blamed for getting us lost, though the truth of the matter is that it's never been my fault yet. (See the Blackburn chapter if you don't believe me.)

Anyway, we'd had a bit of a nightmare at the team's training session with 'Joseph', who I'll get to in a minute, and we were heading back to the hotel to get the rest of the work finished, get some dinner and hopefully see Manchester United get turned over by Real Madrid. Then we got lost. Completely wrong direction. Heading for Spain. Different country – apparently.

I exited the motorway and pulled up alongside a local guy who was minding his own business. I put Shaz's window down and gently prodded her to ask the guy for directions to Santo Tinso, our base, 40 km, south of Oporto.

"Hey wee man, do you speaka da English 'n that?" She enquired gently.

Needless to say, by the time we got back to the hotel they were setting up for breakfast, Manchester United had beaten Real Madrid (but not by enough to go through) and we still had a load of work to finish.

But getting back to Joseph - the stadium chief-something-or-other – here was a guy who just couldn't get his head round the whole UEFA Fair Play idea. It was a completely alien concept to him.

All we wanted to do was what we always do and that is stay behind when the rest of the broadcast media are kicked out of training to film the players going through their paces, and then record a quick five-minute programme for Celtic Replay to set the scene for the following evening's game.

Security was tight and Martin O'Neill from the centre circle sensed it before we did. We were being chaperoned by a couple of security guards and as the manager shouted over to see if everything was all right I couldn't think why it wouldn't be.

Then Joseph arrived like a man possessed by the devil, shouting and screaming in my face about us crazy English (crazy isn't the word he really used and I can't repeat what he said although he genuinely thought we were English).

I sensed he wasn't terribly happy with me for some reason and he demanded we leave "his""stadium immediately, and even got the police and more security guards to see that he got his way.

He would have got his way had he just put his mind to it and not fallen for the Barlanark bravado bluff – he was six feet thirteen and I can't even fight sleep – though he didn't know that then.

Only a few minutes before all of this, the BBC were mysteriously pulled off-air during a live report back to Queen Margaret Drive. It wasn't really a mystery as I'm sure everyone has worked out by now.

Anyway, Joseph calmed down, we were allowed to stay but opted to leave on a point of principle as soon as he said we could carry on.

As you can imagine I was dreading going back to face him the next night but as things transpired I never saw him again until after the match – none of us did.

By that time though we were celebrating being in the final, interviewing our players on his pitch and in his tunnel and generally having the run of the gaff.

Joseph was a broken man. A bit excitable but a broken man nonetheless. I offered him a hand of friendship and he accepted. If only I could learn to be just as magnanimous in defeat I'd be a better person all round.

And if only everyone could behave the way they did when my good friend Pete St John belted out 'The Fields of Athenry' at the home leg, we'd all be better people.

 Celtic FC v FC Porto

Estadio Olimpico, Sevilla
Wednesday, May 21, 2003
Kick-off: 20.45 (CET)

Chapter Nine

FC Porto: So near yet so far

by Jim Craig

FOR admirers of 'the beautiful game', there had been worrying signs in the return leg against Boavista in Porto. On the night, every spectator, whether in the stadium, or watching on TV, would have acknowledged that Celtic was the superior team. What really bothered our fans, though, was the pragmatic play of the Portuguese side, their determination to hold out at all costs, to slow the game down, to stop the visitors by any means. It was not attractive but was effective, and it very nearly worked.

From my own viewing point, in the Webcast studio on the first floor at Celtic Park, I felt we would never break through. Our commentator Tony Hamilton is normally one of the more calm practitioners of the art but even his voice was breaking occasionally. Beside him in the Estadio do Bessa, Tosh McKinlay had abandoned all thoughts of giving an unbiased summary and was cheerleading the team on. And as an unofficial and unrehearsed background to their commentary, an occasional scream from our producer, Margot McCuaig, could clearly be heard.

Beside me in the Glasgow studio, while I endeavoured to remain cool, calm and collected, my colleagues were showing signs of pressure. Frank McGarvey was giving his rapid-fire commentary on the match, telling us what the players should have been doing rather than what they were doing. The trouble was, nobody was listening to him.

Our Web Administrator, John Cole, normally a civil, well-educated personality, went ballistic over the referee's decisions, questioning both his parentage and his allegiance to the fortunes of our chief Scottish rivals. And Bertie Auld jumped up and down from his seat, occasionally roaring at the screen as

someone failed to live up to his expectations. Just the normal scenario for Celtic fans watching their team on TV.

As time went on, the Hoops raised their game, increased their percentage of possession and lay siege to the Boavista goal. However, with the scores still tied at 1-1 from the first leg, and the minutes ticking by, the fans were becoming very worried. They were happy with their team's possession and drive but goals were required and they were not looking likely.

And then, in the 78th minute, Henrik struck, latching on to a blocked pass before cutely adjusting his balance and sending a left-foot shot past the flapping arms of Ricardo in the Boavista goal.

All over the world, the Celtic fans went delirious … and continued the celebrations right up to the final whistle. Once that was blown by referee Ivanov, the euphoria increased. The bars in Glasgow did roaring business, champagne glasses were filled in every corner of the Celtic world and toasts were proposed to the team and the management.

As the Celtic party flew back to Glasgow in the early hours of the morning, to be met by a substantial and delighted crowd, the rest of the fans slipped into the sleep of the contented, their dreams no doubt centred on the UEFA Cup being paraded around Celtic Park.

By the following morning, though, reality had kicked in. Oh! We were all delighted to reach the final but the league title was another of our aims and we had an appointment on the Sunday with Rangers.

At lunchtime that Friday, along with a number of my colleagues, I attended one of the manager's press conferences. He does three of these. One, which I usually take in, is for TV and can be seen in the evening broadcasts; he then gathers with the daily newspaper guys for the second; and meets those working on the Sunday press separately. He's a clever fellow, is Martin O'Neill. Every week, at these press sessions, he gets hit by varying questions, most of them topical, some pointed, a few unbelievably nonsensical! But Martin deals with them all in the same fashion.

One of my former teachers would be delighted that I can still remember some of his advice. In my first year at secondary school, as part of the English curriculum, Mr Hill conducted classes where the precise meanings of various words and expressions were defined. One of these was circumlocution, the dictionary definition of which is 'an indirect way of expressing something'. No Celtic boss has ever used circumlocution to greater effect. Whatever the topic, Martin calmly takes it on board, defuses any possible bombs and defines his answer efficiently and effectively. That's why there is little controversy at these particular press conferences.

That Friday's gathering should have been a dawdle. After all, less than 24 hours beforehand, the club had reached the final of the UEFA Cup. Yet, that did not prove to be the case, with the Celtic manager receiving some sharp questions and the conference going on for twice the usual time. The reason was quite clear. No matter how well Celtic were doing in Europe, on the domestic front they were still eight points behind archrivals Rangers, admittedly with one game in hand. So, after some congratulatory comments about the club's fine show the previous evening, the atmosphere changed as the forthcoming Old Firm contest was discussed and dissected. Martin O'Neill was obviously tired but kept his composure in spite of the probing questions. It was clear that everyone present thought that anything less than a victory for Celtic would hand the title to Rangers. Being a realist, the Celtic boss' own views might have been heading in the same direction; quite rightly, though, he was not going to be drawn publicly in saying so.

Some 48 hours later, as the teams came out on to the Ibrox pitch, 49,740 fans forgot the grey skies and drizzle to give both sides a rousing welcome. Some 7,000 Celtic guys and gals were in the Broomloan Road stand, dressed for the occasion not only in the hoops but also in sombreros and sunglasses. Just before kick-off, more than a few beach balls made their way down the pitch towards the Rangers contingent. It was a message from the Celtic fans. Their team was heading for Seville … and they wanted their rivals to remember it!

If they were happy before the kick-off, by half time they were delirious! Goals by Alan Thompson, from the penalty spot, and John Hartson had given their heroes a 2-0 lead against a Rangers side showing indifferent form.

Shortly into the second half, Ronald de Boer pulled one back but the Celtic midfield always controlled the play and Rangers' forwards received little service. As the final whistle went, three quarters of Ibrox fell silent; at the other end, sombreros and beach balls were thrown in the air. And in households throughout the Celtic world, they marvelled at four wonderful days.

As usual, I watched the game in the Webcast studio at Parkhead. The tension before the match was almost palpable and did not let up throughout the 90 minutes. I found it hard going; others were worse. Over at Ibrox, Tony's voice kept breaking, Tosh showed his bias, Margot shouted at everyone in blue. Beside me, Frank gabbled away, John ranted about the ref, Bertie fired some verbal volleys…and I sat calmly and tried to maintain some order. No wonder my hair is going grey, or is it white?

By Monday, the mood was quite clear. Yes, the league was important…but the UEFA Cup final was winning the thoughts of the fans hands down. The coffee shop on the first floor of the main stand at Celtic Park was transformed into a 'Tapas Bar', with all kinds of Spanish (or was it Mexican?) mementoes on the walls; the daily web broadcasts now began with the camera focussed on a calendar showing 'only XYZ days to go'; and the broadcasters on these shows all wore sombreros.

I found that quite difficult, sitting on a backless high stool, trying to balance a huge sombrero on my wee heid and talk interestingly at the same time. But all the different activities must have struck a chord with the Celtic faithful. When I checked with the Superstore in the first week of June, I discovered they had sold 3,667 sombreros, 19,000 T-shirts, 1,198 mugs, 4,383 scarves, 2,970 flags and 1,065 beach-balls, not to mention the 60,000 new strips currently being displayed all over Scotland, Britain, Ireland, Europe, the Americas, Africa, Asia and Australasia.

As the Estadio Olimpico in Seville got the once-over (and a disapproving one at that, especially the pitch) from the press and TV, the Celtic management tried to keep the players' minds focussed on the league run. And after the boost of the Rangers game, they rose to the occasion. Good away victories at East End Park (4-1) and Fir Park (4-0) were followed by home wins over Hearts (1-0) and Dundee (6-2). The team could do no more; they had taken the title race to the last match of the season. The rest was up to Rangers.

In the week before the big match, two special editions of the *Celtic View* previewed the occasion, as well as providing a free beach ball! In the first, interviews were run with stars like the ex-Spurs keeper Pat Jennings and Cup-Winners' Cup medallist John Hewitt. Two pages were devoted to the delights of Seville, under headings like Sights/Activities, Cuisine, Shopping and Arts/Culture; on another two, fans were given a comprehensive guide to Spain, Seville and the plans for entry to the stadium.

In the UEFA Cup Souvenir edition, chief scout Tom O'Neill cast his eye over Porto; ex-Celt Alan Rough discussed the possible contribution of Rab Douglas; there was a review of previous winners of the competition; both Neil Lennon and Alan Thompson anticipated their involvement; and a UEFA Cup quiz whetted the appetite.

As in previous weeks, a selection of useful Spanish phrases was offered. As I walked through Glasgow one day and noticed the plethora of bulky frames bursting out of the new shirts, I suspected phrase number nine 'Quien se comio toda la Paella?' or 'Who ate all the Paella?' might be the most apt!

Under the heading, 'Fans' Eye View', representatives from the Celtic Supporters' Association, the Affiliation of Registered CSCs and the Association of Irish CSCs looked forward to Seville. The tone in each was unmistakably positive, even if their names had been 'Latinised' for the occasion.

Eduardo Toner, of the CSC, was remarkably prescient: "I don't think there is a stadium, anywhere in the world, large enough to accommodate the Celtic supporters who want to be present at this, our first final for 33 years, and it now looks like those travelling without a precious match brief will outnumber the lucky recipients of a ticket by about two to one."

For the Irish CSCs, Miguel Kelly looked ahead - and back: "So, let's celebrate these good, good times. While we're at it, let's not forget to raise a glass in memory to Jock and Bobby who were with us last time we reigned in Europe and who, no doubt, will be watching from above."

And Pedro Rafferty, for the Affiliated CSCs, gave us all some sound advice: "These games do not come around too often so take the opportunity to enjoy yourself and if we get the result, we hope Seville will see the biggest party that has ever been, not only there but possibly in the whole of Spain."

But the final word in the build-up to the match must surely go to the manager. In reply to comments from Porto's boss Jose Marinho that his side would have little to fear from the Scottish Champions, Martin O'Neill was both diplomatic and positive.

"I'm sure he's entitled to be confident," the Celtic boss said. "He has gone and won the Portuguese Championship quite easily and Porto have beaten quality teams to get into the final. I'm not too bothered about that. We will give it absolutely everything and hopefully, on the day, it's good enough.

"We're there and as the week progresses we'll give it more thought. I'm sure the Celtic fans will party whether we win or lose the game, but we're not going there to make up the numbers. We want to try and win the game. It's a hard game. It's exciting to be in it and with 20 minutes to go against Boavista, if you had said to me then that I'd be getting ready for the final itself I'd certainly have taken it. The goal finally came and then it was the longest 12 minutes of all our lives and it was great to see it through and now we can go to Seville and enjoy it."

The Road to Seville

The Bhoys and Ghirls in the Newsroom all travelled to Spain at different times. Margot McCuaig and Tony Hamilton plus camerapersons Des O'Hara and Sharon Gillespie went out on the Sunday prior to the match. They were all involved in putting out the CelticTV programme from the players' hotel on the Monday evening. This show contained footage from all the various rounds in the campaign and had guests like Martin O'Neill, Billy Connolly, John Hartson, Johan Mjallby, Magnus Hedman and Bertie Auld. It came over as very professional and was well received throughout the world.

Journalists Stephen Sullivan and Alison McConnell had also booked into that same hotel, their brief to file daily reports on the Website and amass some material for what we all hoped would be a rather boastful and euphoric *Celtic View* after the final.

I travelled on the Tuesday morning. We were putting out a Webcast for the match. I would host this from the stadium, joined there by Tony and Margot, and also John Cole and Tosh McKinlay, both of whom would fly out on the morning of the game. Back in Glasgow, our technical expert Peter VanDal, would be one of the few inside Celtic Park that evening but, as he supports our chief rivals, he would probably enjoy the peace and quiet!

On my flight were directors, club ambassadors, distinguished guests, wives of players and coaches, investors and well-known supporters. All my ex-team-mates were also on board; the guys forever known as the Lisbon Lions (I often wonder what we would have been called if the 1967 final had been played in Brussels, for instance, or Rome or even Warsaw? If we had lost, I could think of a very apt word to fit in after that last capital?).

They were all on their best behaviour in such distinguished company and the flight passed uneventfully, the plane landing in Jerez Airport around midday. We then travelled by bus to our base, dropping some Celtic fans at another hotel en-route. A young lady had slipped into the seat beside me and we chatted along the way. She looked to be her early 20s, had already been to Blackburn and Stuttgart and was now looking forward to Seville.

From her description of the two previous trips, she must have had some stamina. She seldom seemed to use her hotel room in those two towns very much but she could give me chapter and verse on the qualities of the bars and drink in each place.

As she descended from the coach outside her hotel, she shouted up the bus to me, "Jim, if I see you in Seville, I'll buy you a drink!" This brought a burst of ribald laughter from the rest of the boys but I made a mental note to check the inhabitants of the city's bars before I went in. The last thing I need is to be drunk under the table by a pretty 20-year-old! Can you imagine the headlines; 'Lisbon Lion can't last the pace!'

When the rooms were allocated in our hotel, I found myself once more with Joe McBride. I have regularly shared with him over the years and find him an easy room-mate. He does, though have one infuriating habit. We can be lying in our respective beds, having a chat, when he suddenly says 'goodnight' turns over and drops off. As quick as that! As one who takes much longer to fall asleep, it can be quite galling.

After unpacking, we went back downstairs for some lunch, then accepted an

THE FINAL COUNTDOWN: *Celtic and Porto line up before the start of the UEFA Cup final at the Estadio Olimpico in Seville*

A SEA OF GREEN AND WHITE: *The Estadio Olimpico was packed to capacity, with three quarters of the ground full of Celtic supporters*

IN THE SHADE: *John Hartson was ruled out of the UEFA Cup final because of a back injury, a cruel blow for a player who'd done so much to help the Celts get there*

TOUGH CONTEST:
In the gruelling Seville heat, Celtic gave as good as they got against the Portuguese champions

THE LONGEST WALK: *Bobo Balde's second yellow card of the night saw him dismissed, a cruel blow on a night when Porto's time-wasting and play-acting spoiled their win*

THE CRUELLEST BLOW: *Derlei's late winner denied Celtic a possible penalty shoot-out*

invitation from Martin O'Neill to visit the playing party. This involved a walk of perhaps two kilometres down the main avenue in the blazing sunshine before reaching the cool of their hotel, or more importantly the bar. Everyone in the Celtic camp seemed to be in good spirits and we returned to our own base feeling confident that they would do the business.

The town centre of Jerez was in the opposite direction to the team's hotel and after changing; we headed there for dinner. Celtic strips were everywhere, obviously not as many as in Seville itself, but still in substantial numbers. The reception they gave us was astonishing. Fans from all over the world vied to have their photo taken with us; others wanted us to sign shirts, old magazines, even the programme for the UEFA Cup final. When we dined al fresco in a square, we were surrounded by hooped shirts at every other table but they gave us privacy and we appreciated that.

At one point, loud cheers startled the non-football folk in the piazza. They heralded the appearance of John Hartson and Tommy Boyd, neither of whom would be appearing in the final the following day. In spite of the efforts of the chosen side to make them feel part of the adventure, players in their position do feel out of things and I'm sure the welcome they received throughout the town helped their morale. Certainly, John Hartson was left in no doubt of the fans' appreciation of his efforts this season.

After the meal, we all attempted a rather shaky version of the Huddle but I'm afraid the Rioja was beginning to have an effect and it turned into a shambles. Back in the hotel, the party continued at the bar but me and my room-mate retired early – McBride can't cope with late nights at his age!

The following day dragged, to say the least. An early breakfast (at McBride's age you can't sleep too long); a walk through the beautiful centre of Jerez; coffee in a pavement café watching everyone rushing off to work (at least the men were; the girls walked more sedately and were much better to look at); an early lunch in the bar of the hotel; a short rest in our rooms; then time to take the bus to the stadium. This proved to be a minibus, ample for our needs, as our number was less than 20. We had been joined that morning by Kathleen Murdoch, Bobby's widow, who had been on holiday in Portugal and had taken a train over for the match.

On the way, my mobile rang. I could hear a voice saying, "Jim, it's Ian Jamieson," (a member of our PR staff) but I couldn't hear anything else. Little did I realise how crucial his unheard message was! As we reached the outskirts of Seville, we began to see a few Hoops shirts. On our seemingly tortuous route through the city to the stadium, the number of fans increased; by the time we reached the Estadio Olimpico, they were everywhere, vastly outnumbering the Porto support.

Once the driver had parked the bus, our party received tickets for the Hospitality Suite at one end of the stadium. While they set-off in one direction, I made my way to the other end, where I had noticed a sign for 'Press Accreditation'. As I made my way through the Porto fans, my mobile rang. Again, it was Ian Jamieson and this time I heard his warning quite clearly: "Jim, you'll need your passport to identify yourself!"

I kept walking but my heart sank. My passport was safely ensconced in the safe in my room, some 30 miles away; there was no chance of my getting hands on it before the kick-off. When I reached the appropriate window, I explained to the UEFA representative that I was a member of the Celtic FC media team and gave her my name. Then came the moment I had been dreading, "Do you have any identification?" No, I hadn't, I had to admit. I pulled out my wallet but, although my credit cards had my name on them, they do not have a photograph. So, rightly, she refused to let me in. I moved back outside, into the blazing sun, and considered my position. I came up with a few different ploys, going back each time for another chat with the lady rep. But she wasn't for budging and at 6.45pm (with my broadcast starting at 7.30pm) I was still out in the sun.

Then, to my delight, I noticed a friend of mine approaching, a journalist with one of our Sunday papers. I have known him for a number of years but he must have been really surprised when I gave him a cuddle plus a kiss on the cheek (he had a beard, too!) and explained my predicament.

Once he received his own accreditation, he agreed to go to our position in the press box and find one of my colleagues. Within minutes, the figure of Tony Hamilton could be seen approaching the door (how handsome he looked, I thought! although perhaps that was just panic showing through?) and within minutes, I was seated at my post, halfway up the main stand.

From there, the view was astonishing. Even one-and-a-half-hours before the start, a large crowd was in place, most of them in Celtic colours. As they were entertained by dancers and a pop group, we brought the scenes to the support throughout the world. Our programme also had the goals from every previous match in the cup run; interviews with the manager, Alan Thompson and Stilian Petrov; and predictions from Margot, Tony, Tosh and John. Naturally, they all thought Celtic would win but, in almost an unofficial tribute to the quality of Porto, they all went for a one-goal victory.

As the kick-off approached, the numbers increased. One end of the Estadio Olimpico comprised Porto supporters; the rest was populated by Hoops fans, displaying banners from all corners of the world. A huge roar went up as the teams came out for what seemed like interminable pre-match activities; the latecomers scurried to their seats. Eventually, the players took up their respective positions and a nice contrast was to be seen, the green-and-white hoops of Celtic against the blue-and-white stripes of Porto. Referee Lubos Michel of Slovakia blew the whistle at exactly 7.45pm and the match got under way. In the following week's *Celtic View*, Stephen Sullivan described the action.

"The conflicting mix of pride, anger and crushing disappointment which left lumps in throats and tears in eyes as the curtain was brought down on last Wednesday's UEFA Cup final has not yet subsided entirely, for players or supporters. As a spectacle, Celtic's 3-2 defeat at the hands of Porto was as mentally and emotionally draining as one could possibly imagine.

"Yet, if one thing had been confirmed by the end of 120 enthralling minutes of action, it was that Martin O'Neill had been justified in claiming pre-match that, while fans may be able to create an occasion, only players can make a football match. After all, while the magnificent Celtic support did certainly proved themselves once again to be peerless, it was the efforts of O'Neill's players that ensured this final would be remembered as a classic.

"And, of all those who felt that an injustice had been visited upon them, no-one had greater cause to feel aggrieved than the incomparable Henrik Larsson, who - for all that he has regularly scaled lofty heights in the Hoops - has never

performed better or more inspirationally than he did last Wednesday. No-one, save perhaps the mercurial Deco, had a greater influence on the match, and were football a just sport, neither the Swede nor Porto's brilliant Brazilian would have ended on the losing side.

"Deco spent much of the match leading Celtic's covering midfielders on a merry dance, and it was he who helped Porto dominate an opening quarter-of-an-hour which saw Rab Douglas called upon to make a string of solid stops. Yet it was Larsson who came closest to breaking the deadlock during this period with one of his better free-kicks, one that flew round the outside of the wall and required to be held competently by the erratic Vitor Baia.

"With half-time approaching, the signs appeared to bode well. There was now an element of genuine composure to Celtic's play and, though they had still to produce that final decisive pass, the space afforded to Didier Agathe offered encouragement that Larsson would soon be supplied with ammunition to shoot the Hoops into the lead.

"It was then, however, that the pendulum swung back towards Porto and, in first-half injury time, the Portuguese champions broke the deadlock. Frustratingly, the opportunity for them to do so only arose as a result of a careless mistake by Bobo Balde, one which was snatched upon by Deco, who measured a brilliant cross towards Dmitri Alenitchev at the back post. Not for the last time, Celtic had allowed the Russian to steal in unmarked and, when Douglas could do no more than parry his stinging left-foot volley, the ball drifted across Balde for Derlei to side-foot home from an acute angle.

"Celtic wasted no time in striking back with an equalising goal, however. With less than two minutes of the second half played, Agathe looped a speculative cross towards the back post and Larsson somehow managed to climb and angle his header back across Baia and in off the inside of the keeper's left-hand post. It was the Swede's 200th goal in Celtic colours, and yet hopes that it could prove the spark for the Hoops to go on and win the match were severely dented 10 minutes later when another moment of defensive hesitancy saw Porto re-take the lead.

"Deco was once again the man to take advantage, displaying the vision to spot Alenitchev making an unchecked run through Celtic's defensive ranks and the ability to find him with a pass which merely required to be diverted past Douglas.

"Failure to adequately clear one's lines was not confined to players in green and white, thankfully, and just three minutes later - following an outrageously long time spent celebrating - Porto's Carvalho headed over his own crossbar when there did not appear to be sufficient pressure on him to justify it. Thompson then swung in the resultant kick and Larsson, left criminally unmarked, bulleted in a header which Baia got a hand to but could not prevent hitting the back of the net.

"The UEFA Cup was now back up for grabs and, for long parts, it appeared that Celtic were the more likely to claim it. That was, however, until Balde received his marching orders five minutes into the first period of extra time after earning his second yellow card with a mis-timed tackle on Derlei. From that moment onwards, Celtic were always likely to struggle to hang on and, with just five minutes remaining, their hearts were broken when Douglas spilled the ball to the feet of Derlei, whose shot spun agonisingly off the big Scotland keeper and away from Ulrik Laursen on the goal-line."

The Road to Seville

CELTIC 2   PORTO 3
Larsson 47, 57   Derlei 45, 115
                  Alenichev 54

CELTIC (3-5-2): Douglas; Mjallby, Balde, Valgaeren (Laursen 65); Agathe, Lennon, Lambert (McNamara 76), Petrov (Maloney 104), Thompson; Larsson, Sutton
Substitutes: Hedman, Sylla, Fernandez, Smith
FC PORTO (4-3-1-2): Baia; Ferreira, Costa (Emanuel 71), Carvalho, Valente; Alenichev, Maniche, Costinha (Costa 9); Deco; Derlei, Capucho (Ferreira 98)
Substitutes: Nuno, Peixeto, Clayton

BOOKED: Celtic – Valgaeren 8, foul on Deco; Lennon 59, foul on Derlei; Petrov 112, foul on Deco; Porto – Derlei 116, time-wasting; Alenichev 119, foul on Larsson; Ferreira 119, time-wasting
SENT OFF: Balde 95, two bookable offences (foul on Deco, foul on Derlei); Valente 120, two bookable offences (foul on Agathe, foul on Thompson)
REFEREE: Lubos Michel (Slovakia)

On the day after the match, the Scottish press gave went to town with their coverage. The *Daily Mail* praised Celtic's commitment: "The indestructable team ethic had seemed for so long set fair to help them bridge the Parkhead generation gap. They did, indeed, have the spirit of the 1967 Lions but, in the 115th minute of their 15th game in Europe, destiny deserted them. In the final analysis, they didn't quite have enough in the tank."

However, there was sympathy for the club's plight: "John Hartson's absence proved costly, the searing heat was a factor and Celtic's marathon run in Europe ended within agonising sight of the giant silver trophy."

And the performance of the man-in-the-middle did not gain universal approval; "Slovakian referee Lubos Michel had a terrible night. His control was questionable as the Porto players repeatedly pulled the wool over his eyes and there was even a half-time bust-up as the teams went down the tunnel."

The Herald's correspondent was equally scathing over Porto's tactics but also gave a pointed rap to Celtic: "In a match sprayed with bookings there was much acrimony in the air, and some absurd play-acting from Porto, especially in the second period of extra-time when Victor Baia, barely touched by a Celtic player, hit the deck as if he had been knifed. O'Neill later rightly expressed his loathing for this, although Celtic did not perform like angels.

"Lubos Michel, the harassed match referee, had no option but to red-card Balde in extra-time after a ruthless plunge at Derlei. Joos Valgaeren and Alan Thompson also perpetrated tackles of considerable venom, and Celtic last night had to be careful not to depict themselves as innocents. It was a match, in fact, which teemed with life."

The reporter did recognise, however, both the quality of the match and the performance by the sides involved: "After 33 years awaiting another European trophy, Celtic ransacked the emotions and jangled the nerves before going down to Porto amid considerable mayhem last night. After two hours of gruelling, draining football, a goal by Derlei, Porto's prince of poachers in this UEFA Cup, finally killed

off Celtic in the second period of extra-time. It was a long and exhausting night, and the Scottish champions may feel a bit bitter, but Celtic were beaten by a more artful team. Before bemoaning their loss it would be remiss not to highlight much of Porto's imaginative play, under a coach, Jose Marinho, who now has a European prize for his considerable reputation."

The match stats give an idea of just how close it was.

Celtic		Porto
2	Goals	3
3	Shots on Target	11
4	Shots off Target	6
30	Tackles	30
5	Corners	5
33	Fouls	24
4	Offsides	2
259	Successful passes	413
171	Misplaced passes	175
60%	Pass completion	70%
42%	Possession	58%

For all those present in the stadium, the presentation of the trophy proved a moment of anguish, as Porto's performance had led to conflicting emotions.

Undoubtedly, they had fine players, well-coached by their manager into an attractive and effective system. It was a set-up requiring pace and touch of a high order, one which could only be employed by classy practitioners. Their performance had much to recommend and admire, yet the play-acting of a few – not all – of their stars left a bad taste. It not only provoked the ire of the Celtic support but it broke up the rhythm of the game, a slowing down not to the advantage of the Scottish champions. That Vitor Baia, the goalkeeper, in particular, did not receive a card of any colour for his reaction to a minor challenge, was incomprehensible.

The referee had some poor moments. I thought his decisions in certain incidents, like tackles and challenges (including Bobo's) could not be faulted; however, he looked less comfortable in dealing with the 'acting' profession. Perhaps, he does not come across much of that in his native Slovakia but as an arbiter experienced enough to be handed a major European trophy final, he should have had the nous to recognise time-wasting.

Where he really fell down, though, was after the Porto goals, when he allowed their stars an extraordinary lassitude to approach their own fans. This again stopped the momentum of the play and left the seething Celtic players waiting around for the re-start. As Porto received the trophy, a chorus of boos rose up from the Celtic support, an unfortunate but understandable reflection of their feelings. That Porto probably deserved their win may have been the considered view of many supporters over the days that followed; but, straight after the final whistle, their reprehensible, cynical and unsportsmanlike behaviour over-shadowed their talented show and I'm afraid I fully sympathised with the Celtic fans.

Our own guys gave their all, in conditions anathema to Scottish-based players. We found the quick movement of Porto difficult to cope with yet twice came back from a one-goal deficit. For this, though, we have to thank the genius of Henrik Larsson.

That word is often mis-used and can be applied to many unworthy talents. Still, if we consider the dictionary definition of 'genius'- a person with exceptional ability- then Henrik really does deserve the accolade. Throughout his Celtic career, he has repeatedly demonstrated skills of the highest order, showing a particular aptitude for goalscoring, that most difficult of the footballing arts.

In Seville, he showed the predatory instincts of the great striker. His 200th and 201st goals for Celtic both came from headers, in situations where the odds were not in his favour. To see him at the end of the match (and caught in the papers the following day), touching the runners'-up medal round his neck while gazing wistfully at the UEFA Cup, was a heart-breaking sight. No player ever deserved a winner's medal more. And the Celtic legions were quick to acknowledge the contribution he, and his team-mates, had put in to the match.

In fact, in his report for the *Celtic View*, Stephen Sullivan summed up the feelings of many when he pronounced his 'Champagne Moment': "The sight of the Celtic fans standing with scarves aloft at the end of the most disappointing of matches was as poignant and awe-inspiring as any moment in Seville."

Unfortunately, as all this was going on, I was still linking the Webcast from the press box. As an evening of tension and excitement, it could not be faulted; for a programme designed specifically for Celtic fans, the ending was anti-climactic. However, we did describe everything, even the moment when many Celtic hearts were breaking, as the Porto captain, Jorge Costa, lifted up the trophy we all thought was destined for Parkhead.

Before we finished, though, and even with the pain of defeat still in our minds, we were keen to stress to our listeners what Celtic had achieved during the season. The Hoops' record in European competition since the late 1970s had been deplorable. Indeed, the last time we had still been into Europe beyond the turn of the year was back in 1979/80 season. Since then, Aberdeen and Dundee United had been more successful than us in the 1980s; while in the 1990s, it was left to Rangers to keep Scotland's name alive, although not always successfully, in the Champions League.

After the disappointment of losing out to an under-rated Basel side and the blow of demotion to what the top clubs regard as the lesser tournament, the players and management could have wilted. But, they did the exact opposite, putting their hearts and souls into the task and going on an excellent European adventure. Once the pain has diminished and time heals, a reasoned assessment of our campaign will show that we had anything but an easy passage.

Certainly, the contest against FK Suduva was a walkover but to beat top sides from well-recognised leagues like Blackburn Rovers, Celta Vigo, VfB Stuttgart, Liverpool and Boavista was a remarkable performance. Unfortunately, the words of the old expression 'nobody remembers who's second!' can be very true. That we lost in the end will initially take some gloss off the outcome, but as time dulls the disappointment and allows the brain to give a more clinical review of the season, the achievement by the manager, coaches and players should receive the fulsome credit it deserves.

After pointing that out and ending the programme, we moved out of the stadium as quickly as possible, through the Porto fans, none of whom thankfully showed

any triumphalism; indeed, they all seemed keen to leave the city and head back to their own country.

As my Webcast colleagues made for their bus back to Jerez, I headed for the Hospitality Suite in the hotel at the other end of the stadium. Mercifully, I did have a pass to get in and soon joined my ex-team-mates in the lounge, where we greedily took in some cool liquid and reflected on the night's play.

The three Porto goals were the subject of much discussion, with varying comments thrown up over the role of the Hoops defenders. Still, I thought everybody was fairly calm, considering what we had just gone through. In the same lounge, the players' wives looked stunned, the club ambassadors appeared thunderstruck and our celebrity fans showed bitter disappointment. It was not the happiest of Celtic gatherings.

From there, we headed for the bus park, where chaos ensued. Hordes of fans were wandering up and down, looking for their appropriate vehicle. As more than a few of my group have problems walking too far, we were not happy chappies. However, thanks to good work by John Maguire, the Celtic Pools director, we managed to board the relevant vehicle and head back for Jerez.

It had been an unbelievable day. We had all been privileged to be present at one of the major occasions in Celtic's history, one which brought back memories of two similar matches for the team of the '60s and '70s. As we made our way along the quay of the Guadalquiver river through the heart of Seville, groups of fans in the Hoops were heading back to their own hotels, sitting in cafes or even on the pavement, still full of good humour.

For the group of players known as the Lisbon Lions, receiving recognition from the fans through the years has been a most rewarding experience. They have given us many good times in various corners of the globe and we are always happy to meet with them and attend their functions. We rightly acknowledge them as a credit to the club. In Seville, though, they surpassed all previous expectations.

For a club to have a travelling support of some 80,000 plus, most without match tickets, for any final is astonishing. When that same support, even in the bitterness of defeat, can drown their sorrows without causing a single problem to their Spanish hosts, it deserves the highest praise. Let's hope UEFA recognises their sportsmanship.

TONY HAMILTON'S EUROPEAN DIARY
Part 8: Proud to be a Celt

IS there one endearing memory of this trip, I ask myself. The answer is no – there are volumes of them for so many tens of thousands of people who travelled in all sorts of ways from every corner of the globe just to be in the city.

The pictures of the guy at the airport wearing the Hoops with the words 'My wife thinks I'm out for a loaf' on the back summed up the occasion.

As did my brother Michael (the new half-time guy; the one who looks like The Proclaimers – both of them) getting a cheer as the Celtic fans inside the ground recognised his voice when he welcomed them to the stadium.

And also, at a personal level, it was mixed in terms of the build-up and obviously mixed after the result. The things that stick in my mind from the game were how proud I felt to be a Celt and how honoured I am to work for this club.

As we made our way to the mixed zone at the end of the presentation ceremony, I bumped in to my better half Lynne, Patsy – Lynne's sister and my two Bhoys Anthony and Michael. (All of whom incidentally had the foresight to get tickets from Uefa.com, while regretting they too never returned the Away European Registration Scheme forms which came with their season books.)

Anthony, at 13, was coping with the result as best he could while Michael, nine, took off his scarf as we met and asked me to give it to Henrik Larsson when I got back to the hotel.

Talk about being choked?

Just as a by the way, I should explain how my Bhoys and not my three Ghirls got to go to the game with the UEFA tickets we had. Kimberley, 15, was in the middle of her Standard Grades and sadly couldn't travel and Kelli, 16, who works at Celtic with me on match days, is earning enough to buy her own tickets!

But Elaine? Little Elaine, seven, is a cracker. For a moment I did consider her for one of the briefs. But only for a moment.

I told her that as she was preparing for her Confirmation to the church she would have to think about a sponsor. "Can I have Carling?" she asked. I realised there and then that there would be enough nutters already in Spain without me exporting another.

She went to her aunt's in Manchester for a couple of days. We told her it was Seville and it was winter. She believed us.

Anyway, I've digressed for the last time.

If you had told me that come May 2003 I would be commentating for Celtic on a European final I'd have thought you were mad. In fact, having read this far you must be mad...

Ordinarily, it would have been the most dramatic thing I'd ever done when you consider that other Scottish commentators can be in the game for 30 years and never see their team in a European final. (Well, it is 31 years since Rangers last appeared in one...)

The drama for me, however, came 48 hours before a ball was kicked in anger

at the Estadio Olimpico. CelticTV had produced and presented eight pay-per-view events throughout the season, all of which were centred around live matches.

The plan was, and is, that we would endeavour to find a way to have a regular magazine-type programme on the Sky platform and beyond, which was made up of live chat, recorded interviews and action.

I suggested we do it live from the team's hotel in Jerez, 90 km south of Seville on the Monday before the Wednesday showdown.

Remarkably, my suggestion was given a blessing from the manager and my gaffer Iain Reid and before I knew it I was in Jerez on a reconnaissance mission with Denis Mooney, who helped us with the production, and our trusted and cool engineer Bob Aitkenhead.

With two weeks before the event we were in Spain checking out the hotel and meeting up with the representative from the Spanish OB company, Frenchman Thierry Hun. (Real name by the way).

At that point everything was clear in my mind. It would be no bother, I told myself. We survived Lithuania so this would be a breeze.

But by the time the opening credits were rolling and I was stuck out in the open by the pool with Bertie Auld and Margot, I was ill – I mean really ill.

So ill, in fact, that I thought I was going to do a Tommy Cooper impression and die live on the telly.

Des shouted "break a leg" minutes before. If there had been a choice I honestly would have broke my leg again.

I knew that if this went belly-up it really would be all over. There would be no other crack at this TV malarkey – I could say adios to my career with much confidence.

However, as things turned out, it went swimmingly.

Wee Bertie was outstanding as he always is, the response from the viewers was excellent, with over 1,000 e-mails coming in as we went live, and we even managed to get Billy Connolly to do the last half hour of the two-hour event.

Margot sweet-talked Johan Mjallby and Magnus Hedman to also do live interviews and along with the manager, who had agreed in advance, Alison dragged on BBJ Hartson, who appeared despite his exclusion from the final because of a back injury.

The consummate professional indeed. But that's enough about me.

Seville was our people's final. It was a chance for ordinary punters like you and me to take our ordinary families on an extraordinary adventure.

It was also the chance to send postcards from Seville to every Rangers pub in Duke Street. I didn't realise that you could spend that much money on postcards – although Des never sent any.

Most importantly though it was, I believe, what we were due for being faithful through and through. Personally I'd like to take this opportunity to not only thank my mammy and my agent but also to thank that Swiss pub team. They did us a right good turn and I don't care what they're called…

Oh, and Des – if someone's reading this for you please remember, I'm only serious. I love you like a brother – just not one of mine.

Chapter Ten

From Suduva to Seville: Fans' memories of a great UEFA Cup campaign

ONE of the best parts of the trip to Seville was the Spaniards. At least 20 school children aged around five/six all filing out in one of the back streets and chanting *'Celtic, Celtic'* at the sight of our Hoops was fantastic!

They all seemed very happy to see the Celts in their city. One of them even offered to swap his school shirt for our new Hoops shirts…Needless to say, we declined his polite offer, but God loves a trier!

KATE McALLISTER

My memories of Seville will live in my heart forever, or at least until next season and we progress even further. The sea of green and white flowing up to the stadium was amazing.

Alas the result did not go the way we wanted, but walking fairly quietly back to our hotel, a lot of Spanish folk who where in the street cafes stood up and applauded us. It made the hair on the back of my neck stand up and I was nearly in tears.

AVRIL McIVOR

I WAS one of the lucky ones – I had a ticket for the most amazing game of football I have ever witnessed. Celtic were amazing, the fans were incredible, we can all hold our heads high.

The story of my ticket purchase begins with an e-mail from a Liverpool fan who contacted my friend at the largest broadsheet newspaper in the country. No names mentioned to protect the innocent. This Liverpool supporter bought six tickets for the final before they played the Hoops. He then contacted my friend, looking for the best way to sell his tickets to genuine Celtic supporters at face value. This was duly done and I became the owner of one of these tickets.

When you hear of tickets trading for up to £1,000, this act of genuine

European memories

generosity by a fellow football supporter makes you believe in the humanity attached to football. Hail! Hail! to the Hoops and one very amazing Liverpool supporter.

THOMAS KERR

THE father of my daughter's friend drives a taxi. He shares the driving with a boy named Mark, who is a mad Celtic fan and decided after the Boavista game he was off to Seville. He booked up immediately on the Internet despite being a tad worse for wear.

On Tuesday May 20, he got his bag packed and checked his tickets to note that when he was inebriated he had indeed booked a holiday to Seville but for the June 20. As he scrolled through the months the alcohol had misdirected his fingers.

So, with the tickets being non-transferable and non-returnable, he had to look forward to a quiet two-day vacation in Seville on June 20!

TONY BYATT

I WAS in Portland, Oregon in the United States, visiting my girlfriend's family for Easter. Desperate to catch the second leg of the semi-final against Boavista, we found our way down to Kell's Bar, where, surrounded by fellow Celtic die-hards, we literally felt the earth move.

As Larsson slotted away yet another Euro wonder goal, an earthquake rattled our pint glasses to the edges of our tables. Is there no limit to that man's powers?

CRAIG BELL

I WAS born on May 22, 1967 so I know the big triumph just from books and video footage. Thirty six years later the Bhoys fought for a similar achievement and I'm sure that it's okay with everyone reading these lines that we can be proud of both our team in the Hoops and our supporters.

Our lads had an uphill struggle and did prove that it was no accident seeing them reach the big final again. Ice-hockey 'fitba' is the most popular kind of sport in my home country and there must have been millions of Czechs listening to a well-known local commentator saying: *"And now you can see probably the best football supporters on the Globe."*

I'm more than sure that he was pretty right. There's no need making further comments. I was proud of all of you. And what's more I did get the special 'antsy' feeling that I hadn't had in years. All of a sudden I felt as if I had moved back into my carefree schooldays, as if all those everyday troubles were suddenly gone and that's what it is all about. Thank you Celtic.

OTA KOPRIVA, Prague

I'M from Glasgow but I live and work on a small island called Bermuda in the middle of the Atlantic Ocean. There is a Celtic supporters' club here. On Wednesday I went with my friends who are Portuguese to watch the match at Flannagan's Irish bar. I had my face painted and my hair sprayed green.

The local newspaper is called the *Royal Gazette* and the photographer was there. He took a lot of pictures and took loads of names to use on the sports pages. Well, can you imagine my horror on Thursday morning when I find myself on the front page of the *Royal Gazette* looking like I'm about to start crying as Jose my Portuguese friend jumps around at the final Porto goal. Everyone in the island I know has called me and I'm getting copies for my family in Glasgow.

It's a funny/sad picture which highlights my agony at the loss but Jose's delight at Porto winning.

CAROLYN BUTLER

IT was your duty to be there. It was a pilgrimage to the city of Seville, Spain on Wednesday, May 21, 2003. It was like renewing your vows to love and cherish till the day you die.

I will never forget the songs, heat, atmosphere, second-half, airlift, walk to the city centre and back for the game. The singing of the *Fields of Athenry* before the game had me weeping with emotion, as were others around me. So good for the soul.

ED BROADLEY, Glasgow

WHAT an unbelievable few days! Did you see the guys in the paper? One of them was carrying what looked suspiciously like Da Vinci's Last Supper but Martin O'Neill replaced Jesus and the players, the apostles. It looked like it was in an amazingly ornate frame. Did he carry it across Europe? Did he buy it in Seville? And who is Judas?

Also, is it only me or did the Porto fans not know how to celebrate? I ended up trying to rouse them and show them what a smile looked like, did a little dance and they rallied for a second. When I enquired as to the reason for their demeanour, more than one fan said, "Oh we are tired. It has been a long day." Another said, "It is okay for you fans from Celtic. We are very poor but you have lots of money!" Aye! That'll be right!

JIMMY O'DONNELL

FOR Celtic fans here in Birmingham, who for reasons couldn't be in Seville, the place to be was Ruskin Hall, Aston, where the No.2 Birmingham Celtic Supporters watch their beloved Bhoys play throughout the season.

A huge party was organised and everyone had a great time. Over 200 Celtic fans from all over Birmingham descended on Ruskin. We had face painters on hand to create Hoop-style faces and, in some cases, heads. People wore wigs, sombreros, and beach balls were bounced about.

One young lady, who will remain anonymous even bared her boobs, to which I said, even when we were down and out we were well supported. We were all very sad but very proud of our Bhoys. They were magnificent, a credit to club, and supporters. Our party went on well into the night.

MARIAN DOWNES

I'M 17-years-old and have been a season ticket holder since 1995. I have been the mascot twice for Celtic and I can tell you one thing – the game in Seville has been the best and most tense game I've ever been to.

I would like to thank all the Bhoys and Ghirls who made my trip to Seville a great time, especially when we were all in the square. I knew when I saw everyone

European memories

in Seville that we are the biggest club in the world and not just Europe. The highlight of my day, apart from the game, is when me and my dad and his friend were walking to the Cathedral we noticed a group of Spanish school children and a bunch of Celtic fans.

The children were chasing after the flags the Bhoys had. My dad's friend gave a little boy his Celtic scarf and his eyes lit up. It touched me. The Celtic fans taught the children how to say Celtic and they were all singing *'Celtic, Celtic, Celtic'*. A couple of Porto fans went behind the children and were shouting 'Porto'. All the Celtic fans and Spanish children were shouting 'Celtic'. We all had such a great time.

I would also like to thank the Porto fans for being so friendly, and especially all the Spanish people in Seville who were great hosts and made everyone feel welcome.

NICOLA MACKIN, G.P.O. CSC

FOR me the highlight of the season has to be the goal scored by John Hartson against Liverpool at Anfield – superb interplay between John and Henrik before the big man takes a side-step away from a defender before unleashing an unstoppable shot passed the helpless Liverpool keeper.

Fantastic goal, fantastic celebrations, brilliant result. I was jumping about my apartment like a loony, much to the amusement of the guy who was cutting the grass outside. It was a great run in the UEFA Cup which we all enjoyed here.

PAUL TIMLIN, Fresno, California, USA

LIKE many, many other fans, I had two out of the three, though some had the less important two. I had the flight and the ticket but no accommodation. It wasn't the most pressing of matters given the comfortable climate in which we could sleep with the stars as our blanket.

Anyway, myself and my four friends found ourselves on the stairs in a slight alcove of the local museum – a snug if you like – some four hours after the dust had settled. It was here we bedded down around 4am, hoping for a two-hour kip, followed by a traditional 'Scots On Tour' breakfast of McDonald's! We managed a decent sleep, given the circumstances, and woke just before 6am to the sweetest smell imaginable – fresh-baked bread and coffee.

The owners of a local cafe had noticed us when they arrived to open up for business and had such a fantastic first impression of the Celtic fans from the previous day, and from the game itself, that they decided breakfast was on them. They couldn't do enough for us – coffee, tea, toast, fruit, croissants, fresh juice and even a paper (okay, it was the local equivalent to *The Metro*, but still!) which showed the Celtic fans as we know how they can be – inspirational.

We tried to leave something for their trouble but they wouldn't have it. Instead they provided a cracking breakfast for five hungry men for the price of a Celtic scarf and sombrero for behind their bar. The Seville people were fantastic; the Porto fans we met were fantastic.

Is there a following anywhere like us? Approximately 75,000 travelling to a foreign country with no trouble and a boost to the local economy to tide them over 'til the next time we get there.

JOHN ALLAN, Airdrie

The Road to Seville

I AM from the Jock Stein Celtic Supporters' Club in Hamilton, Ontario, Canada. My memories of this year's accomplishment are ingrained with much emotion. Unfortunately for our family, my brother passed on last year and there was great outpouring of support for our family throughout the world of green and white.

With Celtic on route to Seville I applied some of my connections and sent my parents to Spain to be part of this great event. They did not have tickets to the game but my dad wanted to be with all the punters in Seville. They travelled for half the cost which elated my father (he is still Scottish with his pocket book). I watched the game in Canada at our club, figuring that our family deserved this – our Terry would work some magic up in heaven and land us a trophy that would, somehow for sometime, attempt to fill the void in our family.

Since my dad was already in Canada by 1967 he questioned whether or not he should spend so much to go, but having worked his entire life raising and supporting six children I reassured him that he worked all his life for a chance to witness something that he has raised us all to respect.

Unfortunately Terry must have beaten St. Christopher at golf that day and our Celtic lost, but in all the joy of watching my mother and especially my father set off for Spain in hope of glory was an award in itself. They needed it. Well done Bhoys, the Sexton family thanks you.

PETER SEXTON

AFTER being in Seville with my father and two friends and it being the first European final in my lifetime I remember walking along the side of the Hoops HQ next to Seville Cathedral.

To my amazement, I saw a Spanish priest walking out of the Cathedral wearing the black shirt and collar and a pair of Celtic shorts, while whistling *'Hail! Hail!'* I must say it was the funniest thing I have ever seen in my life.

MICHAEL CULLEN

I WILL tell you one of my greatest memories from Seville. This came after our defeat to Porto but I think this ultimately shows the love and dedication our supporters have for the club.

I watched the game on the Big Screen that was situated near the river. After the defeat, me and my pals went down to the riverside and sat in silence with our own thoughts about what could have been. All was silent for a few minutes until, in the distance, we heard the anthem *'You'll Never Walk Alone'*.

We looked on in pride as we saw the huge Celtic support walk across the bridge from the stadium back into the centre of Seville singing this song. It shows the belief and pride this support has for the club and is a sight I will never forget until the day I die.

DARREN NEAL

WHILE standing outside a bar only 100 yards from Flaherty's by the Cathedral in Seville, a local Spaniard came up and congratulated me on the atmosphere we had created and the friendliness of all our supporters. Long may this continue.

LESLIE PURCELL, Coventry

European memories

I WAS one of the hundreds who were camped out at the Cathedral in the centre, along with my best friend, and I saw hundreds of funny and incredible scenes. The amazing thing was that at no point did I feel scared or vulnerable in a foreign city in the early hours.

I saw dozens of fans sleeping with their mobiles visible beside them and no-one had touched them. Children as young as two or three, draped in flags, asleep on the pavement. Walking around town at four or five in the morning brought its own experience. Many fans stopped cars that were not taxis and demanded to be taken to Portugal or Malaga because they missed their connections. Some of the banter was hilarious.

My favourite story, however, involves my very last experience of Seville. I was the last to get on the plane to Bilbao after taking photos with my friend Damian. As I climbed the steps, the man who was driving the truck which carries the luggage to the plane climbed the stairs and asked if he could have my hooped shirt. I was not sure, but he then said he would swap it for his Real Betis shirt. I was then encouraged by the air stewardesses and pilot to swap it.

The air stewardess and pilot said they would hold the plane while the guy went to get his strip. He raced off. Those carriers normally go slow, but not this time. He came back with his strip 10 minutes later. I don't know if you have seen their strip but it is hideous. However, it was clear he was desperate for the Hoops. I duly took my top off and swapped it. The cabin crew applauded and I took my seat. It was a great way to leave Seville. We clearly won over the city.

JOHN-PAUL MORRISON

I WOULD love to share with you a couple of moments from my trip to Seville that will live with me forever.

Firstly, while enjoying the sights and sounds in one of the many squares in the city, I noticed a man standing alone wearing an unusual hooped jersey which, by judging from the words on the front, suggested he was not from the UK. I engaged in conversation and it turned out his name was Stefan, from Germany. He told me he was with a group of six other friends all from Germany who came to Seville for the game.

I asked if he had a ticket. 'No,' he replied but added, 'but we just had to be here.' Tell me what other club in the world can attract people like Stefan 'who just wants to be there'? Secondly, while crossing one of the bridges over the river towards the stadium at around 6.30pm to attend the match, we could see there was a 'pleasure cruise' in the distance travelling towards us.

As it got nearer we could hear it was Spanish schoolchildren who were on the boat and they were chanting in their own unique style *'Celtic, Celtic, Celtic.'* Just a wonderful moment. While losing is heartbreaking, which has now only hit home, I am sure that, in defeat, we can claim our greatest victory – Glasgow Celtic are the greatest football club in the world.

HUGH MEECHAN, East Kilbride

I AM just another Celtic fan who was lucky enough to be at all the home UEFA games as well as Blackburn (away), Stuttgart (away) and, of course, against Porto in the final.

This has been the best season I have experienced in all my years as a Celtic supporter, the pride I feel right now is hard to describe. I have spent over £1,000 just getting to Spain and if I could do it again I would. The team and, more importantly, the supporters were magnificent. I maintained the same philosophy from the start of our Euro journey to the end, which was 'give us a fighting chance' and the team certainly gave that and much more.

NEIL LAFFERTY

FROM Sevilla, gracias amigos! I am a 32-year-old TV sports researcher from Sevilla and just wanted to let you know that I lived the UEFA final, the big party, with the Celtic supporters, and I will never forget it.

Celtic may not be the best team in the world, but, for sure, Celtic fans are the best. Drinking peacefully, singing, holding conversations and making friends with locals made up your visit card. All the Sevillanos and the Spanish press appreciated your noble and outstanding qualities with a sentence: 'Hats off to Celtic'. No matter the defeat. You, Celtic, left the sweetest taste.

From now on I assure you that there are many more Celtic supporters in Spain, and I am one of them. I hope to travel to Glasgow soon and see a match. Yes, 'the Celts were here' and we did care! Thank you and Congratulations!

ANGEL M ROLDAN MOLINA

I'M a citizen from Seville and I'm really impressed with the Celtic supporters. All are very good people. Everyone in my city speaks about your very good education. Thanks for your stay in Seville.

Seville will be always with you, Celtic of Glasgow and Seville. Now there are lots of shirts of Celtic in Seville and of the Real Betis in Glasgow. I'm really happy with the Celtic shirt. You are more than a football team. The people of Celtic are in the heart of us. Thanks Celtic, I'll see you in Celtic Park (The Paradise).

MARCO

GLASGOW Airport. Got to check in desk. Found out I had my daughter's passport instead of mine - PANIC! At 5am I phoned my wife who saved the day by bringing my passport to airport

BOBBY THOMSON

I'M a new Celtic supporter, having gained appreciation for the Bhoys watching them win the championship last year on Fox Sports World. The more I watched Celtic, the more affinity I had for the team.

It has been great watching this year's team achieve the success that it has. The victory over Liverpool was especially satisfying. I think Fergie put it best – "this team's no fluke, look at the string of victories they put together to make it to the final – Liverpool, Boavista, Blackburn. All impressive scalps to take in Europe." The only thing better would be if the cup was at Celtic Park.

RUSSELL DE PINA, Houston, Texas USA

MY name is Mateo and I live in Seville. I would like to thank all the Celtic supporters for their behaviour in our city and to support them to push the best team in Europe back to Seville in 2005 for the Champions League final.

WHO'S THAT BIRD?: *BBC Scotland's Jackie Bird mingles with the Bhoys in Seville*

European memories

Sincerely, all the Sevillian people are delighted about the way that all the Hoops have invaded our city, in a peaceful way and with smiles, beer and happiness. A big amount of people in Seville now know who's the best team all over the world and our souls are now linked to Celtic people.

MATEO GONZALEZ ZAMBRANO

This year, I had a Maths Higher exam the day of the UEFA Cup final and a Computing one the day after. When my dad told me three weeks before it that he was going to Seville for the match, I was absolutely gutted!

All his pals kept saying, "Oh ,I bet you wish you were going to Seville!" So can you imagine how angry I was, when, on the night before he was to fly to Seville, he turns round and says he's been pulling my leg for three weeks! Never mind, I'll be getting my new shirt out of him for that one!

AMY HAGGARTY, Dundee

I TRAVELLED to the game with my best friend from Orkney – a Rangers fan. We both grew up there and have been friends for nearly 20 years.

We arrived in Seville on the Tuesday at midday and once we checked into our hotel we headed into the centre of Seville to do a bit of sightseeing, but once we found Flaherty's that was it - we met up with another 10 friends from Orkney – four of whom were staying in the same hotel as us and the sightseeing got canned - the rest of the day was spent mingling with the other fans around the Cathedral doing our bit to drink Seville dry. I didn't broadcast the fact that my mate was a Rangers fan but everyone from Orkney knew and accepted him, no questions asked

All of the above is fairly run of the mill. However, on the day of the game we obviously began to get even more excited. Both myself and my friend were speechless at the sight which greeted us in the centre of Seville – we thought Tuesday was awesome but Wednesday was unbelievable.

I was apprehensive about how my friend would react at the game. I knew he would behave but in what manner would he cheer us on? It wasn't long before I found out. He sang his heart out but obviously picked when to sing and when to just clap and cheer. His comment on going to the final was, 'I am a Rangers fan but, more importantly, I am a Scottish football fan and this is bigger than Celtic versus Rangers – this is Scotland versus Europe.'

Later, when we scored, he jumped and cheered like the rest of us but even that was nothing compared to what happened when Henrik scored our second. I wouldn't have believed it unless I had witnessed it with my own eyes. He was out of his seat faster than any other Celtic fan in the stadium and the jubilation that was evident from his actions and his facial expressions told me I was right to bring him.

I sat through last year's Scottish Cup final with him at my house and he was ecstatic when they scored at the end but even that paled into insignificance compared to the sense of joy he showed when Henrik equalised. When the final whistle came he was a dejected as any true Celtic fan – he felt cheated and robbed but again he came out with a comment which astounded me. 'Celtic may well have lost the UEFA Cup final but they have put Scottish football back on the map and they have won the hearts of the people of Seville. The fans have been immense and made me proud to be Scottish. They have also made me jealous and envious of Celtic

The Road to Seville

Football Club as a whole. Being a Rangers fan and seeing this, I can honestly say that the Celtic fans are probably the best in the world.'

He went on to say that, had it been Rangers in the final, he couldn't see the Rangers fans turning up in such numbers and also does not believe that the atmosphere would have been anywhere near as friendly or as overwhelming.

I haven't named him as he I'm not sure he would be too happy about what I have told you - I'll have to check - but what I will say is that a Rangers fan and a Celtic fan travelled together to Seville. We laughed, cheered, got drunk and cried together but both agree that although we lost, our trip to Seville will remain one of our best memories, something we can look back on and share with our children and grandchildren. A trip which will never be forgotten.

ANDY CROSSLEY

MY father and I travelled to Seville for two magical days and two even better nights. We lived it up like kings in the same hotel as the likes of Billy McNeill, Jim Kerr and a host of TV reports/journalists.

Like so many ticket-less fans, we watched the game in our hotel as we rejoiced in what we thought/hoped and prayed would be for Celtic to take the upper hand and the glory.

But alas it wasn't to be, and as the final whistle blew I began to cry, leading to my father to follow suit. As Porto celebrated their victory, two fans watching this show of emotion came over, began hugging both my father and myself, explaining in broken English 'No worry. You win next year'.

One of the Porto Bhoys then gave us his scarf as a memento, something I will cherish my whole life.

It was the next day and with the mother of all hangovers, my father explained to me that it was one of the greatest moments of his life, to share an experience that he had shared with my grandfather some 33 years earlier.

I can only hope that some time in the not so distant future, I can carry on this 'tradition' with my child, in what I hope are tears of joy.

Like I said I can imagine there are thousands like this story after all Celtic fans crying at the end of 'that' game wouldn't have been far off commonplace but for me it will remain as one of those 'tell-your-grandkids' stories.

CHRIS McCALL, Shawlands

I WAS in Seville. Do you recall the guy at the fountain with the Indian Head? Dress, kilt and drum? (more later)

On the way home, we were flying from Madrid. The BA flight was cancelled and we were all taken to a very posh hotel. Can you imagine 30 or so fans, most with strips on, some very drunk, walking into this upmarket five-star hotel? Anyway, the Chief (Indian headdress guy) had apparently been at Madrid Airport all day and missed two flights because he kept getting into company and missing his flights. He heard we were all being taken to this hotel and just totally chanced his arm and bluffed his way on to the coach.

He got a slap-up meal, a bed and bath. After the meal, the Bhoys ran up a bar bill (signing for drinks 'Henrik Larsson, James Bond, Frank Sinatra, Lisbon Lions' etc). It came to hundreds of Euros. The poor, naive staff tried to get some money back the next morning and it nearly got quite ugly but, of course, a couple of the fans came clean and paid up.

The Chief said his goodbyes at the airport and wandered off, muttering he really must try to get home. I'll never forget the sight of these guys sitting at a table in the restaurant, nudging shoulders with business types, the Chief pride of place at the head of their table, plates piled high with food, and all lording it up. (You know what I mean, sampling wine, swishing it round their mouths as if connoisseurs– "Naw gie's a try o' that white"). It was the first decent meal they'd had for three days. They were loving it.

Even some of the stuffed shirts were killing themselves. This hotel had expensive artworks, pottery etc dotted round the place. Nothing was vandalised or stolen, just a couple of drinks unaccounted for. We have the funniest fans in the world.

MAGS

WHEN he scored only two minutes into his comeback, the whole pub thought Henke would lead us to a convincing victory over our friends from Liverpool.

Yet it wouldn't transpire that way, and a 1-1 draw seemed to suit the Reds of Merseyside. An exam the following morning prohibited me from joining the locals in O'Rafferty's pub, North London, for the second leg at Anfield. Despite the bravado aimed at my girlfriend – a staunch Scouser – the general feeling was the UEFA run may finish beside the Mersey. Yet, as has come to be expected, Martin O'Neill's men refused to be affected by the hype of the second Battle of Britain.

As half time approached, the Hoops were still in the tie when Djimi Traore committed a cynical foul on the man himself, Henrik Larsson. Alan Thompson, on his famous left foot, was favourite to take it. As decisive as the strike was, it was only equalled by the indecisiveness of the Liverpool wall. As the low drive sailed under the leaping Reds, it was clear the goalkeeper had no chance. The Hoops were ahead on the night, but more importantly, on aggregate, and had scored the vital away goal to match Emile Heskey's at Parkhead.

After the break, it was the Celts showing the composure often attributed to teams from south of the border. Liverpool huffed and puffed with Gerrard at the centre of most moves, yet Bobo and the Bhoys stood firm and limited their opponents to few opportunities. Then came a moment of true class from the Welshman who has endeared himself to every Celtic fan's heart.

In fact, my girlfriend's dad had phoned just prior to a Celtic move. I could hear him confidently proclaim a draw was on the cards and extra-time would follow. Yet as that arrow of a shot bulleted past the hapless Dudek, I could almost see him put the receiver down! In fact it was lucky he did, as the yelps of joy would probably have deafened the poor lad! The semi-finals were calling, just as her father had been two minutes prior. The sense of pride surrounding the team that night was immense yet not unfamiliar and indeed stuck with the boys throughout the campaign despite the final result in Seville. As well as this, the bond between both sets of fans, singing in unison to *'You'll Never Walk Alone'*, was a lasting memory few will forget.

DARRAN HANNON

I WAS unlucky and could not make it to Seville because of my Higher exams, but I have some fond memories of that Wednesday night. I headed into Glasgow to soak up the atmosphere, which was brilliant, even Yates' Wine Bar had Hoops fans hanging out the door!

The Road to Seville

The Garage nightclub had a queue which wound its way around the block so I entered a pub called Firewater which, by kick-off, was crammed full of fans in green and white! When the goals went in, the beer was launched into the air and the roof dripped for the rest of the night. The people around me were great and even after going 3-2 down, we still managed to get the rest of the pub to sing again and at full time our rendition of: *'You'll Never Walk Alone'* could stand alongside even that inside the stadium!

PAUL DOWNIE

WATCHING the Bhoys over the last few months has been a joy. It was very hard for me to accept they got into the final. This is because I am in Australia travelling. This has meant that I had to get up at 3.30 in the morning to watch their games.

Everyone was telling me I was mad but watching us do over Liverpool in their own backyard was great, especially because I have a few Liverpool supporters as mates. I won't forget Alan Thompson's free kick. Also beating Blackburn was a great achievement, especially the game at Ewood Park. All my mates couldn't believe the atmosphere at Paradise. I told them we are one of the biggest clubs in Europe, we can win this cup!

Watching these games over here is strange. I watched the Boavista games in an Irish pub, full to the brim. What an atmosphere at four in the morning.

Although we lost the final, no blame could be put on Bobo's shoulders; he has been outstanding this season. The team are all winners. What an achievement.

KRIS SHIELDS

Liverpool v Celtic ... My brother, Brian and I were watching the second leg at home with our friend Adrian, who is a huge Liverpool supporter. Right from the start when we heard *'You'll Never Walk Alone',* we knew we in for a good time.

Before the match started Adrian was talking trash. He said that Celtic would never score at Anfield and that Celtic were a Fourth Division English team at best. When John Hartson scored that beauty my brother and I went crazy. After we calmed down we turned to see that Adrian had almost sunk into the couch. He was speechless. However, Brian and I were not. By the end of the match Adrian was wearing green and white! In fact he never took it off for the rest of Celtic's run. I think that his opinion of the Bhoys has changed for the better.

It was a magical day for us and ultimately we thank out granddad for that. Living in Canada, where hockey is everything, most kids don't live for football like we do. We have our granddad to thank for that and we think of him every week when we watch Celtic on the telly.

ROBB WATSON, Niagara Falls, Ontario, Canada

ONE of my favourite memories was after the final – although not funny it brought a tear to my eye. When we got back to our hotel (yes we were one of the lucky few – but did not use it) the families on the street were out singing *'Celtic, Celtic'.*

We went down and were drinking and singing songs into the early hours with some people we had met in Madrid and Dublin on the way over. Suddenly, at about 5am, a bottle of champagne was produced. Everyone wanted to know who the flash git was, but the barman (who we had come to know as Anto or, as his mother liked to call him, Antonio) was trying to tell us in his best English that it was on the house as a token of his appreciation.

I think we had drunk enough in that bar to send all his kids through college and pay off his mortgage even though it was only 80 cents a glass of beer! I can't remember what time I left the bar at but it was definitely bright out.

GRAHAM BURKE

I TRAVELLED to Seville with my father Bernard and older brother Jeremy, after only deciding to go the day before when we managed to score a ticket that had been given up on a few weeks earlier.

As our dad didn't make the final in Lisbon, we thought it only right that he get our only ticket, while Jeremy and I spent the day on the beer looking for the best place to take in the game. This was to be the first journey to Europe with the Bhoys for any of us and it certainly was one trip we will never forget.

The banter and laughing started as soon as we left the house in Greenock at 6.00am to make our 9.00am flight from Glasgow. Glasgow Airport was a sight to behold! Hoops as far as the eye could see and the sound of *Hail Hail* ringing out every few minutes! The flight was full of banter from the Captain announcing his name as 'Dickie Bird' on the way out, to shouts of "Well done driver" after a bit of a shaky landing.

The fact that, when I asked for two beers an hour into the flight, I was told there was no more drink on board as it had all been consumed has to be mentioned if only to highlight the fact that the atmosphere on the plane was jovial and friendly throughout, with absolutely no trouble at any point. This was to be a familiar point throughout the day!

Walking from the plane to the tarmac was like entering an oven, and at this point the mood got even better, if this was possible, as by now everyone knew that this was to be a memorable day for so many reasons. The walk from the bus park into the town lasted for around 60 minutes with the ever-increasing Hooped army processing through streets and squares to meet up with friends and generally explore this welcoming city.

The locals looked to be in awe as they stood, stared and applauded us everywhere we went. Upon reaching the Plaza Nueva, I had a lump in my throat at the sight of at least 15,000 Celts having an absolute ball! We proceeded to make our way to the Cathedral area, where we spent the rest of the day, and after paying our respects inside, we took to the streets outside to have a few beers and generally join the ever-increasing party. The sight of the whole area being filled with Hoops and flags will stay with us forever as will the sight of locals leaning from the balconies to join in the party!

A salute must go the Bhoys carrying the painting of the Last Supper with Jesus and the Apostles replaced by Saint Martin and the team like a shrine throughout the city streets. One of many side-splitting moments, along with the two blokes carrying the life-size cut out of the King arm in arm!

After our dad had departed for the game we set about finding our spot to watch the game, and after about 90 minutes searching we came across the big screen in the public park where more than 20,000 Celts had gathered to do the same. The slagging of Martin Geisler from Scottish TV while he was completing a live broadcast was another hilarious moment!

Much has already been said about the game itself, but the general consensus was that the team had done us proud again and no-one I spoke to had any regrets about being there to sample a totally unique atmosphere. I think the fact that UEFA have confirmed that this was the largest ever travelling support on the continent proves once and for all that we are the greatest fans on the planet!

SIMON DEVENEY, Greenock

THERE were so many memories from a fun-packed week, it's hard to remember them all. I'd like to initially mention my good friend Paul McNally, originally from Stirling, who has lived in Madrid for 10 years. He and his wife (Irene – not pronounced Irene as in Scotland, as she's Spanish!) put me and a friend of mine up for a couple of nights and arranged a superb 'olde' Spanish apartment for us in Seville.

The only impact was the old lady who rented out the apartment was slightly deaf and blind at a youthful 85-years-old, and to get her attention you had to buzz her three times only as she knew it as a code of someone she'd know!

Of course, armed with a map (supplied by Irene) we go to the accommodation with our bags and our prized possessions – our tickets – and lo and behold there are 12 buzzers to chose from. Within minutes we had a dozen locals and pet dogs etc... all around us offering to help – none speaking English and the pair of us trying our best Scots on them, until a local passer-by came back and read our instructions and we were sorted in a fabulous apartment near the Aveniua de Palmeras.

The one thing that made us think was the real sense of loyalty and community displayed the local Sevillians, not only helping us, but also in protecting the old lady. It was also amazing on the day we left the apartment to head back to Madrid we saw kids in the local school playground sporting their new acquired Celtic tops. Here's hoping the next Raul grows up wanting to play for The Bhoys!

We had a spare bed in our apartment, so I tried to contact my good friend from Toryglen, Henry Cannon, to tell him I could put him up for free for the night. He declined as he wanted to sleep at the Cathedral. Of course, when I met up with him in Madrid, I asked him why on earth did he want to sleep rough when he'd the chance of a bed. He stunned me by stating, 'I'd never slept in a box before!'

I was impressed by meeting guys merrily drinking their worries away up until Friday in Seville. "When's your flight lads?" I asked.

"It was yesterday, but the wife is giein' me pelters, so ah'm staying here till she cools doon!"

The amount of folk who were trying to make their own amazingly planned ways home armed only with 50 Euros to their name and "How do I get to Portugal?" but in fairness, plenty of Bhoys bailed them out, which is the spirit of this club through and through, and it's why I'm only overcome with emotion thinking about these experiences rather than languishing about the results.

My mate Paul, who is fluent in Spanish, read the reports from all over Europe hailing Celtic, their fighting spirit and absence of 'professionalism' that Porto resorted to! I never thought I could love this club anymore than I did, but I do.

GERRY McGEACHY, Celbridge, Republic of Ireland, (ex-Stirling)

European memories

MAY 21, 2003 ... What a fantastic sight, standing at San Sebastian near the fountain looking down the street and watching several thousand Celtic supporters sing their hearts out to *'You'll Never Walk Alone'*.

It made the hairs on the back of my neck stand up. I took a photo of the scene at the time and processed it when I got back home, and when I looked at it closely, there in front of me, just a few steps down the fountain, was my cousin who I was supposed to meet up with in Seville but didn't manage to do so until after the match. What a surprise he got when I showed him the photo.

TOM NOON

THE memory that will last forever is that my friends and I became almost obsessive about superstition. My brother and I watched the Blackburn game at Ewood Park in the Corn Exchange in Gordon Street – a 2-0 victory.

As the pub had two big 'hard-to-miss' screens it was decided that we would go there for the next game we were in town for – Stuttgart away. There was now five of us, sitting at the same table. 5-4 aggregate victory. The table was becoming lucky. Liverpool at Anfield. Five again in the pub, same table, same chairs, same positions. I had to sit to the left of the table, and my brother to my left. 2-0 win. Boavista away. However, there were two men sitting at our table, as we entered the pub an hour early for kick-off. We needed that lump of wood.

Five minutes to kick-off and they were still there, with their pints half-full, despite saying they were leaving before the game. In a flash, some of our group leaped from their chairs. The two men upped and left, and another gathering of fans ran to command 'our' table. Luckily we got their first. Once we arranged the chairs accordingly, everything was in place. Celtic won 1-0.

For the final against Porto, my brother and I took half days from work to ensure that we were in possession of the Holy Grail. The rest of the crew came in after five, and we were all set. Correct table (littered with umpteen glasses), seating ordered properly, nothing could go wrong. It was our destiny. We lost. Damn that table!

GARY SHIELDS

THE thing that will most stick in the memory from our great run in Europe is what I think is the essence of being a fan of the Bhoys. In the final, after a big-hearted display from Larsson and co, it wasn't till the end of the night that we showed how amazing our fans are.

When FC Porto took centre stage to collect their medals and the trophy, it wasn't the Porto fans that could be heard sing their anthems but they were drowned out by our fans singing *'Over and Over'*. The line from that song which rung so true is *'Faithful through and through'* and I will never forget that as long as I live.

DANIEL THOMAS BROWN, Corby, Northants

A GLASWEGIAN by birth, I have spent most of my life in Canada. I am currently in Toronto. To get access to the game at my work I arranged a cable TV feed into a video server in another company building, I then arranged to access that video server from my own building (office).

Over the phone the local technology team tunes in the correct sports channel. I had the game on my computer monitor and boosted the sound with available speakers from the Technology department. I watched the game from my desktop computer in my office in its entirety.

My working colleagues, most of who have a shallow knowledge of the beautiful game gathered around. Canada, a land of immigrants, ensured that any Portuguese representation within the company began to filter into my office as word got round. By the second half my office was full; both teams had their supporters.

Although Celtic lost, their work effort was commendable. As for the winners, Porto and the Portuguese, I say enjoy. The fans enjoyed a wonderful game and Celtic were as deserving as Porto to take the cup.

DAN SIMONINI

My favourite moment was in the final when Henrik Larsson headered the ball, not only once but twice, to score two goals. Hail! Hail! Larsson.

BEN (aged 8)

MY memory was at the end. My son Conor was crying. I said, 'don't worry, there will be more finals'.

He said, 'Dad, it will take them another 33 years.' He cried himself to sleep that night. Hopefully it won't be another 33 years. Na Ceiltigh Abu.

GARRETT MULLEY, Dundalk

I TRAVELLED with my son by car from Lisbon to Seville – seven hours on the day of the match – through rural Portugal and Spain to spend the most emotional overwhelming six hours of my life in Seville, mainly in a park watching a big screen.

My most poignant memory is after the match, of a man, maybe 70-years-old, wearing a bunnet, bare-chested, walking along the line of completely exhausted Celtic fans, hundreds of us, saying 'See you next time, son (or hen)'. Forty years after watching my first Celtic game I sat at midnight in a city 2,000 miles from Glasgow, in 24 degree heat, knowing there will be a next time because of people like him.

As we drove up the motorway – the quick way back – we met loads of Porto fans and although it's easy to be dignified in victory, more than one fan said there should have been two cups tonight, so impressed were they by Celtic. I've just watched the game again for the first time and I'd like to thank the Celtic team for enabling me to enjoy a party, meet old friends, make new ones and make me and my son proud to be football fans and most importantly, Celtic fans.

JOHN SCOTT

MY family and I had booked a holiday in Wassenaar in Holland before Christmas 2002. It was all arranged and paid for, with our departure from Newcastle on May 13, returning on May 25. At the time these dates were of no real significance as our run in the cup was nothing more than an exotic dream!

I was 'tipped the wink' about match tickets going on sale on the UEFA website between the Liverpool games so I gave it a go. The servers were crashing all about the place with the demand on line being so high. I enlisted the help of my brother, Kevin, to try to secure the briefs for the final.

You were getting so far through the booking process only to be dumped out by a message asking for a page refresh. We were constantly on the phone to each

MAY THE FORCE BE WITH YOU: *Even the local police appeared to be getting into the spirit of the final and declaring their support for the Bhoys and, below, Simple Minds frontman Jim Kerr*

other, exchanging stories of how far we had got before being dropped. Three hours later my phone went and it was my brother in a frantic state! "I have reached the ordering point and they want a credit card number!"

"Gie them one then!" I screamed. My brother then explained in a few choice words that he did not own a credit card. So with my details and his computer we ordered the maximum six tickets that they allowed per person. The fight was over and it had been a hard one. I sat back and yelled, my eyes were nipping and my mouse finger had developed some sort of arthritis! We had the tickets so what the hell if we went out. I could flog them to my Scouse mate. I proudly told the wife I was the owner of six UEFA Cup final tickets.

She looked blankly back at me over the top of her novel. It could have been tickets to an Abba revival concert as far as she was concerned. "When is this final?" she asked, getting increasingly more sceptical when the penny dropped that this was football I was on about, "and where is it?"

I informed her that it was in Seville sometime in May. "Remember we're on holiday in May, you better check." On to the UEFA website I went, praying that I would not have to tell her that our family holiday was to be interrupted. "Doh!"

The news did not go down too well and the fact I had just put £180 on our credit card made things worse. I explained my game plan of selling the tickets to my Scouse mate if we were unsuccessful and the wolves were away from the door for that moment at least.

"You said Liverpool would beat you," said my wife Anne but she was happy that I was elated at conquering the mighty Reds. I explained that there was another hurdle to overcome in the shape of Boavista and those things were not cut and dried yet. Anne phoned from her work as I danced across the living room floor after the result in Oporto. She had finally realised that destiny was to take me away from her on our holiday. How could she argue with the 'V for victory' that was our destiny?

I made my arrangements to get to Seville over the Internet and flapped like a budgie as the flights were eaten up and the prices hiked up. Fortunately I found a connection which would get me to Spain – 'Amsterdam - Zurich - Malaga' – on Swiss Air. Seat booked on the Renfe train from Malaga to Seville and it was mission accomplished! The holiday was great and my daughters, Molly and Rosie, were having a ball unaware of the trek I was about to undertake on the morning of May 21.

The Tuesday night in Wassenaar was one of the wettest imaginable and the drumming of the rain on the caravan roof was incessant. On a night where sleep would be difficult I found it impossible! My alarm clock was set for 3am to allow me time for a 7.25am plane from Schipol to Zurich. My attire for the whole duration was to be a long-sleeved Hoops, Celtic tartan kilt, sporran, kilt socks & Cat boots. I drove the 20 miles or so from my campsite to the long-stay car park at Schipol and took the courtesy bus to the terminal.

At 5am I was the only Celtic fan in the place and the kilt drew some astonished looks from the commuters. It was the first time I had been through airport security wearing a kilt and let's just say the frisking was interesting! One of the security staff, an Ajax fan, handed me back my sporran with the words 'good luck tonight' in a genuine way only football fans understand. I was bursting with pride

The Road to Seville

as I embarked on the first leg of my flight, thinking that the Dutch are not such a bad race after all. This was quickly reversed as I boarded the plane and found one of the arrogant sods had pinched my widow seat!

Landing in Zurich was my first visit to Switzerland and I was unsure as to the reception my attire would attract. It was the same as in Holland but I was now not the only Celtic fan around and Hoops were here there and everywhere, but mostly at the bar! I adopted the usual talk to anyone and everyone that arises at European away fixtures.

Three guys and a girl from Cardenden told me of their Fiat Punto that awaited them at Malaga Airport. There was a debate about where the accelerator would be in conjunction with the other pedals. I set them straight about where the pedals were on a left-hand drive car! Two beers later and we were off to Malaga.

For previous sins (I guess) I was seated next to a nice American couple from Philadelphia. The small talk started very early into the flight with the Yanks not wanting to seem ignorant. I was quizzed on my kilt and informed that the gentleman's Gran was from Glasgow. His knowledge of all things Glaswegian ended there!

"Where are your club going?" he asked, looking at all the Hooped jerseys on the plane. I told him it was Celtic and we were off to play in the UEFA Cup final. "Do you play in the kilt?" he asked. I just about fell off my chair and quickly composed myself. His wife then asked me what position I played for the team! Here I was in economy class on Swiss Air dressed in the kilt, not in the best of shape, going to Malaga for a train journey to Seville and they thought I was one of squad! The fact I had Larsson on my back but told them I was of Scottish Irish descent must have totally confused the hell out of them further! Nice people but if your sport does not last four hours with regular TV ads they just don't get it!

As I left the plane they wished me well but I knew they were totally confused. Hopefully they saw the game that night and were enlightened. Although I expect they would say, "That's that Larsson bloke we sat next to on the flight!" Americans, you've got to love them!

Malaga to Seville was a journey that seemed to take forever. I was meeting the lads at the Santa Justa train station and eventually at 4.30pm we met up. Seville was scorching and our pale pasty skins were hidden from sight as much as possible. The gallons of ale were replaced with gallons of water. I did not want to miss this one and the thought of being 'air-ambulanced' out of Seville two hours before kick-off scared me off the booze.

Our first mistake was to queue for a taxi for about an hour. Our second mistake was then to queue in traffic in the taxi for about an hour! Well at least the air-con was on! A few refreshments, however, did pass my lips as kick-off approached, supplied by entrepreneurial young Spaniards selling beer out of ice buckets on the road to the stadium.

The information leaflets indicated a 3km walk to the stadium but it seemed like 30km! The game itself is now history and although tinged with the sadness of defeat was still an awesome event to behold. The elation of a victory would have been indescribable but in actual fact, the event was indescribable anyway.

After boozing till 5.30am in various bars around Seville, the train station floor was my bed for an hour, which then became the train. I wrapped my scarf round my

European memories

napper and dreamt of what had passed. It truly had been a pilgrimage of love. The return journey was a carbon copy of the previous in reverse. Similar looks at Zurich and Amsterdam but there were three subtle differences. I smelt a lot worse, I was walking like John Wayne and no Dutch boy dared steal my window seat now.

STEPHEN McGINNIGLE

MY name is Lisa Robinson, and I'm a Celtic fan based in Birmingham. As soon as Celtic beat Boavista I was trying to get a flight from Birmingham to Seville for the game, for a reasonable price. By mid May I had conceded defeat, and accepted that I would go to Birmingham and watch the game.

On Friday I received an email, from Celtic, offering fans a day package from Prestwick. This was my chance, I was to find out whether I could go on Saturday. It wasn't looking good, as I didn't have a ticket, but when I got the call the whole of Birmingham knew where I was off to! My mam drove me from Birmingham to Prestwick.

We left at six o'clock on Tuesday night. I knew it was going to be a special time when we arrived and saw the amount of people swarming around the airport at three o'clock in the morning. I couldn't believe my eyes when we arrived in Seville. It was a mass of green and white Hoops! I was travelling alone, so I was relieved when I got chatting to two men, Bill and John, who didn't seem to mind me tagging along.

The atmosphere was amazing. I have tried to explain to my friends back home, but my words do not do it justice. I haven't stopped talking about it since I got home on Thursday at about 5pm. I didn't sleep. I couldn't. I didn't want to miss a moment of this piece of the Hoops history.

The Spanish, and the Portuguese, really took us to their hearts, and everybody seemed happy enough to be engulfed in a mass of Hoops and tricolours! I could write all night about the fun, the friendliness, and the atmosphere, but I just wanted to say thanks to all the players, and Martin O'Neill for getting us there, for allowing it to happen, and creating the biggest footballing party ever!

LISA ROBINSON, Birmingham

My memory will be standing outside my flat in Shoreham-by-Sea, west Sussex, and proudly watching the front of my flat covered in green white and orange. I'm proud of Celtic and all its clan.

PATRICK McAFEE

MY father, my younger brother and I arrived in Benalmadena, Malaga, on May 19. We met up with my two uncles and two cousins, along with two other friends. All in all there were nine of us staying for the whole week. And what a week it was!

We partied non-stop from the Monday night right through to the Saturday. Benalmadena is around two hours away from Seville and it was the nearest accommodation we could get.

In the middle of the resort there was the '24-hour square'. It was a sea of green + white every night from about 10 o'clock onwards. The bars and nightclubs were packed with wall to wall Celtic strips and outside on the actual square as many fans sang, danced and boozed the nights away with all the favourite Celtic songs. On the

The Road to Seville

Tuesday night the place was jumping and a guy with bagpipes had the place rocking and that set the tone for the whole night and into the morning.

Fans were coming straight out of the pubs and into taxis heading for Seville, which cost a cool £180 but no-one seemed to care! We hired a coach along with other fans for the Wednesday morning and set off at 12 noon, arriving in Seville around three o'clock after a stop-off on the way there. None of us had a ticket and the word was that they were going for between £500-750. We wandered round Seville and every turned corner had a sea of Hoops fans chanting away.

We walked to the ground and had a look around just to say we had been there, then decided to get to a decent place to watch the game. We eventually came across the big tent full of fans, which was just a 15-minute walk away from where the Celtic buses all congregated. We were in there for half past four and gave it big licks until kick-off. It was a day we will never forget. Celtic were fantastic and the fans spoke for themselves! The tent made as much noise as Celtic Park on an Old Firm day! Porto, great team, but they know they cheated their way to that UEFA Cup.

We arrived back in Benalmadena on Thursday at four in the morning and even that night and the next two, there were still hundreds of fans on that square, deflated but it didn't take much to get us in jubilant mood for we knew Celtic had done us proud! We left Spain on Saturday night and even in the airport it felt as if you where walking through the Gallowgate!

DARREN BOYLE

MY best memory of Seville was the day after the game. There were still thousands of Celtic fans going about singing and having a good time (I would have loved to see it if we had won).

There were nine of us sitting outside a Spanish bar at the Cathedral and the waiter – a Betis fan – asked my friend George for his Celtic hat to which he obliged. Then after a few moments he came out with a round of drinks for the whole table. While in Seville I have never been so proud to call myself a Celtic fan. We just sat there singing all day and the waiter called his family and told them to come down and see us all just singing and dancing. They all loved the Hoops

JAMES FEELY

MY father, my son and I travelled over with the staff from Celtic Park on the day of the game. Despite lack of sleep everyone was in great spirits and once we arrived in Seville it was absolutely amazing to see the tremendous support who had travelled across the water to see the Bhoys.

A sea of green white and gold was a sight to behold forever. The organisation and order was excellent both for travelling and at the stadium - sore feet were the only problem but you can live with that. The Porto fans, Spaniards and, of course, the Celtic fans all did their nations proud and should be applauded. The singing in the streets and in the stadium had to be heard to be believed - I will never ever forget my trip with the Bhoys in Seville. What a story for my grandchildren.

LORAINE PHILLIBAN, St Mungo's Shamrock, Alloa

My memory of my time in Seville is when sitting in my wheelchair on the bridge with my brother Peter watching the tour buses and the horse and carts full of Celtic and Porto fans together going around Seville to the tune of *Hail! Hail!*

European memories

It was a sight to see. It wouldn't happen here if the final were in Glasgow. If only the Porto players acted like their fans …

JOE CLARK, Chapelhall

I FOLLOWED the Bhoys to Seville with my husband and my son (14) and my daughter (4). Both the men had tickets but the girls did not and I was apprehensive about being left to watch the game alone. I need not have feared. I was so well looked after by the Celtic fans in the park where we watched the game – I was really with family anyway!

I was so overwhelmed by what I saw and what I heard and witnessed in Seville it will never leave me. I have never travelled to an away match abroad before but I felt so proud to be a Celtic supporter and was so glad to see so many Porto fans sharing the moment with us all.

Well done to every supporter who spent their hard-earned cash to travel to Seville. The score was the only down point in a truly memorable occasion. I was moved to tears on more than one occasion that day.

LINDA AITKEN

I DECIDED to go to the final as I felt that I just had to be there. I spent three days trying to book up for Seville but to no avail. On the fourth day I managed to get booked up with my partner to go to Torremolinos from May 19-23.

When arrived we decided try and book up for a bus or train to Seville but were told by umpteen fellow Hoops fans that all of them fully booked, so feeling dejected, thinking that we had come this far and the only way we were going to get to the game was if we paid 200 Euros each way for a taxi. Just as we were going to give up we happened to bump into two Bhoys, Andy and Davie, and asked if they knew where there were any buses leaving from. They said that we were in luck. They had just hired a car for the week and they a couple of spaces left. So we later met up with the Bhoys at the Irish bar, The Bailey, to finalise the details. We decided to leave the following morning as we had heard there was a concert being held at the Prada San Sebastian.

We arrived early afternoon in Seville and all had a brilliant day. Myself and my partner both found out that both Davie and Andy were two of the best guys you would ever like to meet. After the game we had nowhere to stay that night so we got talking to another Bhoy who told us about a campsite on the outskirts of Seville. We left about 12.30am and got lost trying to find it a couple of times. Eventually we had to follow a taxi to it, and arrived a the campsite around 2.00am in high spirits.

We then spent half-an-hour filling in paperwork for the campsite. We thought that was it, then the Spanish guy took us outside and pointed to the grass and said, "You put tent there."

All of us looked at each other bemused, before realising that the guy had thought we had a tent, but we didn't! He didn't have any tents to hire so we all had to go the car and sleep. After spending a couple of hours tossing and turning we headed back into Seville about 6.00am and were left gobsmacked when we drove past Flaherty's Irish bar to find about 200 people sleeping on the nearby Cathedral stairs. Some were lying on the stairs, some had managed to get hold of a mattress and one even had a tent sloped down the stairs. We then slept in the car for another short while until the place woke up again.

The Road to Seville

The day of the game was one of the best days of my life and something I will always remember, I must have spoke to what felt like one million Celtic fans and, of course, a couple of Porto fans as well.

Although we didn't bring the cup back the team did us proud and had it not been for a very dodgy referee, we would have, as we had Porto under the cosh.

MICHAEL NELSON & ALISON LYTTLE, East Kilbride

On the way back through the town after the final whistle I was stopped by a slightly lost Celtic fan who asked: "Hey big man. Can tell how tae get tae that big roon square?" I wonder what response he would have got if he had asked a Spaniard?

JOE PORTER, Glasgow

The best part of our trip to Seville was at the end of the game. When Porto went up to get the trophy all that could be heard was 'Over and Over'. This showed that the Hoops have the greatest fans in the world and they fully deserved their standing ovation.

STEPHEN & NATALIE FERRIER

I WAS one of the lucky ones to get tickets to the match in Seville. I went with my sister and my mother. It was the most fantastic experience of my life. Never have I been so proud of Martin and the Bhoys and ourselves - their army of amazing Celtic supporters (in Seville, Glasgow, Ireland, Sweden and everywhere else) as that day.

We invaded the stadium the same way we invaded Seville – we were everywhere! After the match, Martin and the team walked first to the 'Celtic' side and then to our side ('neutral') and applauded us while we sang *You'll Never Walk Alone"* with all of our hearts and whatever was left of our voices.

We walked the long walk back to the city of Sevilla, tens of thousands of us in silence. We were sad and in our own thoughts, but with our heads held high. To the very end, everybody behaved well as no-one wanted to bring shame to the Hoops.

I thank God for letting me have been a part of it all. We met fun, fantastic Celtic supporters from all over the world and were there to support the best team in every way we could. I am so proud to wear my Celtic shirt and to be one of you all. You are fantastic supporters.

To Martin and the Bhoys who played so brilliantly for us – keep your heads held as high as we do. You deserved that trophy, but you have something that all the trophies in the world don't match. You have the best and most loyal supporters and we will follow you anywhere!

SUSANNE (from Sweden)

I HAVE been a Celtic supporter all of my life, I'm a pensioner and the proudest moment of the European tournament was the Celtic fans in Seville.

They did us proud, the team were great also. I hate the expression, 'glorious in defeat.' We are the best supporters in the world, every time we go abroad. Seville and the world saw it.

NANCYMAC

European memories

Sevilla ... May 21, 2003

Brilliant! Awesome! Outstanding! Electric!
Drama! Excitement! Celtic Majestic!
We'll chant a few songs, jump up and down
'C'mon the Hoops!' can be heard through the town!

In at the airports, massive big queues
People mysteriously off work with the flu!
Touch down in Espana 34 Degrees heat
'a'right there Pablo' to the locals we meet

In at the fountain it's all green and white
The Spaniards can't believe all these wonderful sights
Buses, mopeds, cars, lorries and vans
we here for the fitba, and to top up our tan!

To try and explain is an impossible task
there's so many great stories from everyone that you ask.
I'm privileged to have been there and I will never forget
the scenes that I witnessed and the people I've met.

The team have done so well under Martin O'Neill
We deserved to win it, I strongly do feel.
But it wasn't to be and we will always recall
How Henke and co., they gave it their all

We came in our thousands to cheer on the Bhoys
We all feel the hurt but remember the joys.
Home we will go - New York, Donegal
tell all the people that we've had a ball.

As the song we all know says as I bid you adieu
Over and over we will follow you!

DANNY FERRY

THE moment the Bhoys went in for the Huddle I was so proud to be there. I had been to Blackburn Rovers, Celta Vigo, VfB Stuttgart and Boavista and now Porto in Seville. And I enjoyed every moment of them.

Martin and the Bhoys did us so proud with every kick and save of the ball. With tears in my eyes at the final whistle this is the day I will never forget. Walking back looking for the bus to the airport feeling down thinking nothing will make me smile for a long time and who should I meet my favourite player Paul McStay and my smile was back. And the best memory I will ever have is when Henrik scored the goal to take us into the final and me, Brian, Danny and Paul all doing the huddle with tears in our eyes.

CAROL-ANNE HAFFIE, Linnvale Shamrock, Clydebank

The Road to Seville

ON arriving in Madrid on May 20, I got the train from the airport to the city centre where I was meeting my brother, Aidan, who had flown from Sydney for the game. We were extremely excited about the game and particularly proud of ourselves as we had had complete confidence the Bhoys would go all the way and had reserved tickets on the Internet after the Celta Vigo game.

Unfortunately my flight arrived bang in the middle of rush hour, I got on to a packed tube and as the doors were about to shut, five Spanish guys barged in and surrounded me. I couldn't move, and panicked about my wallet, passport, tickets etc. The tickets were in my trouser pockets, with a double button.

You can imagine my dismay when the train emptied, my pocket had been opened and the tickets gone! Fortunately the story has a happy ending! A cousin of my wife's was at the game, he had heard what happened and rang my mobile at 4.30pm on the day of the match to say he'd got two spare tickets. You can imagine my joy and relief and gratitude!

CONOR CAHALANE

THE day started at 6.30am, travelling from Mijas Costas for a two-hour drive, five of us crammed into a Fiesta. On the road, flags out the windows, a few songs to get us in the mood, although that didn't really need to happen as all of us had been on a high, the anticipation, the emotion building up inside. The day had arrived.

On the road we passed and were passed by bus, car and even mopeds of Celtic fans determined to be part of the day of our lives. Eventually we arrived in Seville, and there it was – Paradise, the sun a modest 22 degrees, street loads of Celtic fans.

The figures being touted around range from 80,000 to 150,000. Nothing would surprise me. One thing's for sure, Seville was not ready for this. The day was spent having a few drinks (just a few as we wanted to remember the game). There was no need to get drunk, you were simply high on emotion.

Celtic fans with tickets made sure they where secure. One guy even had his ticket surgically taped to his belly. Johnny Bonkers was his name but there was nothing bonkers about his actions as every fan knew the significance of this day and what it meant to have a ticket. It was time for the game. We walked three miles through the town over to the river, stopping only to get light refreshments as the heat now had reached 33 degrees.

The stadium was not a patch on Celtic Park but one fit for the occasion. As for the game ... well every true fan knows the injustice of that. The aftermath, depression, sadness, the feeling of losing your most precious thing. However, all credit to the players for being the true winners in our eyes, the fans for their singing, partying, and their best behaviour.

KEVIN McMENAMIN

I MADE the trip to Seville with 99 others from the Kirkshaws Club in Coatbridge. What an amazing experience. About 15 of us spent Wednesday walking around the city just tasting the history and taking in what was happening and what we were so proud to be part of.

Every street was packed with fans in green and white. I spoke with Scottish, English, Irish, Americans and Australians – a truly international affair. I attended the game with three others and joined with all other Celts in experiencing the highs and

European memories

lows of the match. So proud of our team but so frustrated at the result and the wasting tactics of Porto and lack of control from the ref.

It was difficult to leave the ground at the end as, despite the result, we just did not want the experience to finish. Once outside we shared our experiences with other fans and shook hands with Porto fans.

MATTHEW COSTELLO

FRIDAY, May 16, I got the news I'd been longing for. My friend in Glasgow had secured a ticket for me. Next stop try to get flights to Seville, Malaga or Faro – no chance. All sold out. Check the Internet for scheduled flights. BMI have space on the flight to Alicante. But that's over 400 miles away. Never mind I've got time. I'll book it up.

I arrived at Heathrow Airport at half past nine on May 20 and joined the queue at the BMI check-in. I knew there would be many other Celtic fans travelling to Spain but what I saw astounded me. Almost all the passengers among the two to three hundred people waiting to check-in for their flight were wearing the Hoops or their yellow away tops.

Very soon I got chatting and found that a few of them were travelling on my flight. Eventually got checked in, the chap at the desk told me he had been checking in Celtic fans since 6.30am, some to all points in Spain and some even to Paris and Amsterdam. They were making their way by bus, train, boat or any other means possible. When we got through security, the transit lounge was a sea of green and white. The fans were enjoying themselves but were still mindful of other travellers. A credit to the club and themselves

We eventually arrived in Alicante at a quarter past three in the afternoon, I had pre-booked a hire car and made my way to the desk and got the formalities out of the way. The staff knew where I was going as they had hired cars all day long to the hoards of fans travelling to Seville. They wished me well and wished the Bhoys good luck. Down the A7 to Murcia. I passed, and was passed by several cars displaying Celtic colours. On to the E-15 then the N-92 to Granada it was the same. Wherever I stopped there were Celtic fans. We had sandwiches and coffee with the locals. They made us really welcome and again wished us well. Then on to the final 300 plus kms to Seville.

I arrived at around 10pm. I could not believe my eyes. Driving down the main road heading towards the Plaza de Espana. A sea of green and white just like the Gallowgate or London Road on matchday, only hotter. The temperature gauge in my car read 34.5 degrees and it was 10.15pm.

I was guided to a parking place, close to the Avenida de Portugal by a local policeman, where I was permitted to leave the car until Thursday. I cannot recall such friendship shown to football fans in any other country or city I have ever visited, and I have been to many. I shall return to Seville, someday, to see its beauty and to visit their fantastic people again. I have many other delightful memories of this fantastic trip, the majority of them involve our great fans. My main memories, however, will be the trip to Seville itself and an incredible night spent in the company of my fellow fans, some really brilliant Porto fans and a small group of Real Betis fans who joined us at the Party in the Park.

HENRY E GIUSTI, Yateley, Hampshire

The Road to Seville

WENT to Seville on Tuesday – brilliant. At Charlie & the Bhoys – some atmosphere. Got tickets for the game – thought the Bhoys played magnificent. I felt cheated but proud!

My feelings are probably like the rest of the Celtic supporters; you know it was an experience that will be hard to capture again. We may not have lifted a cup this season, but we have memories and experienced something that no other team possibly could. That, to me, means a hell of a lot more.

The day was made extra special for me because my partner Stephen, proposed to me on the afternoon before the game outside the Cathedral, in the midst of it all! What a day to remember!.........Of course, I said 'YES!'

We're getting married next September 2004, and the reception will hopefully be at Celtic Park. It goes without saying that Stephen and the rest of the wedding party will be wearing the Celtic tartan!

KERRY McLAUGHLIN

MY wife Katrina, my son Paul, my sister and myself went to the square where the Henrik mobile was parked on May 21. We met an observer from UEFA who said he was absolutely astonished at the passion and numbers of the Celtic fans and enthused that this was what UEFA stands for, fans enjoying the occasion and supporting their team without upsetting any of the local cultures.

He said, in fact, the Sevillians had told UEFA how sorry they were to see the Celts go home. We left this new recruit to the Celtic fan club shaking his head and smiling in awe of the whole situation. Well done fellow Celts you are a credit to this great club of ours and I have no doubt we will be back.

IAN, KATRINA, PAUL & ISOBEL McGUIGAN, East Kilbride.

THE highlight of our trip was that we were in a five-star hotel in Fuengirola. When we arrived on Tuesday night there was a pianist (it was very posh). Luckily enough there was a piano player among us who treated us to some great Celtic tunes!

The SAGA holidaymakers were delighted! They sang and they danced along with us! It was brilliant. They were there for a quiet holiday, but they soon found their youth again, and they had the times of their lives! There were 140 Celts in the hotel. Everyone behaved impeccably, the only down point was that one of our crowd fell asleep on a bench outside the hotel and found that when he awoke he had lost his size 6 trainers and socks! … and that they were replaced by a nice pair of size 9 trainers! (No socks!) He laughed; we laughed, what a time! Shame about the blisters in Seville!

GARY, NICOLA, SCOTT, ALISTAIR, CAROLINE & ANGELA.

I WAS amazed at the people I met while in Seville, After leaving my mobile at home and not being able to get in touch with the people who I had arranged to meet, including my uncle who was coming from Canada, I was standing in the main square with approximately 20,000 other fans singing *Walk On.*

My uncles (one from Glasgow and one from Canada) walked right up to me and we were able to spend the rest of the day together. In almost every bar and street corner I met either a colleague from work or some very old friends whom I had not seen in nearly 20 years. I had my photo taken with Darren Jackson and Tosh McKinlay. I met Greg Hemphill *(Chewin' The Fat)* and to cap it all, Tommy Burns on his

LOVE IS IN THE AIR: *It's a memorable Seville trip for Kerry McLaughlin as her partner Stephen proposes in Seville on the day of the game ... Now she'll never walk alone!*

I'M ONLY HERE FOR A SUNTAN: *One Hoops fan goes topless in sunny Seville while, below, Celtic fans can't hide their disappointment after losing in extra-time*

way in to the stadium. The whole day was a fantastic experience – result excluded. The Bhoys, both fans and team, did us proud and we can walk with our heads held high.

TONY DAVREN

Seville Dream
So off we went on tae the bus,
the Seville wives left in a bit of a huff,
about 1,500 hundred miles to go,
I cannae wait till the Bhoys' show.

We didnae stop singing till we reached northern Spain,
and then only tae joke about the Gers in the rain,
we're laughing and joking, we're drinking and song,
you're looking around you, and you know there's nae wrong.

Proud to be part of the biggest movement of folk,
it makes your Man Uniteds and Liverpools look like a joke,
we are the best behaved supporters, but everyone knows,
that ye cannae fight in yer flip flops, you'd break your bloody toes.

The game was unbelievable and they put us tae the test,
and by the end of the first half you'd of thought they were best,
but when Henrik scored the first of his brace,
you knew we were putting forward a far better case.

Out of the game and on our way home,
I'd never felt part of something and yet felt so alone,
We'd been robbed in that game, and now suddenly I'm sober,
It's been a great time but our Seville dream's over.

And what if we end up with nothing this year,
we've still been better than them, and that's no fear,
it's been a great season, and we should all be so proud,
So let's hear it for the Bhoys, and sing it out loud...
Hail, Hail the Celts are here…

IAN ROBERTS

I WAS in Seville with my fiancé James and my sister Alison. My fiancé had a ticket for the game and we went along for the atmosphere, and it was great. The best memory I have is driving down to the fountain to find somewhere to park the car and seeing a sea of green and white, dancing in the fountain and singing their hearts out.

We soon found somewhere to park and joined in the party. We're from Coatbridge and it was really surreal to think we were in a foreign country and meeting so many people we knew – it was like being down the Whifflet after a big win over Rangers! We did our partying before the game and then went on to the park to watch the game on the big screen. It was great, obviously apart from the score. We were the strongest team, without a doubt. We made our own chances for our goals, but it was defensive errors that gifted the goals to Porto. The Celtic team should be very proud of themselves; they are winners in our eyes anyhow. Porto are a good team themselves and it was disappointing that they had to resort to feigning injuries and diving etc. but I suppose they could afford to do that when they were winning.

I'm still so glad I went, no regrets, even though we had hours of travelling to do. We drove to Manchester (3 hours) then flew to Alicante (2 hours) then drove from Alicante to Torremolinos (5 hours). Then the next day to Seville (2 hours) and then I drove home that night (2 hours). On Friday we drove back to Alicante (6 hours this time) and stayed there the night before flying back to Manchester the next day. It was only when driving back from Manchester that we got lost! We didn't lose our way once in Spain and come back to this country and can't find our way home — typical! So in total, we were driving for about 22 hours!

NICHOLA REYNOLDS

EVERYTHING went to plan on the outward journey to Seville, with flights from Glasgow-Stansted-Heathrow-Frankfurt-Madrid all running smoothly. In fact, after spending an enjoyable night in Madrid the night before the game, and then enjoying the smooth AVE train service to Seville at 8am on May 21, everything was looking good.

Unfortunately, our return flight from Madrid was due to leave at 6,50am the morning after the game, and with no night trains we had made plans to rent a car. However, when we attempted to pick up our car, we were informed that our booking hadn't been processed and that we needed a credit card to hire a car which we didn't have. So we knew that we were in a sticky situation. Nevertheless we made sure we enjoyed the carnival atmosphere in the city and quickly forgot about our problem. After attending the match (extra-time not helping) we tried to flag down a taxi. It has been well documented that this was a lost cause. So we were resigned to sleeping in the Santa Justa train station until the morning.

We managed to get a taxi to Malaga and luckily we all got on to a flight to Luton, and by the time we arrived, we were informed that our connection flight from Stansted was running late. Spurred by this we made a mad dash via taxi to Stansted where we were informed that our flight had been closed and we couldn't get on. This was a complete nightmare added to the pain of the Estadio Olimpico, so after a journey to central London and then a six-hour train journey to Glasgow we made it home, mentally and physically drained, floundering bank balance but nevertheless a totally memorable experience with pride for our wonderful Bhoys beating in our hearts.

JOSEPH CAMPBELL

MY most outstanding memory from the trip was when my son Keith, his pal Brian and I entered through the turnstile at the Porto end (We managed to buy tickets on the day of the game – 400 Euros!)

There awaiting us were two guys from Glasgow in security vests! They told us that they had wandered into the stadium on the previous afternoon and pinched the vests, as they didn't have any tickets! Standing bold as brass, they were

European memories

directing the Porto fans to their seats as cool as cucumbers. We could not stop talking about it all that night and every time I see them in my mind I just burst out laughing. Pity about the result but what ambassadors we were for Scottish football!

JOHN

The memories

We stop in a small tapas bar, an old man walks up and smiles
he starts whistling the Celtic song, through HIS NOSE!,
we walk on and laugh for miles

Triumphant in defeat, we swarmed the Seville streets
Not a sight of the celebrating Porto fans
who like their team, took the weight, off their feet

Partying till the wee small hours, the biggest support ever seen in Europe
The World Huddle alive, proud, partying, having fun, but without a UEFA Cup

Meeting pals from all over the planet, some not seen in years,
sombreros and beach balls a bouncing, loads of sangrias and beers

All praise to the Great Glasgow Celtic , 80,000 not a single arrest
Here's to Martin, and Henrik, and Lenny, our club's still clearly the best

GERRY McGONAGLE

I HAVE been a supporter for 40 years now. I am from Glasgow originally but live in Sydney where there is a great supporters' club. I watched the game in Hong Kong where I was on a business trip and when asked about the result the next day, all I could say was that I was as proud as ever to be a supporter of Celtic Football Club.

The Bhoys did us proud and can stand tall after their courageous efforts. I can imagine how they felt after the game, as I, like many others I'm sure, was totally deflated. However, there's always next year and after a display like that, we can all take heart for a bright and successful future at Paradise.

JOHNNY MILLER, Sydney, New South Wales

MY wife and I have just returned from a week in Torremolinos, and we both went to Sevilla and to the final. I got two tickets for the final from uefa.com when they went on sale and said to my wife, Kathleen, that I'd take her to Spain for her birthday, which happened to be on May 21.

Torremolinos was full of Celtic fans when we arrived on Saturday, May 17, and each night we went to the square. Every night more and more fans would congregate in this square and drink and sing till the sunrise. There was no trouble whatsoever. It was just one big party. This gave me an idea. On May 20, we made our way to the square as normal and each time I saw someone I would tell them to spread the word that it was my wife's birthday the next day, at midnight the first song to sing was *'Happy Birthday'* to Kathleen.

They all said they would but being full of sangria I thought they'd forget. But to my surprise – and hers – sure enough, they sang *'Happy Birthday'.* At first she was looking about to see whose birthday it was then she realised it was her they were singing to. There must have been close to two thousand fans all singing to my wife. Both of us were nearly crying with this sight. This memory will live with me forever. What a birthday present!

Thank you to every supporter who sang *'Happy Birthday'* that night to my wife. Once again, the Bhoys and Ghirls proved they are unique and the very best supporters in the land. It is better to have loved and lost than never to have loved at all.

STEPHEN GRIBBEN (Shamrock Bhoy)

I WAS destined to go to Seville, having followed the Bhoys through thick and thin over many years. I managed to get a ticket from the UEFA website and with search engines going crazy on the web I found a flight to Malaga. Now all we had to do was win against Boavista and final time was upon us.

Having booked a holiday with my wife to Tenerife, we were arriving back to the Kent on May 17 and I was due to go out on the 19th. I could hardly wait. Then disaster – my car was stolen on May 18. I need a car for work, simple as that! Common sense had to rule over my heart and a replacement banger was bought. But I had a few quid left over. Ryanair provided the flight to Glasgow though NOT to Seville, I was surrounded by ardent Celtic fans to see our glory unfold.

We know what happened but we were still Champions in my eyes and in the eyes of the world at large. The icing on my cake was to get a shirt signed by many of my heroes, and as a large part of my season is via the web and the *Celtic View,* I even got Tony Hamilton to sign the shirt! Poor Tony, he was stunned as he mentioned he had never before signed a shirt.

COLIN IRVINE

LATE in the night, after the match, enjoying a few San Miguels beside the Cathedral, I was bemused to see six Celtic fans covered head to toe in dirt and dust.

These guys were not inebriated – well no more so than the thousands of us that put the disappointment of the result behind us to continue the party well into the night. The reason for the appearance of these six fans became clearer when approached in a good and friendly nature by a handful of Porto fans the six, upon contact (handshake) with their Portuguese counterparts, instantly fell to the ground clutching various parts of their anatomy, feigning injuries and rolling around the street.

The Portuguese guys showed a mixture of first bewilderment then upon realisation that this was in reference to the 'playacting' of their heroes, some embarrassment. Then upon completion of the cameo acting of the Hoop Bhoys, they started to laugh along, taking the act in the good nature it was intended.

The Bhoys repeated this act several times during the night. To the credit of the Porto fans, they all reacted in the good manner described above.

I was with my two colleagues (Martin Cassidy, John Costello, both from East Kilbride) in the same location as above. The bar service was excellently provided by a young Spanish lad who seemed to be enjoying the general ambience of the occasion. He had been trying all night to cajole various fellow fans in the bar to part with their hoop tops. At the end of the evening Martin, by this time under the influence of Saint Michael (San Miguel), agreed eventually to accommodate the young lad in the bar.

European memories

Martin swapped his entire strip with the young lad – top, shorts and socks. However, upon slipping on the waiter's trousers, Martin realised they were at least three waist sizes too small. He could not wear the trousers but rather than disappoint the elated Spanish waiter with his new Celtic strip, Martin proceeded through the evening dressed in a wing-tipped white shirt, complete with bow-tie, boxer shorts and his trainers.

As we were only there for the day we had no alternate clothing to offer Martin. As we checked into Seville Airport for our flight home at 6am, Martin was still dressed as above. The Spanish airport authorities gave our friend some funny looks as he proceeded through custom control and on to the aircraft.

MARK KEAVENY, East Kilbride

I WAS heading back to my hotel after the party on Tuesday night, trying to get a taxi along with hundreds of others. After half-an-hour of raising my arm to no avail, I decide to sit down on the kerb of a fountain and take it easy for a while. Around this fountain people were sleeping and chatting as well.

A guy from London came up to me, pretty worse for wear, or at least worse than myself. Anyway, he informed me that he could not remember where he was staying and his girlfriend had gone back to the apartment, leaving him to fend for himself. In the meantime he had jumped into a fountain and bought two giant flags! I had my mobile phone and offered to text his girlfriend to get the street he was staying. Message sent and returned with the name of the street. I decided that we should try to get a taxi and we started walking. Taxis were like gold dust so everyone was flocking to any that stopped.

Eventually, we got a taxi along with an another guy from Glasgow. We were all sitting in the taxi and the driver asked in Spanish where we wanted to go. I announced where I wanted to go, then he turned to the London guy who could not remember where his girlfriend told him, but I remembered for him! Then the third guy from Glasgow announced that a hotel on a hill was his accommodation, which was a good starting point but with a little 'encouragement' about the merits of walking versus being taxied he remembered the name. Off we started, bearing in mind I was staying in the complete opposite direction from the other two.

The London guy I met at the fountain was first to leave after having difficulty getting his flags from the car, nearly poking my eye out in the process. Off we went to the hotel on the hill which was further away from where I was staying! We dropped off the other guy, only for two more Celtic fans appear and ask to share the taxi.

Off we went again back to the city centre. As I chatted to the two guys, one declared that he had come from New York, having just been relocated from Britain. Part of his relocation deal was that if Celtic got to the UEFA Cup final the company would pay for it! I was well impressed! Finally, these guys got out and off we went, taxi driver and me, to my hotel.

During the remainder of the journey I found out that he was a Real Betis support and hoped Celtic won. I arrived at my hotel at 5am.

I also heard a story that some guy nicked a horse and cart from the Costa Del Sol on the morning of the match and was caught on the motorway!!

DERMOT KEANEY

The Road to Seville

I WAS present in Seville as an FC Porto supporter, and I must congratulate Celtic FC fans for the fantastic presence and education, you are an example to the world.

One thing you must be sure, in the future Celtic has one more supporter (and you can say many more) from Portugal, wherever you play I will support your team (except against my team obviously).

Wish you and your team many victories in the future and please never lose your fantastic spirit! Yes is true Celtic will never walk alone ...

RICARDO PEREIRA, Porto, Portugal.

I WAS in a pub when a man walked in after the game and asked the bar to take his top. The man behind the bar was so happy he said, "Is this for me?" and the Bhoy replied, "No, I just want you to wash it and have it ready for me when Celtic come back in 2005 for the Champions League final."

The whole pub bust into laughter and the man behind the bar did not know what to do.

ANDREW DOCHERTY,Bishopbriggs, Glasgow

I am sure you will have thousands of stories like this, but the link across the years from 1967 to Seville was astonishing. I remember so much of being 10-years-old in a black and white world of an Irish family in Birmingham.

My father was laid-back about most things. He taught me that cricket and Shakespeare were a bit pointless, and in the ambivalent way of the Irish, loved the English 'people' but secretly hoped West Germany would win in '66.

Celtic was a different matter. Typhoo Tea provided big card pictures of the players and Tommy Gemmell was one of my heroes. We had never been to Scotland, but that didn't matter. I saw my dad anxious for a rare time. The tension, the relief: football could get no better.

2003: now in middle age – my dad passed on, age 92, a few years ago – I was building up to the game, talking it through with my Scottish father-in-law, convinced it would be 2-1 again. The game unfolded with growing passion and drama and by the time Larsson scored the first, I was 10-years-old again. I know the result was different, but the pride and dignity was just the same.

SEAN McTERNAN

FIRST of all let me start by saying how proud we were of those magnificent Bhoys of Seville. We know how the Bhoys must have felt, out there running for 120-plus minutes.

Living here in Fresno, California, on May 21 we also had 100-degree temperatures, which are not unusual to us ... but put 25 bodies in a 21/17 garage! Wearing big sombreros, I'm sure I lost a pound or two, well maybe naw. Try running in it at full speed for the duration of that magnificent cup-tie, it's hard to even imagine, but none of them looked as if they were out on their feet and would have gone on for another 120 minutes.

The garage Bhoys had two members who were looking for tickets to Seville – myself and Ian McLean – and also Pat Trainer from Vancouver, British Columbia. When tickets started going on sale and for the ridiculous prices from touts who probably have never seen a game in there lives, we thought there was no chance.

European memories

Then our Portuguese satellite maintenance man called me and said he was in touch with a travel agency from New Jersey saying they had tickets. We were right on the phone and the lady told me yes I had two tickets reserved in my name for $640.00 each. Great news! We called BA and arranged flights from Fresno to Lisbon – everything a go.

Then my Portuguese friend called and asked how the arrangements were going and what flight I was on from Lisbon. This we didn't know so he called them, called me back and said he wasn't comfortable with them.

After many phone calls we still did not have the information, although they sent me a fax saying that I had two game tickets reserved for Bill Charters and Pat Trainer. By this time my heart was ruling my brain. I had till midnight on May 19 to cancel my booking on BA to Portugal. At 11.30pm I cancelled. I had been reading all the horror stories about Bhoys being taken to the cleaners back home and around the world, and I felt I would have been one of them. The travel agent called me again on the Monday, saying they had my tickets. When I told her I thought it was a scam they hung the phone up.

The preparations were being made for a garage Bhoys party, locals were calling up asking if they could watch the game with us, and we also found a new pair of Celts from Hamilton who had just moved here to live in Fresno – Marie and Paul Timlin. On the day of the game, we all had the sombreros on, singing and dancing and really cheering on the Bhoys.

The American visitors also cheered them on, and felt disgusted at the end when those cowards walked away with our cup. After the game, the alcohol was flowing freely, and we all sang our hearts out.

When my 10-year-old grandson Devon came home from school he brought one of his wee pals to play, and he said they could hear us all singing when they got off the school bus. The neighbours were asking what's going on. Devon told them Celtic were playing in the UEFA Cup final, which was double Dutch to them. Some neighbours came round as they knew we were partying for something. The only thing was they had never heard a singsong going on at 2pm in the afternoon. We may not have been in Seville but I'm sure Martin O'Neill and the team all heard the garage Bhoys cheering them on from Fresno, California.

BILL CHARTERS, Fresno CSC, (home of the garage Bhoys)

I have attended all the home UEFA cup games, but my fondest memory was the Liverpool match.

I was already hyper with the event and just couldn't stop jumping and singing. This was before the teams even emerged! But what made that night so special was the appearance of Gerry Marsden to sing *'You'll Never Walk Alone'*.

Normally, I get a lump in my throat just watching all the Celtic scarves hoisted high, but to see the whole ground, away end included, all united in one song was overwhelming.

One fan standing next to me turned, with a tear in his eye, to say how wonderful the sight was. What was funny about that was that this guy was six feet round the neck and not someone you'd want to bump into on a dark night! That shows you just how emotional these events are.

ANDY PERRATT

The Road to Seville

ALTHOUGH I had been at San Siro for the cup final in 1970, I could not get to Seville because I had three daughters taking college final exams this week.

So we rented a big screen TV, here in Massachusetts, tuned in to the game live, got the little kids out of school early (the game programme started at 2.30pm local time and school did not get out till 3pm!) Eleven of us cheered the Bhoys on for 120 mins, all of them cried when even Rab ran up to the penalty box for the gallant last minutes. They had all gone to school in Celtic regalia; the college girls met another supporter at University of Massachusetts, an exchange student from Glasgow!

CONNOLLY-BROWN clan, Massachusetts, USA

DESPITE not winning a trophy this season it's been a great year supporting Celtic. My lasting memories are singing *'You Never Walk Alone'* with Gerry Marsden and the Bootleg Beatles in Baird's Bar before the Liverpool game, and also in Seville, where 70-80,000 Celtic supporters drank, sang and behaved themselves impeccably.

No other club, in my opinion, could send that many supporters to a European final. That is why I love Celtic Football Club. It's like a family, we should be proud of all the players, management, staff and supporters.

JACK SULLIVAN, Co. Cork, Republic of Ireland

I MISSED a Maths exam to go to the UEFA Cup final and although we lost, it was still one of the best experiences of my life.

The way that Henrik Larsson brought Celtic back into the game twice was incredible and the memory of that match will stay fresh in my mind forever. I am honoured to say that I supported Celtic in the Estadio Olimpico in a UEFA Cup final.

PAUL McARTHUR, Bearsden, Glasgow

I AM from Dublin, living in San Francisco at the moment, so with the time difference I get to see the games early in the morning – we're eight hours behind here.

The morning of the final I found out that I had to work so I was none to impressed, but only to the grace of God and everything Celtic, the guy we were working for was Irish-American. I explained my situation to him and with a blink of an eye he put the match on in his bedroom and turned the sound up. As we worked away, the American commentator shouting and screaming as the game progressed, I began to work closer and closer to this guy's bedroom and his TV.

I spent a lot of the first-half sprinting into the room as the commentator went mental. I got chills when I saw the amount of Celtic fans in the stadium, it was amazing, The game itself was unbelievable. Larsson proved once again the quality of a player he is by coming up with the goods not once but twice. I thought Alan Thompson was outstanding and all the lads gave 110 per cent. It was just misfortune that got in the way at the end … oh yes, and the diving and time-wasting as well.

BRENDAN CADWELL

I WAS in Stuttgart, watching Celtic in the UEFA Cup. It was the first time that I saw the Bhoys live. It was an absolutely great event for me.

The happiness, the mood, the sincerity, the friendliness of the Celtic supporters

European memories

was so overpowering me, that I'll never forget this event. But the most impressive moment for me was, when we left the Celtic block with all those enthusiastic supporters, they said thank you to us that we support the Celtic team. Never in my lifetime I had such an experience before, and I'm very often in German stadiums to see the FC Schalke 04. I travel home with a feeling of great happiness. And I was very proud that I was supporting the Celtic team in Stuttgart.

ACHIM FRITZ, Obernburg, Germany

HAVING been fortunate enough to have already booked a week's holiday in the Algarve, there was no way we were going to miss the final in Seville. Despite being ticketless we just wanted to be there.

So we – my husband Will, our daughter Niamh (19 months) and myself – hired a car for the day and joined the steady stream of green and white heading to Spain. We spent the day soaking up the party atmosphere and then watched the match on the big screen under the shadow of *The Sun's* bus.

She might not remember it when she is older, but Niamh will know she was there to support her team! Do you think she was the youngest Celt in Seville?

FIONA QUINN

OUR story begins on Wednesday, May 14, 2003, at 6:00pm when we leave sunny Fife heading for Witney in Oxfordshire. After six hours we arrived at my little sister's house, tired and exhausted but at least the first part of our journey was complete.

Thursday was spent relaxing and an evening meal to celebrate my 30th (which was on the 11th and a good excuse for us to head to Spain spending a fortune for a game of football). Friday, May 16 at 4am, I was awoken with shouts of "we've slept in!" I checked my alarm clock and it had been switched off (by me when it had gone off earlier.) Thank goodness John Paul had woken up or we'd have missed our flight. We jumped in the car and hotfooted it to Birmingham Airport for our 7:00am flight to Malaga. We made it in good time and were on our way to Spain!

Arriving in Spain, we waited patiently on our luggage. My suitcase arrived after about five minutes. However, there was no sign of John Paul's and after about half-an-hour, we were starting to get worried. Our first trip abroad was beginning to turn into a nightmare. He looked worried. He turned away from the conveyor to give me a hug and then stopped and walked straight past me. There on the next conveyor – luggage from Cork – was his suitcase. Thank goodness, we were off on our travels again.

We went to the foyer to meet our rep but she was not to be found. We thought that because we were running late, she had left. We found the hire car pick-up point and got our car. Map in hand, we headed to the Costa Del Sol and Fuengirola. What we didn't realise is just how bad Spain is sign-posted. So after two hours of driving about, nervous as hell and constantly trying to drive on the right-hand side of the road, we arrived in Feungirola. An hour later we actually found our hotel!

Our holiday was now looking like a trip to hell as we were transferred to another hotel with no explanation given. Once in our room we thought to ourselves "that's it, we're here, what else can go wrong now?" Then I opened my suitcase and discovered that my sun-tan lotion (oil-based) had burst and emptied all over my clothes!

The Road to Seville

We relaxed in Feungirola until Wednesday and after our disastrous trip from the airport to Feungirola, we decided to plan our trip to Seville in advance. At 6am, the alarm clock went off. We jumped out of bed, and within half-an-hour we were in the car heading to Seville. By 9am, we were there. We spent the whole day in the shade listening to live bands. Seville was unbearably hot. At 6pm, after a great day of singing Celtic songs and meeting old friends and new friends, we headed to the big screen outside the stadium. There we watched the game with thousands of others.

Since returning I have been trying to explain to people what it was like. I find it impossible to describe. The atmosphere that night was amazing. The reception we received from the people of Seville was incredible. With the exception of giving birth to my daughter, it was the best day of my life. To be part of the mass of fans who came from all parts of the globe and all walks of life was something we will never forget.

KAY ROGERSON

It took the greatest team in the world to bring my two brothers and I together. Three magical days in Seville. The heat, the beer, the friendships forged. Let's do it again soon with the Bhoys!

VINCENT McGURK

OUR journey was from Liverpool to Madrid on the Tuesday, and we'd decided to stay the night in the Spanish capital before getting a train for Seville. We had arranged to meet a mate at Madrid Station so we could all travel together to Seville. However, he had not booked his ticket and it looked as though he was going to be stranded.

He went to the Avis office to see if he could hire a car without a licence. At the desk there were two Swiss Celtic supporters and an Irish guy. Between them the Swiss had a licence and my mate had a Visa so they could hire a car. The Swiss were staying in Seville until the Friday and my mate had to leave early the next day with us on the train with no ticket. The funny thing was, my mate was going to be liable for a 500 Euro excess should the car be damaged or not returned to Madrid on the Friday. He did not know the Swiss from Adam but he trusted them because they were Celtic fans. He'll receive his Visa bill soon so, he'll find out if the car was returned or not.

The same friend obviously did not have a ticket for the train back to Madrid on the Thursday. I have to emphasise that these trains were totally different from British Rail. They were more like airlines with x-ray baggage checks and so on. With this in mind he knew he could not skip a journey the way you do back home so he stood at the end of a platform from 5.00am to try and figure out which train would be going to Madrid.

He was there for some time and was beginning to raise the suspicions of rail staff. He quickly brought out his disposable camera, which was used up, and began using the flash pretending to take photos of the Spanish Rail Networks 200mph train. They seemed to accept he was a train-spotter, which allowed him time to cross the track and get on to the Madrid train.

PETER REILLY

European memories

THE Friday afternoon after the game in Stuttgart there seemed to be as many Bhoys out in the main square – Schlossplatz – as there had been in the hours leading up to the match.

The craic was good, sun was shining and beer was flowing and one Bhoy got up and started into *'If you're happy and you know it clap your hands'*, followed by verses *'stamp your feet', 'Shake your head', 'Side to side'.*

Whilst most of us – and the passing Stuttgart public – looked on amused or bemused and applauded the solo artist, at the end he started up again but this time accompanied by his pals, then the next table of al-fresco drinking Celtic fans joined in, then the next table, then the Bhoys sitting on the steps outside the Konigsbau, then the Bhoys spilled out on the grass and so on until there must have been 2,500 Celts singing *'If you're happy and you know it clap your hands',* until the whole square was rocking.

The watching German public were just amazed by the whole craic but delighted at the good-nature of us all and, for me, this just summed up the fun and exemplary behaviour of Celtic fans abroad which leaves the good citizens of the places we visit with nothing but good memories of our 'excursions'.

PAUL HEALY, London

What can I say about Seville that hasn't already been said? Our journey started at Manchester Airport on Sunday, May 18, where we were flying out to Portugal. The sights at the Airport were incredible, with probably about 2,000 Celtic fans already on the move.

We arrived in Portugal to find that it was exactly the same. Everywhere you went you could see Hoops fans. The big day arrived and we travelled by bus from Portugal to the Estadio Olimpico. I was one of the lucky ones who had applied for tickets on the UEFA website. (Thursday, March 13 to be precise – even before a ball had been kicked against Liverpool).

With me on this memorable day were my son Thomas (13), my brother Harry (Rhyl, N Wales) and my cousin Andrew Pearson (London). We had arranged to try and meet up with other relatives on the day, but the mobile phones had all gone down and it was difficult to get in contact with anyone. We knew that another cousin was staying in Portugal but didn't know exactly where. On the way to the Seville, our buses stopped at a service station and lo and behold who did we meet but my cousin Andrew Stewart (Airdrie) who was staying in Portugal. Inside the stadium our seats were situated behind the press box and as we were star spotting again, I met another cousin who I didn't know was going to be there - Brendan Collum (Airdrie) who was sitting about 10 rows in front of us.

We had made a special banner for the occasion to see if we could get it on to the TV screens. Our eldest brother Neil Welsh lives in Calgary, Canada, and it was Neil who started my passion for all things Celtic when I was five-years-old and he took me to Parkhead for the first time. Unfortunately Neil was unable to be in Seville so we thought that the next best thing was to make him a banner with the words – 'NEILLYBHOY - WISH YOU WERE HERE'. When we were at Manchester Airport, Harry spotted Sam Allardyce, the Bolton manager and got him to sign the banner. We then decided to have a competition to see who could get the best signature and it was decided that the competition would be over if we managed to get the greatest captain in history – Billy McNeill. You can imagine my brother's face when he discovered we were sitting behind the press box. Not only did we get Billy McNeill to sign the banner, but also Tosh McKinlay, Murdo MacLeod and Sandy Clark (also an Airdrie man). He conceded defeat gracefully. A big thank you to them all for making my son's day. After the match we were dejected but headed back to Seville with some fantastic memories of a team that had given their all and made us very proud. On the way back we met the members of our supporters' club, the Caritas Celtic Supporters' Club, Airdrie, who were heading back to Torremolinos.

Sitting outside a pavement café in Seville at 3.00am reflecting on what could have been, I noticed a couple walking by and recognised the T-shirt the man was wearing. I chased after him to make sure I was right – he was a member of the Calgary Celtic Supporters' Club and knew my brother Neil. We then made a telephone call to Calgary, to my brother's utter astonishment.

After this we headed towards the Cathedral where the sights will live with us forever. It was like Cardboard City, with thousands of Hoops fans sleeping everywhere and the ones who were still awake very supportive of the team. After spending the night on the streets of Seville we headed back to Portugal the next morning.

Thanks to Martin O'Neill and the Bhoys for giving me the best season I can remember even although we have no silverware to show for it. Thanks also to all Celtic supporters for proving that you can follow football without causing embarrassment to anyone. They were a credit to Celtic and Scotland. To have in excess of 80,000 supporters in one city and not one single arrest being made (even in defeat) made be proud to be a Celt.

KATHLEEN WELSH, Airdrie

I REMEMBER the first round against Suduva and I thought to myself, "at least we made the second round." Little did I realise that it was just the start of the greatest journey of all time.

I was present at every round and was amazed by the fighting spirit of every member of Celtic Football Club. I honestly thought that we would be edged out by a strong defensive Liverpool team but when big John scored that wonderful goal I knew we were going to Seville.

My friend Steve Lowe and I boarded our plane from Glasgow to Malaga and could not believe our eyes. It was a mass of green and white. Even the cabin staff were in the mood, with their sombreros and Celtic scarves waving. It was just amazing to see the sights that awaited us in Seville and the Costa del Sol.

STEVE GILL

IT was Stuttgart that will live with me – missing kick-offs was to become a routine during both legs. For the first leg I was down from Orkney to lecture at Heriot Watt University in Edinburgh - we had come out of a Cantonese restaurant as close to kick-off as my partner could be moved away from her coffee!

We headed up the street to find a pub with screen – looked in the window to check the game was on and found we were 1-0 down! Anyway, I settled in with a pint and hoped for a gritty response! The crowd atmosphere just got better and better as we ended up on a 3-1 win. Inspirational! We flew off on the Friday after to Tenerife for a week for the purpose of celebrating my 40th, which, of course,

European memories

landed on the day of the second leg – February 27. We had a fantastic day out at sea, whale and dolphin watching, drank a few beers and then back to the apartment for a sundowner or three before making tracks for the local big screen pub.

On the way out of hotel we were grabbed by some new pals who were leaving for home the next day and they invited us in for drinks (I couldn't say 'No' apparently!) and despite insisting there was a pint in a pub with a screen with my name on it, we were late getting out! We arrived at the pub and thought there had to have been a mix-up with the scoreboard. Could we really be 2 up? Guess what – the punter who confirmed the score was a Rangers fan, he was not overjoyed but I had the feeling I was going to remember this birthday!

Again settled in with a steady stream of refreshments but what a reversal on the Edinburgh night! The Rangers fan got happier as I (on the Celts going 3-2 down) let out a few choice words which had me elbowed in the ribs by the long-suffering Denise. Anyway credit to the Rangers fan who was genuine on a handshake at the end, wishing us luck for the next round. That was a tough second-half to watch but Celtic made my 40th!

COLIN R BULLEN

MY enduring memory of this season's UEFA campaign was our visit to Anfield for the second leg of the quarter final. The home support made us Celtic Bhoys and Ghirls feel very welcome and both sets of fans ensured a party atmosphere throughout.

I got the clear impression, though, that the Liverpool support felt that with home advantage the tie was as good as won for them. Once inside the ground and as kick-off approached, the determination and ingenuity of Celtic fans was evident in the numbers of Hoops faithful right throughout Anfield – even the Kop had a green and white contingent!

As to the game itself, the players put on a truly magnificent display. Thommo's goal just before half-time was just what the doctor ordered and with time marching on in the second-half, big John's unstoppable, match-winning volley made my joy complete. The final whistle brought an eruption of noise from the Celtic faithful and signalled the start of post-match celebrations which seemed to last almost as long as the game itself. Our rendition of *Hey Jude,* complete with Celtic lyrics was particularly appropriate.

Funniest moment of the trip was the following day when chatting with a young Everton supporter who had been on steward duty at the Kop end the previous night. He was still not sure how he managed to stop himself from celebrating when Thommo's free kick thundered home just in front of him! For me, no matter if nothing had ever come before this game – nor anything since – for those 90 minutes alone I felt proud and privileged to be part of the Celtic family and will never forget that truly wonderful night in Liverpool.

BRIAN DEVLIN, Ballymena, Co Antrim

I got our tickets as soon as they went on sale from the UEFA website, which was before the Liverpool game.

Everything was set for myself and my boyfriend Matthew to fly out to Madrid via Birmingham on Wednesday, May 21 and then stay a few days in Seville, returning on the Saturday. We didn't reckon on the Passport Office totally ruining everything though! Matthew had sent off his passport about three months previously and he had a recorded delivery package on Monday, May 19. Upon receipt of this, he realised that they had returned his old passport so he went down to Newcastle to try and sort it out but to no avail. The flights were non-transferable so I ended up having to go alone. It was a bit scary to say the least, travelling all the way there and then due to a hold-up at the ticket office, I missed the 3pm train from Madrid to Seville, so had to buy another ticket for the 4 o'clock one. Derek and Connor many thanks and I'm glad you blagged your way onto the train.

The guys on the train were brilliant, they looked after me and we sang all the way from Madrid to Seville (just about got my voice back!) I eventually met up with my cousin Vickie at the game, after waiting around the station for an hour and then going via my hotel to dump my bag. Got a couple of hours' kip on someone's room floor on the Wednesday night then went to my hotel. I had to lounge about from 9am until 1pm when I could book in, and the first thing I did was have a good long soak in the bath. My cousin went home on the Thursday and as you can imagine, being on my own I didn't want to wander too far so stayed mainly by the hotel on Thursday.

I went back into Seville via taxi on Friday, and headed to Flaherty's bar where I met two couples who were totally brilliant. Maureen, Mick, Margaret and John, thank you for looking after me for a few hours. I then went back to the hotel and sunbathed in the car park for a few hours as the hotel pool was closed! Got 10am train back to Madrid on the Saturday, met one of the guys from the Heriot Watt supporters' bus and he took me through the metro system and then got to the airport for my flight home. Tommy from Bannockburn who had been to all the games ('67, '70 and this one) chatted on the flight all the way home. Typically though, I survived going to Seville and back on my own and was verbally abused by a Rangers supporter in Princes Street!

CHRISTINE McFADZEAN

WHAT a week! I have never experienced anything like it. We spent a week in Portugal (Albuferia) awaiting Seville and there must have been over 10,000 fans in Albuferia alone that week.

We sang on the streets and in the pubs morning, noon and night and for the whole time we were there, I never saw anyone step out of line because the fans would not let their club down. Every night we would all gather in Erin's Isle or John's Shamrock Bar and sing until the early hours of the morning.

One night while in Erin's Isle with around another 1,000 Celtic fans, three Porto fans came dancing in, they took one look at all the Celtic jerseys and continued to dance and shout for Porto.

We all joined in and sang with them. They could not believe us. One of them, a short smiling man, came on stage and thanked Celtic for having the best supporters in the world and the funniest.

Well, the place went wild. We could not get him off the stage. At one point I think he thought he was Martin O'Neill as we were singing Martin's name. We all hugged and kissed and said goodbye but two minutes later he was back again. This went on for a long time until his two friends carried him out and still he kept shouting 'I love you Celtic!'

European memories

We brought our little two-year-old Bhoy with us and everyone kept telling us he looked like Larsson. As a typical Celtic fan, I did not waste the opportunity and went and got 'God Jnr' printed on the back of his jersey. On the way to Seville that morning there were hundreds of cars, coaches (120 alone from Erin's Isle, vans, lorries, taxis and even bikes … Yes, we saw two Celtic fans on their way to Seville on a bike (did they know that it was over 100 miles to Seville from Faro).

There were about 10 taxis on the route and the drivers were blowing their horns as much as the rest of us. When we arrived in Seville the sea of green and white could be seen from everywhere. The tour buses were full of Celtic supporters waving their flags out the top. Every fountain and pond in the town was full of very hot and happy Celtic supporters cooling off.

The amount of people who played football with our little boy during the day was remarkable. The amount of photos people took of him on was incredible. Lots of men bought him water and fawned him down during the match (Bhoy, it was warm). When the match was over, after a few shared tears, we got up and sang all the way down from the stadium. Porto fans could not get over it. They kept telling us how brilliant we were and nearly apologising for winning.

All the fans we met that week will forever stay in our hearts and memory. I have been to hundreds of Celtic and Ireland matches both home and away, including a couple of World Cups, but I have never experienced anything like I did that week. I can't put my finger on it but it was magical and even though we did not win anything this year, something has happened to every Celtic fan around the world that no amount of trophies could ever achieve.

That week was not only about football but also about family, sharing memories with those you love. All my family was there, from my mammy and daddy, brothers, husband and son. That day brought us all even closer as we know we shared something that only happens once in a lifetime.

Every one of those Celtic fans was part of my family that day and I know everyone else felt the same.

The smile I have on my face as I think of that sunny week we all spent as the largest family in the world singing and dancing, laughing and crying. I'm holding my head up very high now as people stop me to tell my how brilliant Celtic are (which we have all known for years). I don't think Erin's Isle and John's Bar will never be the same again.

To all the extended family that went to Seville thank you for creating something as close to Paradise as you could get. My heart may be a little sad but my head is so proud it could burst. We will never forget the most magical day in Seville. To see so many Spanish kids wearing Celtic strips and swapping scarves with my little boy before and especially after the match is enough to make you cry with pride.

AISLING KANE, GEORGE COGHLAN, RIAN KANE-COGHLAN (aged 2)
(all from Dublin, living in Galway)
and JOEY, JOSEPH AND MAUREEN KANE (Dublin)

JUST outside the ground before the game was a guy dressed in blonde wig, brilliant white track suit, Hoops top, sunglasses, white trainers, huge medallion and gold rings on most of his fingers.

Everyone was looking at him and thinking 'he looks so familiar, who is he supposed to be?' Then he turned around. The name on the back of the tracksuit was 'JIMMY SEVILLE'.

MIKE GILMARTIN

WHILE lying in my bed in a beautiful hotel in Malaga before setting off on the day of the final, I decided to flick through the TV channels to see if there was any reporting on the mighty Hoops or the final.

I came upon a Portuguese TV channel who were interviewing some Celtic fans in Seville. Obviously the reporter was speaking English to the Hoops fans, asking them how long it took them, how much did it cost them and did they have a ticket? Portuguese subtitles were being displayed for the folks back home.

One large Celtic fan then took centre stage, proclaiming he had sold his house, leaving his family back home destitute in order to attend the final. Well, the reporter was overcome by this man's dedication to the Hoops and the story became a main feature of their news programme.

However, the reporter didn't understand the big man's tone and therefore took him at his word. I wonder if the big man knew what a feature he would be in Portugal. In fact they've probably started a collection for him or some sort of Band Aid-like concert or maybe even a charity football match.

Meanwhile, back to the Portuguese TV channel they now had Jorge Cadete in the studio and were helping him relive his Celtic experience by showing him parading round Glasgow in a kilt, then they cut to this lady singing in Baird's Bar *'There's only one Jorge Cadete...'* then back to the studio where, for the benefit of the Portuguese viewers, Jorge then sung his anthem in Portuguese. It was mad. I was half expecting Tony Roper and Jonathan Watson to walk out next!

TONY McCOURT

HAVING been in a 10-year long and happy relationship with my partner Neil, my impending 30th seemed to be an event to look forward. After all, I had surprised him six months previously with a weekend in Amsterdam and 19 friends, what would he do to top that off?

The cup draw against Blackburn did not frighten me, it was another round, which to get through would be a Celtic supporter's dream, but my nightmare. The match was on my birthday. So then, Neil – "who do you prefer, Celtic or me?" Well, the boys in green won hands down and off he went to Parkhead to watch them against Liverpool, leaving me alone and sad on my 30th. A few drinks with my mum and the girls allowed me to forget of the absence of my beloved.

He did make up for it with a surprise party and a balloon flight. Divine retribution struck at the after-party party on the Saturday with a vodka and coke being spilt over his match programme. The corners of my mouth never formed a smile, honest.

CLAIRE BROWNLIE

AFTER flying home to Glasgow from Vancouver to meet up with my dad, we both flew to Madrid and got a train to Seville. Everywhere we went we saw the Hoops. At first we would acknowledge fellow Celtic fans with a 'Hail, Hail'.

However, amazingly it quickly became passé, and walking around in Seville with

European memories

everyone wearing the Hoops became as uneventful as a stroll down Sauchiehall Street. That epitomises how many Celtic fans there were.

My dad has always regretted not going to Lisbon when he had the chance. So when I bought tickets for the final over the Internet before we had even beaten Liverpool in the quarter-finals, we agreed we would go if Celtic made it to Seville. Upon arriving in Seville on the Tuesday night my dad was like a big kid.

I had also bought two tickets for the Celtic Party at the Prado de San Sebastian and before leaving to go there, my dad phoned home at 9:30pm and left a message telling my mum excitedly that he was off to the party. The reason why this has stayed with me is that my dad had a couple of strokes a few years ago and is usually in bed before 9:00pm.

PAUL SUMMERS, Vancouver

I'M a fire-fighter from Garthamlock, and my wife and I planned a week in Torremolinos after the Liverpool game. After managing to swap my holidays in work we were off to Seville my hook or by crook!

My sister in-law and another 20-30 friends and family all did the same. When we got to Torremolinos, all everyone was talking about was getting to Seville. We were told we would not get on any bus or train as they were full. The whole of the Costa Del Sol was panicking because you were not allowed on any coach without a ticket to the final. We hired a car and left for Seville at 6am on the day of the game. With the paranoia of being pulled up, we had our colours and sombreros in our bags hidden from sight.

We got to Seville an hour-and-a-half later with no problems, and were met by a sea of green and white all searching for the party park where the screen was? After soaking up the atmosphere while searching for it, we heard Rod Stewart was in the hotel and my wife, being a huge Rod fan, couldn't resist passing up the chance to meet her idol. We got chatting to Rod and told him how we were stitched up for tickets like so many fellow Celts and that we were badly let down due to lack of money.

So after buying us several drinks and putting the word around for us he came up to us with a ticket! I couldn't believe it and then he said he might be able to buy us another one, but that we'd have to wait and see. I couldn't believe it – spending the whole day and night with Rod Stewart!

He was telling how he had driven around the city to see the fellow Celt fans and how a huge lump came to his throat when he saw the sea of green and white surround the whole of Seville. He said he saw about two Porto fans looking stunned but happy by it all.

Rod then went away to talk to his pal then came back with another ticket for us! Incredible! The best day of our footballing lives! Thanks Rod, you made our dreams and our shoestring budget of a holiday the best ever!

MICHAEL and GILLIAN KIRK

ALTHOUGH we had won the first leg comprehensively, my brother and I decided to make the trip to Lithuania. Vilnius was a tremendous place and the people both in Vilnius and Kaunas, where the game was played, were very welcoming.

On the flight from Gatwick, the day before the game, one of the guys on the plane was trying to buy duty free – nothing the matter with that – but he was trying to pay in Dollars. The flight attendant told him no chance. When the plane landed there was a coach waiting to transfer us to our hotel. Most people were carrying hand luggage so we passed through passport control quickly and on to the coach. We were missing a few bodies and somebody remarked that one of them included the guy with the Dollars.

A wee while passed and then this guy showed up, dragging a big old suitcase. Everybody was asking him what the craic with the case was as we were only going to be staying for a couple of days. He said he had borrowed a Lithuanian guidebook from the library and in that it said you should take Dollars for currency and that there was a thriving black-market for denims. You've guessed it … the suitcase was full of second hand jeans. What makes this story even funnier is in the centre of Vilnius they have Versace and Armani shops. The suitcase with its contents were consigned to the nearest bin.

PAUL BYRNE

THE small matter of a pre booked family holiday was not going to stop me and my nine-year-old son James from being in Seville. Hastily arranged domestic flights provided the transfer from Tenerife to Seville.

Besides the magnificent support, the highlight for James was meeting Roy Keane wandering along the corridor behind the stands before the game. On returning to Tenerife, the Celtic fans who watched the game in the Irish Fiddler told me that when they walked through the streets of Playa de Las Americas after the game, folk sitting in other bars applauded and cheered as they walked by with the Hoops proudly on display.

GRAEME HORNSBY, Thringstone CSC, Leicestershire

A few European memories …

BASEL: Leaving the stadium I said to my friend Paul Craig, "Who wants to go to Manchester anyway, Seville will be far better."

SUDUVA: Didn't go but watched in Heraghty's, then celebrated radio commentary from Ibrox as they were dispatched by the Pollok Juniors of Prague.

BLACKBURN: Loved asking police and stewards if they thought Blackburn would be good enough for the SPL.

VIGO: The morning after the match, Paul had the mother of all hangovers. I said to him at least the day can only get better. You've got it; we were on *'that flight'*. We both gave interviews to SKY and I spoke to Radio Scotland and did our best to get across how ridiculous the pilot had been.

STUTTGART: I was on the day flight so not many personal tales but my mate Phil Harris met Jimmy Floyd Hasselbank at Gatwick on the way home. He congratulated Phil but added that Liverpool would be too good for Celtic. When Phil answered that the same thing had been said about Blackburn, Hasselbank replied that Rovers were not much of a team. Sharp as a tack, Phil said: "They gubbed you 2-1 last week!"

LIVERPOOL: A couple of complimentaries were left for me at Anfield through Terry McDermott but I was not sure if they were under my name or Terry's. When asked my name, I said McDermott and was then asked my first name to which I answered Terry. "There you are, Mr McDermott," said probably the only woman in Liverpool who didn't know what Terry looks like.

PORTO: Stayed in Don Henrique hotel where 18 months earlier I had spent my honeymoon.

SEVILLE: Arrived on the Sunday. My wife, who speaks Spanish, asked a policeman where we could find an Irish bar for the Hearts/Rangers game. After some explanation he told us to get in the police car and then drove us the couple of miles to it. It set the tone for a great few days.

CHRIS O'NEILL

CELTIC 2-3 FC Porto ... It had yet to settle in. The walk from Celtic Park to Glasgow city centre seemed and endless one. As we turned into the Gallowgate the scenes were unbelievable. Celtic supporters all over the street singing and dancing.

What other club in the world could have 100,000 in Seville while nearly 60,000 were still in Glasgow celebrating? A huge step forward for the not so long ago doomed team. It didn't stop there – even right into the city centre it continued. In the kebab shop in Union Street, the fans' pride in their heroes' display was evident. The bus from Union Street to Paisley town centre was that of a team who had succeeded and not lost.

ROBERT HAMMOND, Paisley

TOGETHER with a small band of Hoops, I have been fortunate enough to make the away legs against Blackburn, Celta Vigo and VfB Stuttgart. Fantastic experiences in their own right, surpassed only by Seville, and a rather eventful trip to Trondheim (but that story will only ever be released on a need-to-know basis).

However, our trip to Vigo this season will go down as one of the great adventures of my life as a Celtic supporter. Upon reflection, it was perfect. A fun town, great weather, welcoming people, and most importantly, a great result against a top-five team from arguably the best league in Europe.

The flight from London to Madrid was pleasant enough, albeit after eight-and-a-half hours on the National Express from Glasgow. In Madrid we managed a trip to the Bernebeu, 'football's Mecca' they say. Not quite Paradise, we noted, although, their trophy room is a wee bit bigger!

After a short baggage debacle in Madrid's main airport – which by now must be more than used to the Bhoys passing through – we boarded our flight to Santiago de Compostela, the beautiful medieval capital of Galicia, and supposed resting place of St. James the Apostle, who in hindsight, must have been watching over us! My good friend Michael Brady, a renowned Euro-trip organiser, had neglected to mention in his itinerary that Santiago Airport was some 45 minutes drive from Santiago train station. We landed at 8.35pm, our train, the last of the night, departed at nine.

After a sprint through the baggage court which would have done Didier Agathe proud, we jumped into the nearest taxi, and in broken Spanish and some French which the driver seemed to understand, we managed to communicate that our train left at nine, and that we would make it worth his while if he got us there in time. It was about then that we noticed that our driver, Jose, was heavily under the influence of some strong substance or other. As he sped down single lane country roads at 130km/h, we covered our eyes. As he attempted to educate us about the history of the region, we prayed to St. James.

We arrived mentally scarred, but intact, at Santiago station at 9.01pm, the train was three minutes late. Suddenly 20 hours or so of travelling became a day at the beach, we were one step closer to the Balaidos Stadium, and we were alive, the meaning of which could only truly be appreciated by those who have first-hand experience of Jose's driving. Mick then proceeded to look for some celebratory cervezas at the station bar.

The old train rolled in slowly, then came to a stop. Myself and my other mates Chris and Stephen began loading the luggage on board. There was still no sign of Mick, but we were sure he would be on his way, and we assumed that a long-distance passenger train would stop for at least a minute at each station.

As Mick appeared from the bar with beers in hand, we boarded the train, looking forward to the last leg of the trip with a few cans and a bit of community singing. As Mick got nearer however, the huge hydraulic doors closed. No problem, I thought. The train wasn't moving yet and besides, the driver could clearly see him making his way towards us. The doors would surely have an 'open' button, or lever, everything was okay. That is, until the train started crawling out of the station, with three out of four Glaswegians on it!

Mick, marooned on the platform began to run after the old ramshackle. I can still see the look of disbelief on his face, it actually amuses me now, but at the time, it was a different scenario. He was a two-hour journey from Vigo, with no apparent means of transport, and on top of that, our hotel was in his name! Luckily enough, Mick managed to get a taxi to Vigo – even if it absorbed most of our funds! We went on to have a great time in that city, which I can say is now home to a large group of adopted Galician Celtic fans, some of whom we still hear from.

John Hartson scored a vital away goal on the night, keeping us in Europe, post-Christmas, for the first time in my life. It was a great game, against quality opposition, and the Bhoys came through for us, showing all of the character which has endeared this Celtic team, and its indomitable manager to thousands of us who follow them now, and forever, over and over.

BARRY JOHNSTON, Kings Park, Glasgow

THE memory I have is trying to get to the Cathedral area by cab and having the cab stopped by the police about half-a-mile away due to the crowds.

Then walking down and seeing CSC flags from all over the world – New York, Cork, Geneva, Australia etc… Walking back to the hotel later after the game was like a scene from Vietnam, with bodies strewn on the street.

TIM DUNNICLIFFE, Brighton

My friends arrived on the Monday and were staying in the same hotel as Paul Elliott, Jim Delahunt and a mixture of assorted press and journalists from around the globe.

My friend Brian Small, whose father was on Celtic's books in the 1950s, got chatting to the Bosnian Dougie Donnelly, whose name was Zoran. He was commentating on the match for Bosnian TV. Zoran was very partial to a G&T ice and a slice, so mixed well with my friends, Brian and Jim Agnew, who, over the course of the night, had found out he had two tickets that were up for grabs.

European memories

On the Tuesday night, when I had met my friends, the deal had been done. They had got the briefs. The only drawback was that whoever went would have to be of smart attire and wearing no colours as they were to be seated beside Zoran in the press box as he does his commentary on the game. So Jim Agnew, who had already had a ticket, and Brian decided that the best two from their party were Frank Reilly and Big Roy.

Frank was a bit disappointed as he had just bought the new strip. The Bhoys met up with Zoran on the day of the game, went along with him to the match and indeed were sitting in the press box as Zoran commentated on the match, passing him little snippets about the Celts as the match went on. Jim Delahunt and Sandy Clark looked on in amazement as they went to their seats, hearing Glaswegian voices in the Bosnian press box.

PAUL LOUGHRAN

MY favourite memory of the UEFA Cup run was watching Celtic face Liverpool. I follow both teams, and both games were great. I was not aware that Celtic fans also sang the song *You'll Never Walk Alone*.

When I heard it during the final against Porto I had to smile. Who could lose with such great teams (Celtic and Liverpool) to follow?

DAVID COLE

MY favourite story is from the night of the final itself. Not being able to travel to Seville I, along with others, watched the game at Parkhead in the Kerrydale Suite. What an atmosphere it – was the next best thing to being there.

My brother and I led from where we were sitting (and standing) chorus after chorus of songs. The atmosphere was incredible and when Henrik scored his two goals the euphoria and emotion was unbelievable. In all my 44 years of following Celtic that atmosphere was equal if not better than anything before, even including the glory days in the Jungle. We still talk of it yet despite the outcome.

When the game ended, we stayed on until asked to go and we sang and sang and people were even holding up their mobiles to let others hear the deafening crescendo. At one stage the table behind us in a period of relative quiet urged us on to start the singing again, which we duly did on top of our seats. I also have to say the staff on duty were great and the service was fantastic. I will never forget the night and look forward to many more

GERARD MONTGOMERY

MY best memory on the Road to Seville is from the second round and the tie with Blackburn Rovers at Ewood Park. I live in an area where Celtic wouldn't be the best-supported team.

Although we have some support, it's Liverpool, Arsenal and Man Utd who would have the biggest fan base. I constantly hear the jibes that Celtic couldn't compete in the Premiership, that the SPL has only two teams, that Henrik Larsson can only score goals in Scotland etc. This despite the fact that he scored more goals in the World Cup than Van Nistelrooy, Henry and Owen put together. As soon as the draw was made I was licking my lips in anticipation of the Celts having a chance to prove them all wrong.

The Road to Seville

Following the first leg, in which we didn't give our best performance, we were absolutely ridiculed. From the 'Men against Boys' taunts to the gloating of the Premiership fans, who believe their league to be untouchable, we were mocked from all corners. What they all forgot was that we actually won that game 1-0.

And so to Ewood Park. I travelled over from Ireland to the game, on a hiding to nothing according to a lot of people back home. No sooner were we in our seats than Martin sprung a surprise on us by naming a changed team. Henrik Larsson, Chris Sutton *and* John Hartson in for this one.

All the hallmarks of a team on a mission. The Darwen Stand was a sea of green and white as *You'll Never Walk Alone* was belted out by the 8,000 or so travelling supporters. Let the battle begin.

Blackburn started slightly the better, with Rab Douglas having to make a couple of early saves. Celtic soon began to settle and on 15 minutes were ahead. Sutton played a perfect through ball and that man Henrik was on hand to chip Brad Friedel and give us a priceless away goal.

Even at that stage I couldn't wait to get home and see a few people! The next 75 minutes bordered on total annihilation as the 'Men' were left with a lot of egg on their face against the 'Bhoys'.

Big Chris finished the job off on his old stomping ground in the second half and the last 20 minutes were played in a party atmosphere as the Celts played around with their more fancied opponents. Blackburn left the field dumbstruck and in total awe of their opponents. The singing continued all the way to Seville…

Celtic proved a few points to a lot of doubters that night. Chris Sutton, branded a flop in England, had the game of his life. Neil Lennon, allegedly too slow for the Premiership, dominated midfield. Rab and his defence stood tall against Champions League winners Yorke and Cole. And, of course, the Magnificent Seven showed yet again that he is a world-class footballer who will score goals for fun on *any* stage. On my return home, with my head held very high, insisting that we had proved ourselves to all the doubters, I was greeted with a new 'argument' – It was only a one-off, we hadn't beaten a top team. The usual rubbish. On a March night at Anfield, with one swing of his right boot, Big John took care of that.

MICHAEL McGRORY, Co Donegal, Ireland

THE three days I spent in Seville were all eventful but the day of the match was superb. Down by the Cathedral the Celtic the fans were gathering in their thousands and thousands. The atmosphere was fantastic and we were all in full song just anticipating the day ahead.

It was like a 'Gathering' of Celtic supporters from around the world. On one side of the street was a New York banner and on the other a Western Melbourne banner. In between these, thousands of supporters mingling with each other and making new friends and contacts around the world.

As I was standing outside McDonald's by the river I saw a crowd of Celtic fans walking up the street all sounding excited as it was now 5pm. Lo and behold, the man leading the group was none other than Billy Connolly, looking very grey but very distinctive with the biggest grin on earth. Even the Big Yin couldn't have missed this gathering. This, to me, this showed the pulling power of such a great club followed by fantastic supporters from all around the world. I didn't manage to get a ticket so watched the match on the big screen. At the end of the night we were robbed of the biggest party in football history by a referee with blinkers and a Portuguese side full of skill but also members of their Olympic diving squad.

The result I could handle but when I looked around and saw just how many supporters we had brought and how much Celtic meant to every one of us, I just cried. I wasn't the only one and if I think back even now, a tear comes to my eye.

CHRIS ATKINSON, Burnley

MY mate got up on the Wednesday morning for work, kissed the wife goodbye and wandered along to Glasgow Airport, where he jumped on a plane to Seville. The wife didn't know anything about it till he fell in at five the following morning!

THOMAS MACKIN

My name is Davide Montini and I live in Torino, Italy. From 2002 I am a Celtic fan. From the match with Stuttgart I followed Celtic in their campaign. I suffered watching Anfield match (on the German network DSF). I suffered against Boavista. It was a very great adventure. Next year, I hope Celtic will meet Juventus.

DAVID MONTINI, Turin

I WAS lucky to spend four days in Seville, a beautiful town with fantastic people who took us to their heart. However, I thought a couple of mildly amusing stories from Celtic fans may be of interest.

I was talking to a Celtic fan from Dublin who had just come out of the nearest hostelry – the Spanish café just up the street from Flaherty's. At the bar, he had asked, in his beautiful Dublin brogue, for six pints of lager. He waited five minutes, then the waiter appeared back with a plate of pasta. The guy said, 'No, No, I asked for six pints of lager,' … or similar more flowery words, and the waiter replied, 'Si, Si a plate of pasta.' And so the story went on. Considering everyone was buying lager he was absolutely stunned. He left with neither pasta nor lager.

At Seville Airport, on Thursday afternoon as I prepared to leave, I went to buy perfume for my wife from duty-free. I was standing at the perfume counter behind this guy who was getting served. Then his mate raced up with a lovely looking bottle and said, 'Get this for me, it will be fantastic for the wife … for cooking. Would you like me to get one for you too?' The first guy looked at the bottle and said, 'Aye, definitely.' I looked down at the bottle and burst into fits. He was buying a bottle of olive oil for his wife. He had just been to Seville for who knows how long, obviously had a ball, and instead of bringing back Chanel they bring back Olive Oil. By this stage the guys were in fits too. I would have loved to have seen their wives' faces when they got home.

GERARD DEVANNEY

MY best match was against Liverpool in Anfield. Being from Wales there was no moment like when super John banged that screamer in. I know Thommo did well but I am so sick of the way the that Scottish football gets slandered and we showed how we are well capable of beating anyone, not just in Europe but in the world

NATHAN SAUNDERS

The Road to Seville

MY favourite episode had to be when a large group of Hoops fans positioned at a roadside cafe with their flags, banners etc, merged with a Spanish Demo. The demo was against education cuts and the marching teachers and pupils held the Andalucian colours (green and white stripes) in a banner.

The two groups were suddenly united by their colours. Celtic fans joined the demo and danced and cheered with the protesters. The teachers and children waved their banners towards the fans and the fans had photos taken with them and made as much noise as the demonstrators.

I also enjoyed the bemused look on the face of our Spanish shopkeeper as we purchased our obligatory sombrero in 'Mini Hollywood' (where *A Fistful of Dollars* was filmed) They couldn't understand why a Mexican symbol was being adopted the Escoceses!

The post-match calm was very impressive as many Spanish people class all British people as 'Ingleses' (English) and English football fans have a terrible reputation in Spain. In the tapas bar we retreated to (across from the Scottish bar) it was nice to see Porto fans sitting chatting to Celtic fans

JULIE FAHY

AS a Celtic fan living on the Wirral (over the water from Liverpool) I get my fair share of stick about the SPL. The night when we beat Stuttgart to get to the next round was when it started – the tension, the excitement, the racing pulse. This was such a massive game for me.

For two weeks in school no work was done. It was just continuous arguments about the game, analysing every player on player, Larsson on Hyppia. Owen on Balde etc ... I wasn't on my own, though. Every Everton, Man United and Tranmere Rovers fan was backing me up.

The night after the match I didn't get a minute's sleep. I lay awake all night with a big smile on my face thinking about the next day. Second lesson I walked into the PE changing room to a massive cheer from every non-Liverpool fan. My Hoops were snatched from me and thrust into the air with chants of *'You're not singing any more.'* Walking home from school I bought three papers, including the *Liverpool Echo,* which was a good laugh to read!

ALISTAIR BOND, (age 16), Wirral

On the Tuesday evening prior to the final, I and the rest of our party passed a bank at the square in the centre of Seville. An Australian Celtic fan said to me that the UEFA Cup was on display in the bank but the doors had now closed.

Undaunted we banged the door and after pleading with the security guards we were let in. Here is the result – We all got tickets to the game and enjoyed everything apart from the result. We hoped that the next person to touch the cup after us would be Paul Lambert but alas ...

JOHN TURLEY, Baillieston, Glasgow

I ATTENDED both the Stuttgart and Liverpool away legs and the atmosphere at both of these was amazing. When Celtic reached the UEFA Cup final, like many other fans, I just had to travel to Seville, despite not having a ticket.

The highlight of my trip, aside from the match itself, was the 'Party in the

European memories

Park' at Prado San Sebastian on the eve of match day. Thousands of Celtic fans splashed about in fountains before crowding towards the stage at the front to hear the band. The sea of green and white bounced up and down in the sticky evening heat, with flags swishing and beach balls flying through the air.

As the darkness fell, the atmosphere was tremendous – words cannot describe it accurately but I knew it was perfect and this was exactly the reason why I made the journey to Seville. I'm sure I was not alone in feeling, at that time more than ever, that there was something special about being a Celtic fan. The Spanish police on duty at the party were even smiling and tapping their feet to the music.

JO FIELD

SO much surrounding Seville is unrepeatable, unique, and quite wonderful but for me a memory that will never fade is my arriving at the top of the Geraldo. For those who don't know, the Geraldo is the minaret turned bell-tower of the Cathedral.

When I and my mate, Hugh, reached the top, we were overwhelmed to hear the serried ranks of Celtic fans surrounding the Cathedral become massed choirs, as they launched into *'You are my Larsson...'* It wafted up to us, hundreds of metres above. Heavenly music indeed. The Lord Himself must have had a wee smile.

G. HAMILL

MY favourite memory, is not the day before, or even the day of the final, but the day after. I remember waking up on the Thursday, walking around Seville, and thinking that something was missing.

There streets were relatively empty; the bars were full of … Spanish people! Then it hit me. What I was missing was all the Celtic fans. There were no masses of supporters in the streets.

There was no sea of white and green Hoops. There were no flags and scarves hanging from the windows and tied to the trees. There were no booming voices singing out all the Celtic songs loudly and proudly.

And that is the memory I will take away with me, how the Celtic fans took over a sleepy Spanish city and turned it into a Green and White Fiesta! Fantastic!

STEFAN HONSTETTER

IT was the Friday after the semi-final when I said to my wife I would love to go to the final. My wife of 26 years who is English, asked me why and I explained the final in any European game does not come round very often. With this in mind, she said why don't you go. I didn't really want to go on my own but my son-in-law said he would go with me.

So that was it. Off to the travel agents next day with the wife at my side to ask them about Seville when all of a sudden my poor wife said, "Where is that in Scotland?" I had never once said it was in Scotland. To be honest I never said where the final was, but being the good wife she is, she still let me go.

My son-in-law and I had a great time like everyone else. By the way, I forgot to say the son-in-law is a Rangers fan, so it shows that we can all mix together and, yes, I will have to return the favour if Rangers get to a final one day.

JIM McCABE

The Road to Seville

MY five pals and I had an epic journey to the final. I wish I had time to tell you all the details but essentially, we flew to Madrid via Gatwick, then drove to Albufeira in the Algarve then onto Seville and back again to Madrid. We returned the rental car to Madrid with less than a minute to spare. If we'd missed the return time, we'd have had to pay for the car!

We all felt like we'd lived two or three lifetimes in the few days we were in Spain and there has been no experience in any of our lives to match the one in Seville. We lost, but it actually felt like we won by just getting there and the party atmosphere before and after the game made it feel like we won by a country mile! There simply is no-one like the Celtic fans anywhere. We covered the whole city of Seville like some massive green and white blanket and partied under for the best part of a week – without even the slightest hint of trouble or hassle.

JIM LOUGHRAN, Charing Cross, Glasgow

AFTER the semi-final against Boavista I decided I was going to Seville, with or without a ticket. Having searched the Internet for a flight and a few nights' accommodation I then decided to make a week of it for my girlfriend and myself, so booked a week in Fuengirola.

We were to leave on Saturday, May 17. The Thursday before we were due to go I received a phone call from my cousin Gerald Hendricks telling me he had managed to get me a ticket for the game. He only had one. My girlfriend understood what this meant to me and was quite willing to stay in the hotel. I was over the moon, like an excited child.

We left home on the Saturday morning for a few hours drive to Gatwick Airport all ready to go to Seville, the excitement rising. We spent a few days in the sun and when the day came I travelled to Seville on a coach organised by the hotel. We got to Seville quite early in the morning. I had arranged to meet my cousin in Seville centre. In my haste and excitement I didn't take any sun cream with me, thinking I would be okay as I had a Welsh flag which I wrapped around my legs to offer some protection.

I soaked up the atmosphere in Seville, which was amazing. During the course of the day I could feel my legs burning but wasn't too concerned as I had the biggest game of my life to look forward to. I got to the stadium and took it all in – the flags, the noise and the huge Celtic support. The excitement by now was building up inside me ready to explode. All the while my legs were killing me and I was glad for my seat. The team took to the pitch and my excitement spilled over along with the thousands of other fans inside the stadium. During the course of the match I looked at my legs which were red raw, at which point I started to get concerned, especially when I saw the blisters forming around my ankles.

The second-half kicked off and Henrik scored a goal. I tried to stand to celebrate and realised the legs wouldn't let me. The second Celtic goal went in and again I tried to stand but the pain was so intense, the blisters by now were getting bigger as were the size of my ankles. After a few more minutes I decided to see if I could find some first aid help to perhaps give me some cream or something just to soothe them.

I spoke to one of the security men who summoned a policeman. He told me he was going to call an ambulance, I begged and pleaded not to send me in the ambulance, but he insisted. Three policemen then helped me on to the stairway and told me to wait. An ambulance appeared and, not being fluent in Spanish, I could only say over and over "No hospital, no hospital." The ambulance man pulled my trainers off and started saying "Ay, ay, ay," over and over. The other two ambulance personnel came over and had a look and then invited the policemen to take a look. Over and over I kept hearing "Ay, ay, ay."

I was more concerned about missing the game and the ambulance man assured me the hospital was in the stadium and so I would still see the game, or at least I thought. Whisked away in the ambulance lights flashing sirens wailing didn't fill me with too much hope of seeing any more of the game. Having reached the hospital within the stadium I was stretchered in to the treatment room, trying desperately to find out if they had a TV so at the very least I could still see the game – not a chance!

The doctors and nurses came swarming around me, speaking all at once. Again I was greeted with lots of "Ay, ay, ay," which I can only assume was something like, "Oh my God!" Luckily a lady who spoke English came and stood beside me. She told me I had suffered second degree burns to my legs caused by the effects of the sun. All the while I could hear the fans screaming and shouting. I kept asking what the score was and holding my fingers up asking 2-2. One of the doctors pulled out a camera and started taking photos of my legs. She then pointed the camera at me and took a photo. My legs were treated and bandaged and I was being instructed by the English-speaking nurse as to what I should have done regards sun cream.

One of the doctors was looking at me and speaking to the nurse who spoke English. She asked me about my Celtic shirt – did I buy it in Seville or bring it with me? I told her I'd received it the Monday before I left, saying it was the newest Celtic shirt. She then told the doctor, and I asked if he would like to try it on. He asked for the camera and then asked for my shirt, I took it off and gave it to him and he happily stood and posed for a photo.

I then took my camera and took a photo of him. He then sat beside me, grinning from ear to ear and gave a big thumbs up while another photo was taken. I took the opportunity and passed my camera to the nurse who took a snap for me. I motioned for the other doctors and nurses to join us and so I have a group photo of myself and the staff at the hospital stadium. I heard a roar from outside and asked if someone could find out who scored. My heart sank when the nurse came back and told me it was Porto. I had quite a walk to get to my bus and was caught in between leaving there and then or going back inside. I heard the cheer going up by the Porto fans and realised it was all over, so decided to go.

The English-speaking nurse told me it had been a pleasure to meet the Celtic fans and praised us on our attitude and behaviour. I felt as though I had made a few new friends but left for the long walk with a heavy heart. I at least have my memories of Seville and photos of a very, very pleased Spanish doctor looking proud to wear the Hoops.

ANDREW HOEY

I WAS living and working in Aberdeen, Washington during the earlier rounds and managed to watch the games in Kell's Bar, home of the Seattle CSC.

The kick-off time was usually about noon, Pacific Standard Time. Unfortunately, on the day of the second-leg against Stuttgart, I had an important meeting to attend and therefore could not take the day off to go to Seattle for the match. I had to endure the agony of keeping up with the game on the UEFA website, which meant watching a text commentary which refreshed itself every two minutes. When Celtic went 2-0 up, I began to relax and sat back with an inane grin on my face, which somewhat unnerved my American colleagues.

Imagine my horror as the Germans fought back to go 3-2 ahead on the night. My agony was confounded as, with some 15 minutes or so still to play, I was summoned to the meeting, knowing that another two German goals would knock us out. I contributed to and took absolutely nothing from that meeting, which lasted all of two hours. It took me 45 minutes to drive home, the longest 45 minutes of my life, before I was able to go to the Celtic website and get the final result. Text commentary? Never again.

TOM McLAUGHLIN, Motherwell

LAS VEGAS to St Louis to Chicago to Glasgow to Seville and back, a week I will never forget. Standing to check-in at Glasgow my young cousin walks past, he too on his way to Spain.

Meeting my mum's neighbour, Peter Hickey, the man who used to take me to the games when my father was working right outside the stadium after the match. Just a few memories of the fourth greatest day in my life – after my Bhoys' births and my wedding. Had to say the wedding part as who else would have let me travel halfway across the world without a ticket to see a soccer match?

PAUL BREDIN, Las Vegas Celtic Supporters' Club

Add another country of origin to the list of where Celtic fans travelled from for the game – LIBYA! Well, indirectly, as I work there and was not meant to be at the final due to my work schedule getting me home the Tuesday after the game.

My wife's father died the week before the game. I got permission to get home on the Friday for the Saturday morning funeral. Saturday afternoon I had my flight arranged. Monday at 10.45pm I successfully bid £550 on e-Bay for a ticket then off to Seville on the Wednesday morning.

Words cannot adequately describe the 45-minute walk from the stadium around 2.30pm to meet up with friends in the Bar Espanol in Calle San Fernando. Suffice to say it was easy to see that there had to be at least twice the number of fans who actually made it into the stadium.

JIM McCANN Glasgow.

SOME people have called me the luckiest man in Seville. I was a season ticket holder for many years, but gave it up went I went to work in Germany. I went to Seville with two of my friends, both still season ticket holders. None of us had tickets, but were hopeful of picking some up in Seville.

Both my friends got tickets on the day of the game, but at a price I would not have paid. I walked up to the stadium with them in the hope of a last-minute ticket. I was walking around the stadium hopefully when I heard two people discussing a pair of tickets. The seller was only interested in selling them as a pair, but the buyer only wanted one. The seller moved off and I followed him and offered to buy

European memories

the pair. I bought two 60Euro tickets for 150Euros and found the person who was initially offered them and sold him one for 75Euros. I ended up in the main stand next to the press area in a great seat.

ALISTAIR

Our journey to Seville started in Melbourne, Australia the Friday before and my mate Alex Buntine and I were looking forward to catching up with family in Seville and watching the game on the big screen as we were informed two hours before departure that the tickets that we had bought and paid for on the internet were now not available.

We were sick and the 22-hour flight to London was filled with thoughts of how to pay back the shyster in Hamburg whom we had paid our hard-earned dough to. I was meeting my daughter Kirsty, who is backpacking around Europe in London, and I had to practice smiling before I walked out of customs at Heathrow to greet her. She was as gutted as I was and told me that she had cried for the last 24 hours because she knew how much Celtic meant to me. She had never seen Celtic live but has never missed a game on telly for the last 17 years, bearing in mind that we see Celtic in the middle of the night!

After staying in London until Tuesday, we flew to Madrid as there were no flights to Seville. Alex, Kirsty and I picked up our hire car and headed out of the airport and started on the motorway. After about five minutes of driving I suddenly realised that I had no idea where I was heading. Mild panic set in as we tried different ways of determining if we were heading south, i.e. sun at our backs, Madrid on our left, all the things you learned as a Boy Scout at Auchingillan.

We eventually took an exit and pulled along side a large Mercedes and in our best broken Spanish asked if we were on the right road to Seville. He looked surprised until he saw the Hoops tops and said, "Ah Celteec, follow me" and he turned off the motorway and drove back the other way, finally pointing us to the right road. We had been driving for 45 minutes the wrong way!

We settled into our journey and enjoyed the scenery and finally stopped a few hours later at a roadside service stop where we met two Argentinean truck drivers who knew all about Celtic and our great history. We spent a wonderful 45 minutes with them and gave them two Jock Stein Celtic Supporters' Club tops from Melbourne and got our pictures taken in front of their trucks, one of which had the Sacred Heart on one side and the Virgin Mary on the other side. After forgetting something and running back inside, I was humbled to see the two of them were wearing their new tops and were telling the Spanish locals about their new amigos.

We continued on to Seville arriving around 8.30pm and were overwhelmed at the scenes of green and white everywhere. We made our way to San Sebastian Park for the concert which was an experience we will never forget. Alex found his family from Port Glasgow in the crowd, which was a feat in itself, and Kirsty and I had to leave around 11pm to meet up with Maria Garcia, who was a friend of my brother-in-law's. She had said that we could sleep at her place. She lived right in the centre of Seville and we found her pretty quickly. We assumed that once she showed us our beds that the night was over but she asked us at midnight did we fancy a drink and something to eat, so we then disappeared into the night and joined thousands of Celts on the streets and went to a little Tapas bar across from her place.

The Road to Seville

What a night we had. The food and drink was fantastic, matching the colourful atmosphere. I said to her that she must use this pub a lot as everybody seemed to know her, but she said that they all knew her because of her job which was reading the news on Spanish telly! Kirsty and I kept her going with stories of Celtic until the not so early hours of the morning. By the time we went to bed the sun was coming up and Maria was slightly the worse for wear, (I think it was something she ate!)

We were up for 8am and Alex met me at the scene of the previous night's concert as we didn't want to miss anything and Maria took us to her favourite breakfast place, which was alongside the Cathedral. Thousands of mad Celts were congregating there to start their day of worship. After about an hour we were approached by a Spanish guy who whispered out of the corner of his mouth that he had tickets to sell. After subjecting him to various checks and telling him that life would not be worth living if they were fakes, we parted with our Euros and emerged, singing and dancing, into the throng with our tickets hidden on our bodies, ensuring that we were not letting them out of our sight. I even kissed the scalper on both cheeks (as you do in Spain).

We then enjoyed the sights around Seville, with Maria taking us to various bars along the river. She told me that she started at 3pm to get ready for the news and I suggested to her that perhaps she might lay off the beer a bit. She assured me that she was fine but I wonder what the Spanish thought of their newsreader at 6pm that night because I am sure she would have appeared to be a bit off colour, although she said that the make up department would hide most things!

You know the rest. We walked to the game and back for hours, broke our hearts at the game, but I will live with the memories of Kirsty and I seeing our first live match together forever. We are all extremely proud of our Bhoys and despite the season's end we are still happy with what they achieved.

To all the Celts who made it to Seville, by whatever means, I salute you on the way you conducted yourselves. To Kirsty, I know this memory will live forever and now you know what being a Celt is all about and to Alex, thanks for the wonderful time and your fantastic company.

BILLY McLAUGHLIN, Melbourne

I HAVE travelled a few places to see the Bhoys and was ecstatic to get to Seville. On the day of the game we were dropped off at the stadium about 11.45am and I made my way into the town centre for a prearranged meet with some mates.

Due to the heat and the wife not wanting to walk very far, I decided to pop into a posh-looking hotel to ask if I could phone for a taxi. This hotel was about three quarters of a mile from the stadium. As I approached the hotel entrance, I was stopped by two policemen who asked were I was going. I realised that they were having great difficulty in understanding my accent when another two appeared, By this time it looked as though I was causing a scene but I was only asking to gain entry to phone a taxi.

The hotel manager appeared and in very good English told me to go away. I was having great difficulty understanding what's going on when all of a sudden a camera crew appeared and a coach pulled up, which I could just see out of the corner of my eye.

European memories

It turns out this was the Porto team hotel and the coach was coming to pick them up at this exact moment. As the players came out and went on to the coach it made me laugh that they saw me as some kind of threat me standing there with the Hoops on and the shorts. If only I had kicked a couple of them!

JAMES and PAULINE SWEENEY

I HAVE restarted this letter a thousand times, each with a special moment remembered on the Hoops' Road to Seville. I now must conclude that, besides the overall spectacular performance of The Blessed Martin and the Magnificent 'Tic, my everlasting memory will be of the fans, the 'Fiesta Grande' and the news coverage of the travelling support.

To the watching world, even Satcchi & Satcchi could not have sold us better! My son was there, financed by us for his 21st birthday! Maybe not the traditional gold watch, but memories made of purer gold than any Swiss timepiece! He slept with friends for three nights in a hired Ford Ka and endured a marathon journey of 'Jules Verne meets the Wacky Races'.

If I had trouble knowing where to begin my memories, I now have even more deciding where to end them!

DANN1K

I LIVE and work in Australia, staying about an hour's drive from Melbourne. The final was being telecast at 4.45am on Opencast channel but I chose to travel up to the city to watch it at the Celtic Club in the central business district of Melbourne.

I parked up at my cousin's and we caught a taxi to the club. Up the elevator to the room which was broadcasting the game live on two big screens. A sea of green and white Hoops in the middle of the floor. We all hooked into pints of lager in the wee hours of the morning. What a game! The goals! We were coming from behind all through the match.

And I was hoping for a goal or two which, as we all know too well, occurred. The Celtic Club erupted. Anyway the end of the game came and the result wasn't what we wanted, but you couldn't take away the excitement it had generated. It was about 7.30am and we all staggered out of the Celtic Club, drunk and dissatisfied, but thrilled we were in a final of such significance, the UEFA Cup.

PETER SHARKEY, Melbourne Glasgow Celtic Supporters' Club

AS a long time resident of Hong Kong, it has been a mighty interesting season for us expatriates in a land where there is virtually no Scottish football coverage on local television stations.

The normal situation for the members of the South China CSC is to get together every Thursday night and hope that the tapes will have arrived by courier to allow us to see the previous weekend's action. Not so this season. The combined forces of broadband, CelticTV and pay-per-view, brought many a European game into my wee study at home in the small hours.

The matches v Basel, Suduva, Blackburn, Celta Vigo and Stuttgart followed a similar pattern. Set the alarm clock for about 2.30am, get up and watch the match on a tiny computer screen. It really is quite surreal to be sitting in your boxer shorts, stone cold sober in the middle of the night, shouting away, watching the match while

The Road to Seville

all your high-rise neighbours are fast asleep. Of course, when the matches were over about 4.30am, it was clearly impossible to switch off the adrenaline and go back to bed and certainly far too early to even think about going to the office. The end result was therefore a couple of days of jet lag-type symptoms. (Every two weeks!)

Cometh the mighty Liverpool, Hong Kong TV, with its voracious appetite for all things Premiership, finally took an interest. A slight variation on my usual routine, therefore, and we all headed for the Dublin Jack pub in Hong Kong's Central District at three in the morning to watch as a group on the big screens. Unimaginable joy after the second leg and we found ourselves in a disco at six in the morning drinking beers in celebration. We still made the office by 8.30am, although productivity proved to be non-existent for the rest of the day.

Semi-final time and a decision had to be made. Which leg should I go to? Luckily I decided on the away leg and after a couple of days in Glasgow to get over the long journey, we breezed into Oporto for less than 24 hours, hoping and praying. That last semi-final in 1974 of Ayala and Juan Carlos Lorenzo et al seemed a lifetime away. The suddenness of Henrik's late goal, the agony of the clock running down over the last 12 minutes and the sheer explosion of emotion at the final whistle. Unconfined joy. I didn't even get too drunk afterwards but wanted to soak it up and enjoy every second.

My mobile never stopped as congratulatory messages poured in from Scotland, Hong Kong and elsewhere. Back to Hong Kong, after a successful stopover at Ibrox-on-the-beach, and returned to an even greater lack of productivity in the office. The trip to the final had to be planned quickly.

A couple of nights limbering up in Marbella then 50 of us set off by coach at 7am on the morning of the final, bizarrely ignoring the possibilities of a two-hour motorway journey and opting instead for the four-hour tourist highland route to Seville. Glorious weather and cold beers were never far away and I lost count of the number of people that I bumped into over the course of the day, many of whom I had not seen since leaving Scotland over 16 years ago. It was simply just great to be there and emphasised to me at least; the cruelty of losing in a semi-final which denies everyone the opportunity to assemble in mass for a party at the final. Better to lose in a European final than not to be there at all.

It was a party. Inside the stadium the singing was fantastic, the team gave their all, especially in that second-half and in extra-time. Defeat on the night, yes certainly. Failure, definitely not. We love our team dearly and passionately. Seville was a pilgrimage, a gathering of the Celtic family from all around the world. An occasion to truly savour for all time. Who knows when the next opportunity will arise?

ROBERT GROME, Hong Kong

IT will live with me forever. From Stuttgart, where there were so many, to Seville where there were at least five times more. The party was awesome and a credit to the club as was the performance of the team.

Larsson's second goal will live in the memory forever. So will the Bhoy who gave the Spanish barman his new Hoops top. The barman said, "Thank you senor, is that for me?" "No," said the Bhoy. "I will be back for the 2005 Champions League final so have it washed and cleaned for me."

MARTIN MELDRUM

European memories

WE were in a pub in Seville and the TV was showing a bullfight. Many of the supporters were drawn to the event, watching the matador spear the helpless animal and to the tune of *'C'mon the Hoops'* came the chant *'C'mon the bull'*.

PAT KENNEDY

AFTER the game, my two brothers are walking home, feeling fairly disappointed at the result. On coming across a pub that other Celtic fans were trying to get a drink, one fan shouts to his mate, "What ye wanting?"

Reply: "A pint." "They've only got Vodka left." Reply: "Well then, a pint of Vodka!" … Cheered them up no end.

KEVIN O'NEILL, BURNSIDE

I HEARD a funny story regarding a street vendor in Seville selling Celtic T-shirts. One of my fellow supporters who speaks the lingo told me that the words on the shirt should have read *'Hail, Hail the Celts are here!'*

The Spaniard obviously lost a bit in the translation as it literally spelt *'Hailstones, Hailstones the Celts are here!'*

FRANK MUNGALL

BUYING beer from a local, who was selling it from a shopping bag that your gran used to have, and being handed a pack of sausages at the same time.

It took a while to figure out that he had put them in there frozen to chill the beer. The beer was terrible but the sausages went down a treat.

STEVE WALLS

MY lasting memory is just being in the stadium when Celtic ran out. I just stood in awe. I'm 35 and I just burst oot greetin'. And I also got my photo taken with Rod Stewart as well. Memories forever in Celtic.

DAVID COOTE, Duntocher

IT is now well-documented that there were a number of forged tickets for the Blackburn away game and many people with genuine tickets were refused entry. Myself and four friends were unfortunately among them.

Leaving the ground totally dejected wondering what to do next, we headed down Bolton Road towards Blackburn centre surrounded by rows of houses that would be best described as Coronation Street. The occupiers were standing at their front doors exchanging pleasantries with the Celtic support when, in jest, I asked one elderly lady if it would be possible for myself and friends to watch the game in the comfort of her house. We were totally amazed at her reply. 'Wait there I will ask my husband.'

One minute later we were sitting in their back lounge watching the game live on TV, with the Jack Walker Stand some 50 metres from the lounge window. We will be forever grateful to May and Joe Gilmour of Bolton Road, Blackburn.

May, incidentally, hails from Bridgeton Cross in Glasgow. We were particular grateful for the exclusive use of her kettle and coffee jar and also for her generous hospitality at half-time.

VINCENT HARKINS

The Road to Seville

CELTIC v PORTO
Larsson, Petrov
Thompson, ball
Kicking, passing
Then a fall

Tripping over
Porto's act
All intended
To distract

Agathe runs
Down and up
All he wants
Is to get the cup

Balls flying
Into nets
Everyone making
Lots of bets

Bobo's shouting
Disagreeing
With that man
Who's refereeing

I think that
Porto did cheat
Tripping over
Their own feet

Poor old Celtic
Out in Spain
Didn't even
Win the game!

By KARYN BAXTER (age 11), Newton Stewart
(PS: I wrote this for my dad for when he came back from Seville.)

MY husband and I travelled from Torremolinos to Seville and had the most fantastic time and heard some great tales during our week's holiday. We arrived on the Saturday before the game and had to organise transport to Seville for ourselves and 12 others from the Neil Lennon CSC who were arriving on the Tuesday.

After looking into other forms of transport he decided to get a price for a 55-seater bus and put a note in reception to see if anyone was interested. We then went out for the day, only to return to the hotel at night to find 95 names on the list and lots of pieces of paper under our hotel room door with peoples' names,

European memories

hotels or room numbers on them. My frantic husband then rushed to try and book another bus successfully, then spent three sleepless nights worrying that the buses wouldn't turn up. The sight of 110 people milling about our hotel – the Royal Park in Torremolinos – at 7.30am on that Wednesday morning will stay with me forever. Thankfully the buses turned up and we had a fantastic day, whatever the result.

LYNN KARTE, Stirling

I TOOK my wife to Seville on a one-night trip. After arriving at the coach park at the stadium, the rep informed us that the bus would be there after the game. We made our way to the city centre where we had something to eat and met up with friends and family.

Had a great day (other than result). I went to the game with the men. My wife went to watch it on the big screen with her sister, daughter, niece and friend. After the game we went to get the bus but it had been moved! My friend and I eventually found the bus after about one hour. Meanwhile, my wife was looking for it with my daughter but they could not find it. I went on the bus going to Jerez Airport, hoping my wife would get there, either by taxi or coach.

When I arrived at the airport there was no sign of my wife who, incidentally, had my passport and both mine and my friend's flight tickets. We waited for her but to no avail, so what do I do? I spoke to the rep who informed me that my wife was at Seville Airport with tickets and passport! The British consulate representative got me and my friend on a plane home to Glasgow where the rep had informed me my wife would be waiting.

On arriving at Glasgow at 7am, there was still no sign of my wife. I had no house keys to go home, so I waited on flights from Seville for seven hours. At 2pm, I called home to be greeted on the other end of the phone by my wife who had been put on plane to Prestwick Airport.

I arrived home at 4pm to meet my wife for the first time since before the match.

FRANK CASSIDY

I CAN remember walking with my dad from a restaurant beside my hotel, towards the Cathedral in Seville. The road was surprisingly quiet but you could hear the party in the distance. As we took a short cut up an alley towards the madness there was a group of about 10 men, all decked out in blue and white Porto strips.

But we'd walked too far to turn on our heels and run. As we got beside the Porto supporters they started singing their songs and having a bit of a joke. It was all very light-hearted, not as you would get walking through an alley full of your rival supporters in Glasgow before a European Cup final. So as we were walking away, a man in a Porto strip came running up beside us from them, he said in broken English, "You go Catheeedral? I come with you."

We were walking along the street with this man, who looked a bit worse for wear and had obviously had a night on the tiles. We were worrying about the prospect of bringing a Porto fan into the Cathedral with us as it was our first night in Seville and we never knew how friendly the atmosphere was. I said to my dad, "I hope he's not expecting us to jump in for him," and the man in blue and white, turned and said "Eet is only a gayme!"

The Road to Seville

I informed him it was the UEFA Cup final and it was a lot more than life and death. This comment was greeted with a blank look, the man ripped off his Porto shirt and burst into a rousing chorus of *'Hail! Hail! The Celts Are Here!'* in a rough Glaswegian brogue. He was from Dennistoun and had swapped jerseys with a Porto fan! I thought this summed up the atmosphere of Seville. We were all there for the craic, win lose or draw,

CHRIS WALSH, East Kilbride

THIS was the trip of a lifetime. We set off from Perth, Western Australia, on Sunday, May 18. On arriving at Perth Airport to check in for our flight to Bangkok, we met two Celtic fans in the queue. It was then it really dawned on me how special this adventure was going to be.

On arriving in Bangkok, the first thing I saw was the Hoops, as we came across another long-distance traveller, joining us on our journey to Rome and then on to Madrid. Seville was fantastic. The game was unbelievable. Oh to have won!

The memory that will stay with me forever is sitting having dinner on Thursday night at a Tapas Bar in Seville, still singing the songs and chatting to the locals. A local girl walked towards our table in a green skirt and white shirt. We all started singing *'Verde-blanco, verde-blanco, verde-blanco por la senorita.'*

As she passed our table, she turned to go into her building, put the key in the lock, turned around to us as we stopped singing, and sang *'Hail! Hail! De Celts are here!'*

This brought a huge cheer, and we got her to sit down with us. She spoke very good English and told us how much the Celts had touched the people of Seville, in particular the story of an old, 83-year-old lady who sits down by the river feeding the birds every day.

On the Thursday this little old lady, in her wheelchair, called our new friend over and asked the result of the match. On hearing the score she said she was so sad for these Scottish people, she had so wanted them to win as they have shown so much passion for their team and brought so much joy to everybody in Seville.

The girl in Verde-blanco was actually a one-woman performer of the opera *Carmen,* and had re-worded one of the *Carmen* songs with a tribute to Celtic, and was apparently filmed by BBC Scotland.

ANDREW RIGG

RICH or poor we were all united in Celtic! It was wonderful to watch the thousands of Celtic fans march to the Estadio Olimpico, wearing the Hoops with pride. It seemed like everyone was wearing them!

As I entered the stadium complex it was my great pleasure to have a photo taken with Eddie Jordan (racing car owner). He was, of course, also wearing the Hoops with pride.

At Seville Airport the day after the game, my brother who now lives in Barcelona, managed to have a quick chat with Radomir Antic (Barcelona manager) who was extolling the virtues of the Celtic support and commenting on the wonder of Henrik Larsson. We know how wonderful we are as a support but its great to hear seasoned observers confirm it for us.

KEVVYBHOY

European memories

TOO many memories to mention – all fantastic. The best part was being in the stadium in Seville, standing with my sister Charlotte, arm-in-arm watching the Huddle and the crowd go crazy and flashing cameras. Tears of emotion were aplenty.

Sitting in one of the many Plazas watching local families of Seville join in the party and exchanging Celtic memorabilia with the fans, and their children copying us, shouting *'C'mon the Hoops'* even though they had no idea what they were singing. No other team in the world could create what the Celtic fans had in Seville.

CATHERINE EWING

I WAS in South Carolina with my wife and frantically drove the four hours to Charlotte in North Carolina to join the Celtic Supporters' Club there to watch the game live in the local bar.

Arriving at the bar at 2.30pm (kick-off 2.54pm), we were horrified to find the bar closed and no-one around! Just a few seconds before all sanity was lost, a lovely young girl, Amy, drove up and in her Glaswegian accent, asked if we were looking to watch the final. She then got us to follow her car to a local Irish Bar. We went into the bar, only to find out that their TV was broken! 2.40pm

We ran round to another Irish Bar, Connolly's, just in time to see the teams kicking off. Within 5-10 minutes there were about 20 of the Bhoys in the bar giving an amazing atmosphere. Just after Henrik scored his first goal, the satellite went down! Out came the mobile, and I phoned my mother-in-law in Coatbridge to find out the latest score. She said it was 2-2! Never! So I called another friend in England who also confirmed 2-2. By then almost all the Bhoys were on their mobiles calling home and asking for them to be put beside the TVs! It started belting down with rain outside and we demanded that the bar owner get the satellite fixed. He grabbed his umbrella went out onto the roof and two minutes later the game was back on!

The silence was deafening when Porto scored the third goal, then *'We are Celtic Supporters'* started to ring out in the bar until the end of the game. We may have lost, but in every other respect we won. I have always been proud to be a Celtic supporter, but never more so than in that bar surrounded with fellow Bhoys, whom I had never met before and will always be with me when I recall May 21, 2003.

GERRY MORROW

STUTTGART v Celtic ...I got the call from my season ticket-holder husband to book some flights after the Blackburn game, and to hold accommodation on both possible nights. I did as requested: February 20 – a little expensive, February 27 – cheap or what! After all. He'd been to all the other matches both home and away!

As it happened the Bhoys went to Stuttgart for February 27, so the 20th was cancelled. Bit of a shame, though, because our daughter was at school that week. After some persuading, the grandparents came up trumps (I think they may be Celts anyway, although they won't admit it to me!)

We set off from home to Leeds/Bradford Airport at some unearthly hour, flying with KLM via Amsterdam to Stuttgart. We arrived in Amsterdam at about 9.00am and the next thing is, we are on the port and brandies, as we had rather a long wait before our connection to Stuttgart. When we eventually boarded the flight to Stuttgart, we were surrounded by the Hoops. It was fantastic.

The Road to Seville

The air stewardesses took all the supporters to their hearts and even made a special announcement to wish the 'Celtic Glasgow' (as they do in Europe) all the best for their match. It was a lovely touch and very special to us all on that flight. We could not wait to reach our hotel, drop off bags, and get amongst the throng.

Andy and I have travelled around a lot in Europe, but this was a very special trip. The fans were there in their thousands. There were so many German Celtic supporters too. We had a fantastic afternoon, and it was all topped by me meeting my long lost friend from when I studied in Germany in the '80s, who had bought the tickets for us, but in the Stuttgart End. He posted them to us, as he was not sure he could make the game. He eventually turned up at Stuttgart Railway Station … in a Celtic Shirt.

We had to have a couple of Steins together before heading for the stadium. He took us on the U-Bahn and I recall eating a Bratwurst outside the ground, accompanied by a beer (unbelievable) and then I remember having a very in-depth conversation with Hoopy. This game was a winner all the way. We beat Stuttgart over the two legs, but they won at home and I am so proud to recall the acknowledgements between the home and away support as goals were scored – there were plenty in this game. Every time a goal went in the net, we all cheered for each other and shook hands – it was fantastic. And I remember reading all the fantastic stories in the *Celtic View* from Stuttgart supporters who had really enjoyed the game – to a man they wanted Celtic to go all the way!

My favourite recollections of this trip were the following comments:

'How can they drink so much?' The barmaid in the Dorint Hotel.

'I just want you to know that it has been a pleasure to serve you in our hotel and I hope you come back soon,' Breakfast server in the Dorint Hotel to the Bhoys after the game.

I think the reply she got was something like "my wife doesnae say things like that to me!"

On the bus from the airport terminal to the aircraft from Stuttgart to Amsterdam, the singsong started and a comment was made about Cardiff, (ie: if you sing you may get diverted!) but when they started with *"If you're happy and you know it, nod your head!"* we were creased. I am a Celt, and this trip was very special as it showed the supporters in their very true light.

Meeting in Seville was different again. The calls were coming through on the mobile phones from here, there and everywhere. The guys we met on holiday back in 2002 were ringing to see where we were. They so wanted to be in the crowd. I'm sure I speak for thousands when I say that the time we spent in Seville's Square is one that will never leave me. It was a tremendous feeling to be a part of a very successful football club. I remember the moment when I tried the ticket in the turnstile to see whether it would let me in – it went green and it was okay, but to see the match I had to be in the Porto end while my husband was in his Celtic end. We cheered, with the goals, but it was hard at the Porto end. The Bhoys did us proud. We walked for miles to get back to the centre of Seville and the mobile would not function, but eventually we found our partners.

Thursday was amazing. Tricolours, Hoops and Celtic sombreros all over. We got to the airport and it was bedlam. It was not until the flight lifted off the ground that I realised what we had all come to see, and that was when it hit me… the tears came and I was so sad that we had come so near and yet lost so much! The Celtic army is unique in every aspect.

A CARPENTER, Leeds

BEANN MHADAGHAIN CSC MEMORIES OF SEVILLE

After long trips to Suduva, Vigo, Stuttgart and Oporto, and a little jaunt across the Irish Sea to Blackburn and Liverpool, it was 4.00am on the Sunday before the greatest night of most of our lives. Fifty or so bhuoyant Bhoys and Ghirls arrive at Belfast International Airport, for the first leg of our memorable journey to Seville, via Torremolinos. The craic's 90 and everyone is fresh-faced and raring to go (aye right!) The flight's on time so everyone gets checked in and head straight for the bar.

I didn't realise that so many were afraid of flying. Well, that's the reason most give for having a pint. "Its medicinal," was the cry from the three amigos.

Now the three amigos are a hefty trio (shirt sizes XL, XXL and XXXL) and certainly contributed to the massive rise of alcohol sales on the Costa Del Sol. But rooming with them, was a certain Mr Devlin. It may be no surprise to any that know him, but Liam was sober for all of six hours in the whole week, and that was to see the match. But what a character to have with us – Norman Wisdom, Chubby Brown and Ronnie Biggs rolled into one. I use the latter, cause he must have done a Ronnie Biggs to get here.

Arriving at the Apartments, El Pinar, to find fellow Celts from our native Belfast, (a certain Mr Ward standing at reception, giving Devlin a run for his money) Scotland, England, Canada and America. We were here and what a buzz it was. Allocation of rooms sorted and it's off to the pool (bar) we go. Several hours and an extraordinary amount of 'Cruzcampo' later, the locals of the Costa Del Sol certainly know we've arrived. *Hail Hail, Over and Over, The Fields of Athenry* and a few others, echo over the balconies and down the cobbled streets. Everywhere was a sea of green and, God, did we enjoy it.

It was more of the same fanfare for the next few days as the excitement really got a grip and the anticipation of watching history in the making was almost unbearable. More and more Celts were arriving, including a large number from our own club, and the rooms at the El Pinar were bulging with suitcases, duty free, and sunburnt bodies.

It's here! Matchday and everyone's in reception, fresh-faced and raring to go (aye right!). Coach loaded up and it's off to Seville we go. Every coach, van, mini-bus, car and even scooter was heading our way. Scarves, flags and sombreros hung from every window as the amazing colourful convoy headed inland. A couple of hours later and we were finally there. What a feeling! To be truthful we never really got to see much of the city, as we were blinded by tens of thousands of our fellow family members basking in the red hot heat.

Open top buses draped in flags, dancing, singing, and even two six-foot leprechauns guided us into the city. None of us had ever experienced anything like it. Bus parked up at the stadium and back into the main centre. "Any tickets, any tickets," bellowed from every corner, all sorts of Euros being offered. No thanks; our match tickets were absolutely priceless.

Across the river and into a nice little Mexican Restaurant, just to get out of the heat. *'It's A Grand Old Team'* mixed with locals' car horns resounded around the city, and now and again the faint cries of *'Porto, Porto'* could be heard between verses. As usual the warmth and friendliness offered to opposing supporters was commendable and we received it back in abundance.

The long trek back to the stadium was worrying in the soaring heat, so a horse and cart was commissioned. Seventy Euros one horseman asked! You're kidding? So a short dander 100 yards further up the road and 30 Euros was more acceptable. Passing through the mass hordes in a horse and cart just added that extra touch. A very touching scene. Reminiscent of *The Quiet Man,* with Liam Devlin resembling Barry Fitzgerald's character, Michealin Og.

The match itself was indescribable, so I won't even start. Of what I'm certain that even after the result, no-one in Olympic Stadium would have been anywhere else. Those memories are everlasting and everyone will have there own special ones.

The next few days are ones tinged with a little disappointment, but full of immense pride. The enquiry begins round the pool, 'What a day' ,'Unforgettable', 'historic'; all the superlatives were being used. The best in my view was the Spanish newspaper, whose headline read when translated *'Unrepeatable Atmosphere'* That summed it up, and brought home the great ambassadorial job that we, the supporters, had done.

The party was not over for the Beann Mhadaghain crew and we soon continued with the visits to the local senoritas, sorry tavernas. We ended the week in great style with all the bar staff at the hotel wearing their new Celtic tops on our final farewell.

And then to round it off, the three amigos go and get themselves stuck in the lift. What a laugh that was, like something out a cartoon strip. (XXXL) was animated; (XXL) stayed calm and the small one? (XL) absolutely terrified. It was only a small lift that could take no more than four at a time, so it was well overloaded. It was extremely hot and a long time to be stuck in there, and I was more worried about them drowning (in their own sweat), given their size.

Needless to say the stick given out the next day was side-splitting and rounded off the most memorable of weeks. Thank you, Martin and the team, we can't wait till the next one, not 33 years please. We will always savour Seville.

ANDY KANE, Beann Mhadaghain CSC

Chapter Eleven

Post-match reaction

MARTIN O'NEILL'S POST-MATCH REACTION

"I'm obviously very, very proud of the team, and I'm disappointed. I think the sending off had a big effect because about four minutes earlier Henrik Larsson had been fouled on the edge of the penalty box. But it was a fantastic effort by the players – and the supporters. Yes, I'm disappointed that we lost the game, but I'm very proud of the team and very proud of the supporters.

"The players were immense tonight. They've been immense in victory at times, and they've been immense tonight in defeat. Sometimes you get what you deserve in this game. I thought we deserved more tonight."

On Porto's approach...

"I wasn't pleased with it. I wasn't pleased at all. You saw the reception they got when they collected their medals from our fans and, having been around a long time, Celtic fans are as fair-minded as any in European matches. And you saw their reaction tonight.

"The referee looked very, very young and he will learn from his experience tonight. One of the lessons he should learn is that, when you score a goal, the kick-off should not be five minutes later. That's one, but loads of things were going on tonight. However, he'll learn from the match and hopefully so will we."

On the fans ...

"I was taken aback, yes. We had come out to the pitch about an hour and 15 minutes before the game just to have a look at the pitch, and it was an amazing sight. And it was obviously even more amazing just before kick-off. They're a wonderful support, no doubt about it – there were probably as many outside the ground as there were inside it – and they love their football."

HENRIK LARSSON'S POST-MATCH REACTION

"I just can't sum up how I feel. It's just unbelievable and really tough for me at the moment. We are all very unhappy. This is the final and at the moment I'm very disappointed. We came back twice and we looked the strongest team in extra time. This is more disappointing than Japan in the World Cup. It was disappointing to go out at that time. But this is the UEFA Cup final and to come back twice is hard to take."

ULRIK LAURSEN'S POST-MATCH REACTION

"It was meant to be the biggest thing of our lives but it ended up the biggest disappointment of our lives. We were absolutely gutted when they got the third, especially because we felt we could have prevented it. Nobody said anything in the dressing room because there was nothing we could say.

"It was a massive blow for us when we were reduced to 10 men and I think we were hoping to take the game into extra-time because everyone was pretty tired by then and eleven against 10 was pretty difficult. Bobo maybe had two challenges which he mis-timed and he ended up with two yellow cards. It's never good to get sent off in a final never mind the UEFA Cup final, but there was no way you could blame him for those tackles."

On Derlei's winning goal ...

"I knew it had to have hit something because I had anticipated it going flat across the ground towards goal but it seemed to bounce and skid into the air. I tried to block it but maybe wasn't quick enough to react. The team played well and although they were a bit on top of us in the first half, we came out in the second-half and scored twice and it is so disappointing to then lose the game in injury time."

BOBO BALDE'S POST-MATCH REACTION

"It's very disappointing and it was very hard to hear them in the dressing room after the match. It was a very sad moment for me but I am still not finished and I will come back. I didn't think I played too badly, but that was one of my worst games of this year. The fans have travelled a long way to lose the game which is hard for them. I thought we would go on to win after we equalised, but I didn't think the referee was going to give me a red card. Then I saw his face and I knew then that I was going off which was hard for me to take."

NEIL LENNON: DAY AFTER THE MATCH

"It doesn't feel any easier to be honest and I think the longer it goes on maybe the worse it will get. You don't really have all that much time to think about it immediately after the game because there is still a lot going on and you are with

Post-match reaction

the rest of your team-mates. It's when you're alone at home that it really sinks in. That's when you keep going over and over it in your head and keep analysing every minute of the match. You'd just give anything to have the chance to change it, to play it again and it hurts even more the longer you think about it.

"When you look at the players and the management that are here today, they have pulled this club up by the boots. It was in the depths of mediocrity only a few seasons ago, yet we have just played in a European final, something that no other Celtic manager has led a team to for 33 years. We have given the fans their pride back and put the club on the map in Europe once again."

MARTIN O'NEILL: TWO DAYS AFTER FINAL

"I'm pretty tired, I'm pretty disappointed, but there's also a good deal of pride there because the performance of the team and the performance of the supporters, which was just extraordinary. I think they've done the club proud and I think that they've done Scottish football proud. I mean, there were 75,000-80,000 people there and they tell me that there might have been one arrest if that. It's extraordinary.

On his criticism of the referee ...

"I stand by the comments, absolutely. The referee was very young, he looked inexperienced, and he will learn from the experience – absolutely right. There's nothing to get too excited about there, and I think there was probably only about 50,000 people in the stadium and 17 million watching on TV who agreed with me.

PAUL LAMBERT: Celtic View interview, May 28

"It's still sore, there's no point in me or anyone else denying that, but although this might sound silly to some people because we haven't won anything, I'll still look back on this as an unbelievable season. When you think of the experiences we've had in the UEFA Cup, you wouldn't have changed them for the world. If you could tell me now that we'd have another European final to look forward to next season, with all the consequences that go with that, I'd take it in a second."

DIDIER AGATHE: Celtic View interview, May 28

"As a player it has been fantastic to play against some of the teams we have met in the UEFA Cup this year and I think that as a team we have learned a lot. Hopefully that experience is something we can use next season when we try to get ourselves into the Champions League. We are very disappointed, of course we are, because we came so close to both the UEFA Cup and the title. Although we have ended up with nothing we can't have any regrets because there is absolutely no way that we would swap the UEFA Cup experience because it was fantastic."

PORTO MANAGER JOSE MOURINHO'S POST-MATCH REACTION

"I can say that the best team won. We were also the team who tried most for the win and who played the best quality football. However, honour also goes to those who lost – they lost with dignity. And the supporters were great beforehand, during the match and, I believe, after the match as well."

The route to the UEFA Cup final

 Champions League, Third Qualifying Round
Celtic versus FC Basel (Switzerland)

First leg, Celtic Park, August 14, 2002
CELTIC 3 FC BASEL 1
SCORERS: Celtic – Larsson (pen), Sutton, Sylla; FC Basel – Gimenez

CELTIC (3-5-2): Douglas; Mjallby, Balde, Valgaeren; Sylla, Lennon, Lambert (McNamara 76),
Petrov (Maloney 104), Petta (Guppy 56); Larsson, Sutton.
Substitutes: Hedman, Hartson, Crainey, Fernandez.
FC BASEL (4-4-2): Zuberbuhler; Barberis, Murat Yakin, Zwyssig (Quennoz 38), Duruz;
Ergic (Varele 62), Cantaluppi, Hakan Yakin, Esposito; Rossi (Tum 67), Gimenez.
Substitutes: Rapo, Koumantarakis, Degen, Atouba.
ATTENDANCE: 58,520

Second leg, St-Jakob Park Stadium, Basel, August 28, 2002
FC BASEL 2 CELTIC 0
SCORERS: FC Basel – Gimenez, M Yakin

FC BASEL (4-4-2): Zuberbuhler; Quennoz, Murat Yakin, Barberis, Duruz; Cantaluppi,
Varela (Degen 51), Hakin Yakin, Ergic; Gimenez (Koumantarakis 85), Rossi (Tum 71).
Substitutes: Savic, Rapo, Streller, Atouba.
CELTIC (4-3-1-2): Douglas; Valgaeren, Balde, Mjallby, Laursen (Guppy 46); Lambert (Agathe 46),
Lennon, Petrov; Sylla (Hartson 71); Larsson, Sutton.
Substitutes: Hedman, Crainey, McNamara, Fernandez.
ATTENDANCE: 30,500

AGGREGATE: Celtic 3 FC Basel 3 (FC Basel win on away goals)

 UEFA Cup, First Round
Celtic versus FK Suduva (Lithuania)

First leg, Celtic Park, September 19, 2002
CELTIC 8 FK SUDUVA 1
SCORERS: Celtic – Larsson (3), Sutton, Hartson, Petrov, Lambert, Valgaeren
FK Suduva – Radzinevicius

CELTIC (3-5-2): Douglas; Valgaeren, Balde, Laursen (Crainey 60); Sylla, Lambert,
Lennon (Fernandez 60), Petrov, Guppy; Sutton, Larsson (Hartson 60).
Substitutes: Gould, McNamara, Thompson, Agathe.
SUDUVA (4-4-2): Padimanskas; Kunevieus, Sendzikas, Grigas, Devetinas; Zitinskas (Stankevivius 80),
Suliauskas, Adomaitis (Kraipavicius 75), Sidlauskas (Haciulis 46); Slavickas, Radzinevicius.
Substitutes: Balyns, Klevinskas, Rukavicius, Larcenka.
ATTENDANCE: 36,824

Second leg, Dariaus Ir Gireno Stadium, Kaunas, October 3, 2002
FK SUDUVA 0 CELTIC 2
SCORERS: Celtic – Fernandez, Thompson

FK SUDUVA (4-5-1): Padimanskas; Kunevieus, Sendzikas (Kraipavicius 46), Grigas, Devetinas;
Slavickas, Adohairis (Haciulis 70), Suliauskas (Sidlauskas 84), Litinskas, Larsenka; Radzinevicius.

Substitutes: Balyns, Stankevivius, Rukavicius, Klevinskas.
CELTIC (3-5-2): Gould; McNamara (Miller 72), Kennedy (Smith 52), Crainey; Agathe, Healy, Maloney, Thompson, Petta (Lynch 78); Hartson, Fernandez.
Substitutes: Douglas, Sylla, Balde, Laursen.
ATTENDANCE: 1,200

AGGREGATE: Celtic 10 FK Suduva 1

UEFA Cup, Second Round
Celtic versus Blackburn Rovers (England)

First leg, Celtic Park, October 31, 2002
CELTIC 1 BLACKBURN ROVERS 0

SCORERS: Celtic – Larsson

CELTIC (3-5-2): Douglas; Valgaeren, Balde, Laursen; Agathe (Sylla 81), Lennon, Lambert (Hartson 75), Petrov, Thompson; Larsson, Sutton.
Substitutes: Gould, Fernandez, Maloney, Guppy, Crainey.
BLACKBURN ROVERS (4-4-2): Friedel; Neill, Short, Taylor, Johansson; Flitcroft, Tugay, Duff (Dunn 66), Thompson; Yorke, Ostenstad (Cole 46).
Substitutes: Jansen, Grabbi, Kelly, Gillespie, Douglas.
ATTENDANCE: 59,553

Second leg, Ewood Park, November 14, 2002
BLACKBURN ROVERS 0 CELTIC 2

SCORERS: Celtic – Larsson, Sutton

BLACKBURN (4-4-2): Friedel; Curtis (Gillespie 46), Johansson, Short, Neill; Duff, Dunn, Tugay, Thompson; Cole, Yorke (Jansen 64).
Substitutes: Todd, Grabbi, Ostenstad, Douglas, Kelly.
CELTIC (3-5-2): Douglas; Valgaeren, Balde, Laursen; Agathe (Sylla 82), Petrov (Thompson 77), Sutton, Lennon, Guppy; Hartson (Lambert 69), Larsson.
Substitutes: Gould, Fernandez, Maloney, Crainey.
ATTENDANCE: 29,698

AGGREGATE: Celtic 3 Blackburn Rovers 0

UEFA Cup, Third Round
Celtic versus Celta Vigo (Spain)

First leg, Celtic Park, November 28, 2002
CELTIC 1 CELTA VIGO 0

SCORERS: Celtic – Larsson

CELTIC (3-5-2): Douglas; Valgaeren, Balde, Laursen; Agathe (Sylla 85), Lennon, Petrov, Sutton, Guppy (Thompson 85); Larsson, Hartson.
Substitutes: Gould, McNamara, Fernandez, Lambert, Maloney.
CELTA VIGO (4-2-3-1): Pinto; Mendez, Berizzo, Sergio, Silvinho; Ignacio, Luccin; Lopez (McCarthy 83), Mostovoi, Juanfran; Catanha (Edu 48).
Substitutes: Cavallero, Caceres, Giovenella, Coudet, Jandro.
ATTENDANCE: 53,726

The route to the UEFA Cup final

Second leg, Estadio Balaidos, December 12, 2002
CELTA VIGO 2 CELTIC 1
SCORERS: Celtic – Hartson; Celta Vigo –Jesuli, McCarthy

CELTA VIGO (4-3-3): Pinto; Mendez (Vanger 59), Caceres, Berizzo (Jandro 84), JuanFran; Luccin, Jose Ignacio, Lopez; Edu, McCarthy, Jesuli.
Substitutes: Cavallero, Silvinho, Giovanella, Coira, Coudet.
CELTIC (3-5-2): Douglas; Valgaeren, Balde, Laursen; Agathe, Petrov, Sutton, Lennon (Lambert 55), Thompson; Hartson, Larsson.
Substitutes: Gould, Guppy, Maloney, Sylla, Fernandez.
ATTENDANCE: 26,000

AGGREGATE: Celtic 2 Celta Vigo 2 (Celtic win on away goals)

UEFA Cup, Fourth Round
Celtic versus VfB Stuttgart (Germany)

First Leg, Celtic Park, February 20, 2003
CELTIC 3 VfB STUTTGART 1
SCORERS: Celtic – Lambert, Maloney, Petrov; VfB Stuttgart – Kuranyi

CELTIC (3-5-2): Douglas; Valgaeren, Balde (Laursen 87), McNamara; Thompson (Smith 70), Lambert, Lennon, Petrov, Agathe; Sutton, Maloney.
Substitutes: Marshall, Sylla, Fernandez, Healy, Guppy.
VfB STUTTGART (4-4-2): Hilderbrand; Gerber, Bordon, Meira, Hinkel; Hleb (Carnell 52), Balakov, Meissner (Aundio 76), Soldo; Kuranyi, Amanatidis (Dangelmayr 18).
Substitutes: Ernst, Tiffert, Seitz, Ganea.
ATTENDANCE: 59,000

Second leg, Gottleib-Daimler Stadion, February 27, 2003
VfB STUTTGART 3 CELTIC 2
SCORERS: Celtic – Thompson, Sutton; VfB Stuttgart – Tiffert, Hleb, Mutzel

VfB STUTTGART (4-3-1-2): Hilderbrand; Hinkel, Dangelmayr, Gerber (Seitz 80), Wenzel; Hleb, Soldo, Tiffert (Mutzel 65); Balakov; Amanatidis (Ganea 46), Kuranyi.
Substitutes: Ernst, Schneider, Seitz, Luz, Rundio.
CELTIC (3-5-2): Douglas; Valgaeren, Balde, Laursen; Agathe, Lambert (Maloney 81), Lennon, Petrov, Thompson; Sutton (McNamara 86), Hartson.
Substitutes: Marshall, Sylla, Guppy, Maloney, Crainey.
ATTENDANCE: 50,348

AGGREGATE: Celtic 5 VfB Stuttgart 4

UEFA Cup, Quarter-final
Celtic versus Liverpool (England)

First leg, Celtic Park, March 13, 2003
CELTIC 1 LIVERPOOL 1
SCORERS: Celtic – Larsson; Liverpool – Heskey

Game-by-game

CELTIC (3-5-2): Douglas; Mjallby, Balde, Valgaeren; Smith, Petrov, Sutton, Lennon, Thompson (Guppy 26); Larsson (Lambert 76), Hartson.
Substitutes: Marshall, McNamara, Sylla, Maloney, Crainey.
LIVERPOOL (4-4-2): Dudek; Carragher, Traore, Hyypia, Riise; Diouf (Biscan 89), Hamann, Gerrard, Murphy; Heskey, Owen.
Substitutes: Arphexad, Baros, Smicer, Diao, Cheyrou, Mellor.
ATTENDANCE: 59,756

Second leg, Anfield, March 20,2003
LIVERPOOL 0 CELTIC 2

SCORERS: Celtic – Thompson, Hartson

LIVERPOOL (4-4-2): Dudek; Carragher, Traore, Hyypia, Riise; Smicer (Baros 56), Hamann, Gerrard, Murphy; Owen, Heskey.
Substitutes: Arphexad, Berger, Diao, Cheyrou, Mellor.
CELTIC (3-5-2): Douglas; Mjallby, Balde, Valgaeren; Thompson, Lennon, Lambert (McNamara 73), Petrov, Sylla (Smith 86); Hartson, Larsson.
Substitutes: Marshall, Laursen, Maloney, Guppy, Crainey.
ATTENDANCE: 44,238

AGGREGATE: Celtic 3 Liverpool 1

UEFA Cup, Semi-final
Celtic versus Boavista (Portugal)

First leg, Celtic Park, April 10, 2003
CELTIC 1 BOAVISTA 1

SCORERS: Celtic – Larsson; Boavista – Valgaeren (og)

CELTIC (3-5-2): Douglas; Mjallby, Balde, Valgaeren; Agathe (Sylla 74), Lennon, Lambert, Petrov (Fernandez 78), Thompson; Hartson, Larsson.
Substitutes: Marshall, Maloney, Smith, Crainey, McNamara.
BOAVISTA (3-4-1-2): Ricardo; Turra, Eder, Avalos; Mario Loja, Pedrosa (Oscar 89), Anunciacao, Martelinho; Erivan; Claudio (Cafu 46, Bosingwa 80), Duda.
Substitutes: William, Jorge Couto, Jocivalter, Yuri.
ATTENDANCE: 60,000

Second leg, Estadio do Bessa, April 24, 2003
BOAVISTA 0 CELTIC 1

SCORERS: Celtic – Larsson

BOAVISTA (3-5-2): Ricardo; Avalos; Eder, Anunciacao; Mario Loja, Erivan (Jocivalter 80), Martelinho, Pedrosa (Yuri 84), Pedro Santos; Duda, Silva (Luis Claudio 69).
Substitutes: Andem, Oscar, Bosingwa, Goulart.
CELTIC (3-5-2): Douglas; Mjallby, Balde, Valgaeren (Smith 74); Agathe, Lennon, Lambert (Sutton 34), Petrov, Thompson; Larsson, Hartson.
Substitutes: Marshall, Sylla, McNamara, Laursen, Maloney.
ATTENDANCE: 11,000

AGGREGATE: Celtic 2 Boavista 1

Celtic FC ... 2

3-5-2 formation

Douglas;
Mjallby
Balde
Valgaeren (Laursen 64);
Thompson
Lennon
Lambert (McNamara 75)
Petrov (Maloney 104)
Agathe;
Larsson
Sutton

Substitutes:
Hedman
Sylla
Smith
Fernandez

Scorers:
Larsson (2)

ATTENDANCE: 52,972;   **REFEREE:** Lubos Michel (Slovakia)

FC Porto ... 3

3-4-1-2 formation

Baia;

Valente

Carvalho

Jorge Costa (Emanuel 71);

Maniche

Costinha

Alenichev

Ferreira;

Deco;

Capucho (Marco Ferreira 97),

Derlei

Substitutes:

Nuno

Ricardo Costa

Peixoto

Clayton

Tiago

Scorers:

Derlei (2)

Alenichev

SCORE AFTER 90 MINS: 2-2   **FINAL SCORE:** Porto win 3-2 after extra time

Campaign statistics

ROBERT DOUGLAS

Minutes on park	1110
Goals conceded	12
Saves	33
Saves to shots ratio	73%
Catches	17
Punches	6
Crosses not claimed/drops	2
Clean sheets	5

JONATHAN GOULD

Minutes on park	90
Goals conceded	0
Saves	3
Saves to shots ratio	100%
Catches	1
Punches	0
Crosses not claimed/drops	0
Clean sheets	1

Campaign statistics

BOBO BALDE

Minutes on park	1083
Tackles made	34
Tackles success rate	79%
Passes	329
Clearances	133
Blocks	26
Interceptions	5
Fouls conceded	15
Goals	0
Yellow cards	1
Red cards	1

JOHAN MJALLBY

Minutes on park	480
Tackles made	20
Tackles success rate	79%
Passes	168
Clearances	35
Blocks	5
Interceptions	5
Fouls conceded	13
Goals	0
Yellow cards	2
Red cards	0

JOOS VALGAEREN

Minutes on park	1039
Tackles made	46
Tackles success rate	86%
Passes	370
Clearances	74
Blocks	21
Interceptions	6
Fouls conceded	18
Goals	1
Yellow cards	2
Red cards	0

ULRIK LAURSEN

Minutes on park	568
Tackles made	24
Tackles success rate	71%
Passes	238
Clearances	41
Blocks	15
Interceptions	2
Fouls conceded	9
Goals	0
Yellow cards	1
Red cards	0

STEPHEN CRAINEY

Minutes on park	120
Tackles made	7
Tackles success rate	86%
Passes	48
Clearances	7
Blocks	1
Interceptions	1
Fouls conceded	0
Goals	0
Yellow cards	0
Red cards	0

JOHN KENNEDY

Minutes on park	51
Tackles made	1
Tackles success rate	100%
Passes	30
Clearances	11
Blocks	2
Interceptions	2
Fouls conceded	1
Goals	0
Yellow cards	0
Red cards	0

NEIL LENNON

Minutes on park	1046
Passes made	684
Pass completion	84%
Tackles made	50
Fouls conceded	11
Shots attempted	5
Shooting accuracy	20%
Goals	0
Assists	0
Yellow cards	2
Red cards	0

PAUL LAMBERT

Minutes on park	680
Passes made	404
Pass completion	83%
Tackles made	19
Fouls conceded	8
Shots attempted	3
Shooting accuracy	33%
Goals	2
Assists	1
Yellow cards	0
Red cards	0

Campaign statistics

STILIAN PETROV

Minutes on park	1069
Passes made	465
Pass completion	85%
Tackles made	33
Fouls conceded	7
Shots attempted	15
Shooting accuracy	40%
Goals	2
Assists	3
Yellow cards	3
Red cards	0

JACKIE McNAMARA

Minutes on park	253
Passes made	111
Pass completion	70%
Tackles made	6
Fouls conceded	6
Shots attempted	0
Shooting accuracy	0%
Goals	0
Assists	0
Yellow cards	0
Red cards	0

COLIN HEALY

Minutes on park	90
Passes made	61
Pass completion	92%
Tackles made	4
Fouls conceded	3
Shots attempted	2
Shooting accuracy	0%
Goals	0
Assists	0
Yellow cards	0
Red cards	0

LIAM MILLER

Minutes on park	19
Passes made	17
Pass completion	88%
Tackles made	3
Fouls conceded	0
Shots attempted	0
Shooting accuracy	0%
Goals	0
Assists	0
Yellow cards	0
Red cards	0

DIDIER AGATHE

Minutes on park	894
Passes made	278
Pass completion	78%
Crosses made	41
Cross completion	22%
Shots attempted	6
Shooting accuracy	17%
Goals	0
Assists	2
Yellow cards	1
Red cards	0

ALAN THOMPSON

Minutes on park	864
Passes made	396
Pass completion	71%
Crosses made	68
Cross completion	26%
Shots attempted	11
Shooting accuracy	64%
Goals	3
Assists	2
Yellow cards	2
Red cards	0

STEVE GUPPY

Minutes on park	328
Passes made	114
Pass completion	70%
Crosses made	34
Cross completion	26%
Shots attempted	2
Shooting accuracy	0%
Goals	0
Assists	2
Yellow cards	1
Red cards	0

JAMIE SMITH

Minutes on park	169
Passes made	84
Pass completion	75%
Crosses made	20
Cross completion	10%
Shots attempted	1
Shooting accuracy	0%
Goals	0
Assists	0
Yellow cards	0
Red cards	0

Campaign statistics

MOMO SYLLA

Minutes on park	212
Passes made	84
Pass completion	65%
Crosses made	12
Cross completion	25%
Shots attempted	3
Shooting accuracy	33%
Goals	0
Assists	1
Yellow cards	1
Red cards	0

BOBBY PETTA

Minutes on park	78
Passes made	59
Pass completion	90%
Crosses made	4
Cross completion	50%
Shots attempted	0
Shooting accuracy	0%
Goals	0
Assists	0
Yellow cards	0
Red cards	0

DAVID FERNANDEZ

Minutes on park	132
Goals	1
Shots on target	2
Shots off target	3
Shooting accuracy	40%
Goals to shots ratio	20%
Fouls conceded	3
Assists	0
Offsides	1
Yellow cards	0
Red cards	0

SIMON LYNCH

Minutes on park	12
Goals	0
Shots on target	0
Shots off target	1
Shooting accuracy	0%
Goals to shots ratio	0%
Fouls conceded	0
Assists	0
Offsides	0
Yellow cards	0
Red cards	0

The Road to Seville

HENRIK LARSSON

Minutes on park	886
Goals	11
Shots on target	23
Shots off target	13
Shooting accuracy	64%
Goals to shots ratio	31%
Fouls conceded	22
Assists	1
Offsides	5
Yellow cards	0
Red cards	0

CHRIS SUTTON

Minutes on park	893
Goals	3
Shots on target	5
Shots off target	15
Shooting accuracy	25%
Goals to shots ratio	15%
Fouls conceded	19
Assists	5
Offsides	7
Yellow cards	1
Red cards	0

JOHN HARTSON

Minutes on park	805
Goals	3
Shots on target	12
Shots off target	15
Shooting accuracy	44%
Goals to shots ratio	11%
Fouls conceded	31
Assists	4
Offsides	14
Yellow cards	3
Red cards	0

SHAUN MALONEY

Minutes on park	204
Goals	1
Shots on target	3
Shots off target	2
Shooting accuracy	60%
Goals to shots ratio	20%
Fouls conceded	2
Assists	1
Offsides	1
Yellow cards	1
Red cards	0